Peacemaking and Religious Violence

Princeton Theological Monograph Series

K. C. Hanson, Charles M. Collier, and D. Christopher Spinks,
Series Editors

Recent volumes in the series:

Charles Bellinger
The Trinitarian Self: The Key to the Puzzle of Violence

Linda Hogan
Religion and the Politics of Peace and Conflict

Chris Budden
*Following Jesus in Invaded Space: Doing Theology
on Aboriginal Land*

Jeff B. Pool
*God's Wounds: Hermeneutic of the Christian Symbol
of Divine Suffering, Volume Two*

Lisa E. Dahill
*Reading from the Underside of Selfhood: Bonhoeffer
and Spiritual Formation*

Samuel A. Paul
*The Ubuntu God: Deconstructing a South African
Narrative of Oppression*

Jeanne M. Hoeft
*Agency, Culture, and Human Personhood: Pastoral Thelogy
and Intimate Partner Violence*

Ryan A. Neal
*Theology as Hope: On the Ground and Implications
of Jürgen Moltmann's Doctrine of Hope*

Scott A. Ellington
Risking Truth: Reshaping the World through Prayers of Lament

Peacemaking and Religious Violence

From Thomas Aquinas to Thomas Jefferson

ROGER A. JOHNSON

☙PICKWICK *Publications* · Eugene, Oregon

PEACEMAKING AND RELIGIOUS VIOLENCE
From Thomas Aquinas to Thomas Jefferson

Princeton Theological Monograph Series 120

Pickwick Publications
A Division of Wipf and Stock Publishers
199 W. 8th Ave., Suite 3
Eugene, OR 97401

www.wipfandstock.com

ISBN 13: 978-1-55635-069-6

Cataloging-in-Publication data:

Johnson, Roger A.

   Peacemaking and religious violence : from Thomas Aquinas to Thomas Jefferson / Roger A. Johnson.

   x + 252 p. ; 23 cm. — Includes bibliographical references and indexes.

   Princeton Theological Monograph Series 120

   ISBN 13: 978-1-55635-069-6

   1. Peace — Religious aspects — Christianity. 2. Violence — Religious aspects — Christianity. 3. Aquinas, Thomas, Saint, 1225?–1274 — Political and social views. 4. Llull, Ramon, 1252?–1316. 5. Nicholas, of Cusa, Cardinal, 1401–1464. 6. Jefferson, Thomas, 1743–1826 — Religion. 7. Herbert of Cherbury, Edward Herbert, Baron, 1583–1648. I. Title. II. Series.

BT736.15 .J58 2009

Manufactured in the U.S.A.

To Carol

Blessed are the Peacemakers,
for they shall be called children of God.

Matthew 5:9

Contents

Acknowledgments / *ix*

1 Religious Violence and the Peace Mandate of Jesus / 1

2 Christians Orthodox and Heterodox: Thomas Aquinas and the "Manichees" / 33

3 Christians among Other God-Fearers: Ramon Lull's Dialogue of a Christian, Jew, and Muslim / 73

4 Christians and Other Religions: Nicholas of Cusa's Vision of Global Religious Peace / 107

5 Wars of Christians against Christians: Herbert of Cherbury's Theological Antidote to Religious Warfare / 159

6 Disestablishing Religion and the Waning of Christian Violence: The Political Theology of Thomas Jefferson / 197

Epilogue: Reclaiming the Peace Mandate of Jesus for the Twenty-first Century / 223

Bibliography / 237

Name Index / 247

Subject Index / 249

Acknowledgments

DURING THE PAST SEVEN YEARS, I HAVE BENEFITED FROM MONTHLY luncheon meetings in which I and two colleagues regularly discussed each others' drafts of chapters, public lectures, or other work in progress. In the course of these luncheons, Paul Santmire and Clifford Green—friends, former Wellesley colleagues, and fellow Lutheran pastors—invested their theological wisdom and literary skills in the chapters of this book as if they were their own. I have shamelessly incorporated many of their suggestions into this text.

In addition, most of the chapters were first presented as papers to the Boston Theological Society or the New Haven Theological Discussion Group. Many suggestions from individual members of these two associations have been incorporated in the book and some specific contributions are noted in footnotes.

In discussing Islamic texts and issues, I am indebted to my Islamicist colleagues at Wellesley, especially Professor Louise Marlow, as noted in footnotes.

Beyond these professional networks of support, including librarians at Wellesley College and Harvard Divinity School, I am also grateful for the patience and support of my family, including my grown children and wife. By her example, Carol taught me some peacemaking responses to the anxious and frustrating experiences that often accompany a sustained writing project.

In addition to the circles of friends, colleagues, family, and co-workers recognized above, I also want to acknowledge the research of prior scholars and their publications which provided essential resources for my work. For example, I could not have written chapter three without Anthony Bonner's translations of Ramon Lull's Catalan writings. I am also indebted to Tony for his essays on Lull's historical context and my conversations with him on Majorca. Other published resources are noted in the text, footnotes, and bibliography.

1

Religious Violence and the Peace Mandate of Jesus

> We have just enough religion to make us hate,
> but not enough to make us love one another.
>
> —Jonathan Swift (1667–1745)[1]

THIS IS A BOOK ABOUT RELIGIOUS VIOLENCE AND PEACEMAKING: A
violence fostered by Church leadership and a violence repudiated by
peace advocates of that same Church. Sometimes I describe a bloody
massacre by knights assured of a heavenly reward; sometimes I recount
the struggle of Christians to live peacefully with believers from different
faith communities. In the dramas narrated in this book, the Church is
sometimes the villain, recruiting warriors to kill in the name of God.
That same Church also inspired a political restraint of sectarian violence. In these two stories from the history of the Church, the peace
witness was so interwoven with the outbursts of religious violence that
I could not tell the story of the one without the other. In fact, I discovered many of these nonviolent alternatives only by exploring the violent
contexts that prompted their creation.

In order to illumine the Church's ambivalence on issues of violence
and peace, I will examine a series of European wars from about 1250 to
1650. The conflicts of pre-modern Europe were theologically charged,
as they have become again in the twenty-first century. That is why I have
chosen this period for a study of the Church's struggle with peace and
violence. These conflicts also reflect an alliance of Church and civil gov-

---

1. Swift, *Miscellanies,* 1:273. Swift was not only the author of *Gulliver's Travels,* but
a priest of the Church of England. He wrote the epigram quoted here while serving as
Dean of St. Patrick's Cathedral, Dublin, Ireland.

ernment prevalent during the Constantinian era in the West and still characteristic of most non-Western political-religious relations today.[2]

In some cases, these wars were intra-Christian conflicts within Europe: for example, the thirteenth-century Albigensian Crusade and the seventeenth-century Thirty Years' War. In other cases, the enemies were Muslim: not only in the crusades to the Holy Land but also in the wars with Muslims at the western edge of Christendom (Spain) or eastern border (Constantinople). In all these wars, the contending armies were not merely servants of a civil government, but men who saw themselves as servants of God fighting evil. Such a theological definition of war, as a struggle between the servants of God and forces of evil, was not limited to the pre-modern Constantinian era, as is apparent in the war rhetoric of the present century.

Christians were not of one mind in their response to these outbreaks of religious violence. Some persisted in their efforts to effect peaceful resolutions of conflict even in the midst of church-supported violence. The peace mandate of Jesus—his command to love our enemies—was too prominent in his life, death, and teaching to be disavowed by all who became his followers. Later in this chapter, we will encounter Jesus's peace mandate and repudiation of violence in his Sermon on the Mount. In subsequent chapters, we will hear echoes of Jesus's peace mandate even in those historical periods when the church appeared to be joined more closely to a government's violent policies than to Jesus's proclamation of peace.

The primary purpose of this book is to help Christians recognize and claim both the violence of their religious past and the peace mandate of Jesus. Shortly after the terrorist attack of September 11, 2001, the Christian ethicist, Robin Lovin, challenged Christians to remember their own history of violence.

---

2. During the first several centuries of the Common Era, the Christian Church was a minority religious movement in the Roman Empire, often subject to persecution. After the conversion of Emperor Constantine in the fourth century, the Church was first granted recognition as a legal religion and subsequently became the official religion of the Empire. Other religions, Jewish and pagan, then became the objects of persecution by the government. From the fourth century until the eighteenth century, the Church in the West enjoyed the legal status of an established religion in a changing cast of civil governments from the Holy Roman Empire to the emerging nation-states of Europe. It is this long history of alliances between the Church (in its medieval unity and post-Reformation plurality) and a civil government that is known as the Constantinian era.

No response to this moment in our history that overlooks the
evils in Christian history can be an appropriate Christian response. To treat extremism as if it were only a problem in other
people's faiths calls our own honesty into question.... If we are
unable to admit [our Christian religious intolerance and ethno-
centrism] to ourselves and confess it before God and humanity,
people of other faiths and of no faith will regard Christian calls
to faith as a very dangerous response to the present problem.[3]

In one respect, this book is a response to Lovin's challenge: it provides some details of this violent history for Christians who may perceive killing in the name of God as a practice only of other religions.
Remembering this past is not simply for the purpose of correcting an
often-idealized history, but as a first step to guard against its repetition.

In another respect, the book highlights the continuing peace witness of Christians. I focus on a group of church leaders and theologians,
both clergy and laity, who struggled to establish peaceful relations among
diverse religions. They developed nonviolent procedures to resolve religious conflicts while divesting religious differences of their potential
for fostering hatred. They were not pacifists, but within the limits of
their historical situation, they gave priority to conflict-resolutions that
avoided killing.

The last two chapters explore the transition from the religious wars
of the Constantinian era to the religious peace of the modern West.
The political situation of religion in the American colonies and Europe
changed dramatically in the seventeenth and eighteenth centuries.
Those of us living in peaceful relations with neighbors of differing faiths
should not take that religious situation for granted. The separation of
religion from a government's resources for violence is a bold experiment, not a self-evident or universal condition of human life. Chapter
6 will explore the ending of the Constantinian era in the birth of the
United States and the changing politics of religion in Europe.

Seeking Peace in the Midst of Violence

The peacemaking purpose of past Christians has often been lost because Christians, like most other believers, chose to ignore the violent
episodes of their own history. For example, the theological *Summa* of
Thomas Aquinas is not usually understood as offering a peaceful al-

3. Lovin, "Faith, Ethics, and Evil," 155.

ternative to the violent methods of the first Inquisition. When read in relation to the Church's struggle with the Cathar heresy, however, its peaceful purpose becomes obvious.

In the late medieval era the Cathar movement, an alternative form of Christianity, posed a serious threat to the spiritual authority of the Church and the unity of Christendom. As a result, the Church unleashed a variety of aggressive attempts to destroy the Cathars. The papacy first organized a crusade (the Albigensian Crusade) in which French nobles from the north massacred whole populations of towns in what is now southern France. While this crusade broke the capacity of the nobility in the south to defend their Cathar Christians, it did not eliminate the heresy. In a second effort, the papacy mounted the first Inquisition, whose methods included torture and the handing-over of unrepentant Cathars to civil authorities for execution.

Thomas wrote his *Summa theologiae* during the second stage of the Church's program to destroy the Cathars. However we may regard this magisterial work today, when read in the light of Thomas's own religious situation, it becomes apparent that it was written, in good part, for his Dominican brothers in their mission to convert Cathar heretics. Newly-translated Aristotelian texts provided Thomas with rich resources for this task. Aristotle gave Thomas a naturalism to correct the excessive spiritualism of the Cathars. His arguments for a single First Mover exposed the inconsistencies of their metaphysical dualism. The rationality of Aristotelian thought provided an additional means of demonstrating the truth of Catholic faith.

For Thomas, rational persuasion became the nonviolent means of resolving the conflict with the Cathars: not the mass killing of the Albigensian crusade nor the Inquisition's torture and civil execution of individual Cathar believers. We can appreciate this nonviolent legacy of Thomas's work, however, only as we read his texts in relation to his historical context. Thomas was not a detached intellectual historian, rescuing Greek philosophy for academic purposes. Nor was Thomas a theologian of the future, constructing a theology to guide his Church in navigating her way through all future crises. He wrote his "beginning theology" for the readers he knew: his Dominican brothers in their mission to re-convert Cathars back to the Catholic faith. What is true in the case of Thomas is also true for the four other theologians examined in this book.

Ramon Lull (1222/23–1316) was born and self-educated on the island of Majorca, then recently conquered by Christians from Muslim rule. He became a Christian specialist on Islam, mastered the Arabic language, and studied the Qur'an and other basic Islamic texts. While living in a mixed society of Jews, Christians, and Muslims on Majorca, Lull witnessed many instances of Christian animosity against Jews and Muslims.[4] As a result, he wrote a dialogical theology respectful of all three religions, a theology that could support their peaceful co-existence. Lull also opposed a planned crusade to invade Muslim-ruled territories in North Africa. Instead, he risked his own life traveling to these countries to preach and engage in public debate with Muslim scholars. He repeatedly reminded Church authorities that Jesus Christ had not established the Church by violent means but by demonstrating in his life God's love and peace.

Nicholas of Cusa (1401/02–1464), a specialist in Church law entrusted by several popes with the resolution of intra-Church conflicts, was also an imaginative and prolific theologian. In 1453, Muslim Turks captured Christendom's second capital, Constantinople. It was an event accompanied by an orgy of maiming, raping, and killing Christians. While several popes called for a crusade to set right this wrong, Nicholas wrote a treatise, *De pace fidei* (On the Peace of Faith), that offered a new theology of religious diversity, neutralizing religious differences as sources of hatred. Nicholas' dialogue included representatives of all religions then known, as well as a cast of heavenly powers including God, angels, Peter, and Paul. For Nicholas, the diversity of religions was part of God's plan of salvation; that diversity was also grounded in the multiple ethnic and linguistic differences of the human species. His fifteenth-century text often reads as if it were a twenty-first century theory of religious pluralism.

Lord Herbert of Cherbury (1582/3–1648) was a Christian layman whose professional and personal life was closely bound up with a series of intra-Christian wars. While he was England's ambassador to France, he sought to restrain French military action against French Calvinists (Huguenots) and to win political support for a newly installed Protestant King of Bohemia. He failed in both these efforts, and a religious war of thirty years duration grew out of the religious-political

---

4. For instance, Christians once observed Good Friday by hurling stones from rooftops on Jewish residents below.

struggle born in Bohemia. During the English Civil Wars of the 1640s, fueled in part by theological disputes within the Church of England, his ancestral castle was besieged until he surrendered it. Herbert's political and personal experience of wars, kindled by the mixture of religion and government, led him to propose a new political model of religion, one in which faith and political power were sundered from each other for the sake of peace.

Thomas Jefferson (1743–1826) was a founder of the United States, author of the *Declaration of Independence*, and amateur theologian. He sought a political solution to the religious violence of post-Reformation Christendom. He also recognized that thirteen colonies with different established churches could not be peacefully united in a new nation. He devoted much of his political life to the disestablishment of religion, first in his home state of Virginia and then, assisted by James Madison, in the First Amendment of the United States Constitution. Jefferson thus created a political context for religion, which both allowed and required religious communities to live with each other peacefully. During the nineteenth and twentieth centuries, the politics of disestablishment spread beyond the limits of the United States to provide a model for other nations in the West and Asia.

While Thomas Aquinas constructed the theological concept of religion that provided an intellectual framework for understanding religious diversity, it was Thomas Jefferson who constructed a political system that permitted diverse religions to live peacefully with one another. It is therefore not surprising that in the correspondence of his later life Jefferson repeatedly identified Jesus's command "to love your enemy" as the most valuable guide for sustaining political peace within government and between nations. During his first term as president, Jefferson also assembled his first book of Jesus's moral teaching. It highlighted the universality of neighbor-love in the teachings of Jesus.

All five of these theologians—Thomas, Lull, Nicholas, Herbert, and Jefferson—sought peaceful alternatives in the midst of religious violence. While none were pacifists, all were responsive to the peace mandate of Jesus. They sought first a peaceful resolution to religious conflicts, potential or actual. While I discuss these five theologians individually in their own historical context, they belong to a continuing Christian tradition rooted in Jesus's peace mandate. Nicholas of Cusa copied by hand one-quarter of the writings of Ramon Lull; he also borrowed extensively from the writings of Lull's contemporary, Thomas Aquinas. Lord Herbert's library included works by both Thomas and Nicholas. Jefferson was strongly influenced by two of Lord Herbert's disciples; he was a second generation descendent of Herbert's political theology.[5]

In the Epilogue, I step outside the historical limits of the Constantinian era to examine examples of peacemaking and violence in the twentieth and twenty-first centuries. These examples no longer offer clear cases of religious violence. The Nazi effort to destroy the Jewish people, for example, was no longer religious in its definition of Jews. They were not defined by their beliefs, synagogue membership, or worship habits. Yet, it would be unrealistic to deny the long history of Christian anti-Judaism and anti-Semitism that made Nazi ideology appear legitimate and acceptable to so many Europeans. Similarly, in the beginning of the twenty-first century, the American invasion of Iraq was perceived by many Middle Eastern Muslims as a war against Islam. Some television preachers offered support for the war that seemed to share this view.[6] The official war rhetoric defined this war as a war against evil, which strongly resembled the rhetoric of religious wars.

While the disestablishment of religion was a major step in neutralizing the role of religions in violence, the end of the Constantinian era has not eliminated the religious dimension of warfare. For those living after the Constantinian era, the role of religion in violent conflicts is still an issue with which we must struggle. This is especially true for those of us who are Christian and find our conscience instructed by Jesus's command to love our religious enemies.

I suspect that many other Christians, clergy and laity, belong to this tradition of peace witnesses.[7] Medieval and early modern Christians were not only occupied with crusades, inquisitions, and religious warfare. They also struggled, directly and indirectly, to claim the promise of the Gospel: "Blessed are the peacemakers" (Matt 5:9).

---

5. Charles Blount and Lord Bollingbroke were two of Lord Herbert's followers represented in Jefferson's library and writings.

6. For example, the Reverend John Hagee and the Reverend Rod Parsley.

7. There are several obvious and well-known examples that I have not considered in this study: for example, Saint Francis in medieval Europe and the peace churches in the post-Reformation era (Friends, Church of the Brethren, and Mennonites).

In the chapters that follow, we will become better acquainted with these witnesses to the peace of God and the religious violence that prompted their work. In the meantime, I need to examine a cluster of issues surrounding the particular kind of violence that is, in part, the subject of this book: religious violence.

Issues of Religious Violence

Religious Violence as a Controversial Concept

The concept of religious violence plays a central role in the argument of this book. This is not a book about violence in general; its focus is on the type of violence organized, motivated, and/or justified by the leadership, scriptures, and rhetoric of religious communities. First, however, I will examine the very idea of religious violence. Is the concept of religious violence valid? Is the claim that religious communities may foster violent behavior true, or is the very idea of religious violence nothing but a product of confused thinking? While my research, along with the work of others, has convinced me that religions often do provoke and legitimate violence, many reject such a claim. In the next few pages, I will summarize four types of objections to the idea that religions play a role in fostering violence.

Objections of Political Leaders

Shortly after the September 11, 2001, attacks on the World Trade Towers and the Pentagon, President George W. Bush and Prime Minister Tony Blair most explicitly denied any role of religion in that attack. After his initial error in identifying the "war on terrorism" as a crusade, President Bush strongly separated the terrorist attack of 9/11 from the religion of Islam.[8] In a speech two weeks later, he insisted that the war on terrorism was not a crusade against Islam, for there was no valid link, he said, between Islam and the terrorists' actions. Religions, Bush claimed, were harbingers of peace, not violence; terrorists were only a marginal group of believers who perverted the teachings of their religion to justify their violent deeds. As the President announced in his speech of September 20, 2001, "the terrorists practice a fringe form of Islamic extremism that

---

8. In a speech to the nation on September 16, 2001, President Bush warned the American people that "this crusade, this war on terrorism is going to take a while."

has been rejected by Muslim scholars and the vast majority of Muslim clerics, a fringe movement that perverts the peaceful teachings of Islam."[9] Because "Muslim scholars" and "the vast majority of Muslim clerics" did not approve of the violence of 9/11, the President located the origins of that violence not in the "peaceful teachings of Islam" but in a fringe movement.[10]

Prime Minister Tony Blair echoed this theme, assuring all people that the 9/11 attacks were "no more an expression of true Islam than the Crusades were an expression of true Christianity."[11] According to the claims of President Bush and Prime Minister Blair, it would appear as if the very concept of religious violence is a self-contradiction, somewhat like the concept of a square circle.

I cannot disagree with the short-term value of separating the taint of violence from Islam immediately after the 9/11 attacks. Government leaders in the West rightly distinguished the religion of Islam from this attack so that their American and English citizens would not be moved to lash out at Muslims in their midst. They also hoped that Muslims in other nations might not perceive the war on terrorism as a war on Islam. This political rhetoric was both wise and necessary in those circumstances, but that rhetoric is dangerously dysfunctional for formulating long-term policies. It has concealed the religious factors that inform much of the terrorism of this century. As a result, the response of religious and political leaders of the West has too often been misguided. They have projected on to the terrorists the identity of a nation-state that could be moved to surrender by a military onslaught and invasion. In fact, they were dealing with an amorphous movement of religious radicals whose defeat required quite different tactics. In order to correct this ignorance, it is now time to acknowledge the connection between

---

9. Bush, "Speech Transcript."

10. This political claim concerning the separation of violence from the religion of Islam appears to have derived its intellectual foundations from Mark Juergensmeyer's important study of religion and violence, *Terror in the Mind of God.* Published just the year before the September 2001 attacks, Juergensmeyer made a strong case for the separation of militant violence from Islam. Terrorists might appropriate some of Islam's language of faith, but they did so without the support of duly constituted religious authorities. Juergensmeyer, like President Bush, used the approval of established religious authorities as the criterion for determining whether or not violence was an expression of religion.

11. Blair as quoted by James Carroll, *Boston Globe*, October 9, 2001.

religion and violence, not with reference to one religion alone but regarding the global family of religions.

OBJECTIONS OF SOCIAL SCIENTISTS

For many economists and political scientists, religions do not, and cannot, play a significant role as a causal agent of violence. As Oliver McTernan observed in his research on inter-religious violence in Ireland and Sri Lanka,

> The paradigms [of the social and political sciences] reflect the reductionist approach to conflict that prevails in these disciplines. Reductionists always seek the simplest explanation for conflict. As religion is considered to be a redundant factor in life, an epiphenomenon that is incapable of having its own independent impact on the social and political level, it does not merit, therefore, being taken seriously as a real cause . . . To focus on religious motives, many political and social scientists would argue, is to risk masking over the real cause, which they would claim is more likely to be a mix of grievance and political ambition.[12]

In a recent book, the American sociologist, Rodney Stark, notes that American scholars, by and large, doubt the relevance of religion for understanding matters of social, political, and military importance.[13]

Modern Western culture offers several reasons for this assumption. In part, this claim reflects the materialist tradition of nineteenth-century sociology initiated by Karl Marx. For Marx, religion was an epiphenomenon of history, a result of political or economic changes, but not a cause of such change. In part, this premise reflects the secular politics of the modern West in which the claims of any religion were excluded from public life. In this view, religion may play a significant role in the private lives of individuals, but not in the public sphere of politics and economics. It is this assumption that led so many social scientists to dismiss or minimize the role of religion in the public domain.

As a result of this bias, the role of religion in international affairs has been firmly shrouded in ignorance, just as the role of religion in

---

12. McTernan, *Violence in God's Name*, 18, 23.

13. Stark, *One True God*. "It is widely assumed in scholarly circles that historical inquiries into matters such as the social consequences of monotheism are long outmoded and quite unsuitable" (1–2).

voting patterns had been until recent decades. As Mark Noll and Lyman Kellstadt noted in their critique of social scientific literature concerning the role of religion in American politics,

> Social scientists studying twentieth century politics have assumed, until quite recently, that religion in America is a private affair of little public influence. From this assumption, the conclusions followed that it was not worth studying religion with the same care that sociologists and political scientists directed to race, income, education, and other important social variables. Scholarship in nineteenth century America should have shaken these assumptions, but it took a surge of the Religious Right to alert academics to the continuing salience of religion in public life.[14]

In addition to "the Religious Right," I would call attention to the actions of religious terrorists as a force awakening social scientists to the role of religion in the public arena.

While I recognize the claim that religion is a relatively unimportant cause of conflict, I cannot accept its validity.[15] It is an assumption that has been proven false by historical evidence and by the public role of religions in contemporary America. Jewish, Catholic, Protestant, and Muslim believers have denied the boundaries of modern religious privatism, if they were ever so confined. In many cases, congregations have now replaced precinct wards as the context in which people debate the pros and cons of government policies, including decisions of war and peace. The preachers of radio and television communicate their views of government programs and foreign policy as do the bloggers of the internet. Religion has become very much a part of our public space. While this expansion of the boundaries of faith-talk has been most

---

14. Mark Noll and Lyman Kellstadt, "Religion, Voting for President," 355. See also Swierenga, "Ethnoreligious Political Behavior" in this same book. Swierenga notes that political science studies had recognized religion as a significant factor in voting by the mid-nineteenth century (146–49).

15. The writings of Paul Collier, a World Bank economist, illustrate the assumption that religion does not play a significant role in political conflicts. In his studies of the relative role of "greed" and "grievance" in civil wars between 1900 and 1990, he concluded that greed—the desire of a small group of people to acquire significant short-term gains from the chaos of civil war—is the most important factor in such movements. Grievances concerning sectarian or ethnic issues may play a secondary role in winning public support at home and international patience abroad but they are not causes of the conflict itself (Collier, "Doing Well out of War," 91–92).

dramatic among Christian evangelicals, it is increasingly true for other Christian churches as well.[16]

Objections of Historical Revisionists

Historical revisionists have rejected the application of concepts like "religious war" or "religious violence" to events in post-Reformation Europe usually identified by some such category. In the standard version of European history, the sixteenth and seventeenth centuries are described as a particularly bloody period of civil and international wars provoked and/or legitimated by the Catholic or one of the Protestant Churches. The historical revisionists, however, object to the description of these multiple wars as "religious wars." In their view, the bloody wars of the sixteenth and seventeenth centuries were the birth pangs of the modern nation-state and have little, if any, connection with the religious quarrels of this era.

William Cavanaugh, for example, cites the action of Cardinal Richelieu in subsidizing thirty-six thousand Swedish soldiers then on German territory as evidence of an alliance contrary to religious loyalties: "presumably the Catholic Cardinal was not motivated by love of Luther to support the Protestant cause."[17] Presumably he was motivated by the interests of the King of France in whose service he was employed. If Swedish forces helped to establish a strong and secure French monarchy, so be it. The recognition that nationalist interests may sometimes override religious loyalties does not eliminate the religious interests of such wars. The Cardinal did not subsidize a Calvinist army of 36,000.[18] The Calvinist religious minority in France had been a threat to the unity of the state and the monarchy.

While I note the objection of such revisionists, I do not agree with their claim. Wars are multi-dimensional events in which economic interests, political power struggles, and, in some cases, religious conflicts

16. In a 2004 poll, over one-half of Evangelicals, a third of mainline Protestants, and a quarter of Catholics rated religion as important in their political thinking. Heim, "Voters and Values," 26.

17. Cavanaugh, "A Fire Strong Enough," 397–420. As Geoffrey Parker noted, the destructive role of "confessional politics" in Europe remained a "destabilizing influence" throughout the Thirty Years' War: "the abatement of this major destabilizing influence in European politics was one of the greatest achievements of the Thirty Years' War" (Parker, *The Thirty Years' War,* 219).

18. For a similar argument, see Bell, "State and Civil Society," 425–27.

play a role. To call attention to the nation-building aspect of a war does not eliminate religious, economic, and social aspects of that same war.

Objections of Religious Believers

Religious believers offer a fourth kind of objection to the linkage of religion and violence. When their religion or its founder is accused of violence, they experience it as a deep insult to their own identity. A Danish newspaper cartoon of 2005 depicted Mohammad wearing a bomb with a lighted fuse in place of a turban. The worldwide Muslim riots of 2006 were a typical response of believers to the implied accusation that the founder of their religion was an agent of violence.[19]

In September 2006, Muslim religious and political leaders directed a similar protest against a speech by Pope Benedict XVI. In a lengthy speech on the relationship of faith and reason, the Pope inserted a three-line quotation from the "erudite Byzantine emperor Manuel II Paleologus." According to the Pope, this "erudite emperor" had challenged anyone to "show me just what Mohammed brought that was new, and there you will find things only evil and inhuman, such as his command to spread by the sword the faith he preached.[20] As we will see in chapter two, the Byzantine emperor's critique of Mohammad was not new or original to him, but was a standard stereotype circulating in medieval Christendom.[21]

---

19. To be sure, the entire series of Danish cartoons of Mohammad violated the Muslim taboo against any representation of the Prophet, but the cartoon that made him an agent of violence transgressed an even deeper taboo. These riots responding to the cartoons led to the death of hundreds, the destruction of several Scandinavian embassies in the Middle East, and were accompanied by an organized boycott of Danish products and several European Union exports.

20. Benedict XVI, "Pope's Speech." The need of Muslim traders for trustworthy agents at the ends of their trade routes in Asia and Africa is an alternative explanation for the rapid growth of Islam. Traders were predominantly Muslim, whose economic livelihood required trustworthy local counterparts at the ends of their trade routes. Conversion to Islam appears to have been the best resource available to create honest partners in trade. The African or Asian convert also gained by conversion since all Muslim traders were more likely to do business with a co-religionist.

21. For example, Aquinas wrote, "Mohammad said that he was sent in the power of his arms—which are signs not lacking even to robbers and tyrants—[and he used these ignorant believers] to] force others to become his followers by the violence of his arms" (*Summa contra gentiles*, I 2).

Like the global reaction of Muslims in 2006, I have encountered a somewhat similar response in my teaching from some Christian students when I have spoken of the violent history of the Church. That claim was often met with a combination of disbelief and denial. Few believers welcome a discussion of violence in their religion, though they are perfectly happy to recount violent episodes in some other religion. When I heard repeated claims of Christian innocence of violence from my students, I asked them if they had checked that perception of Christianity with any Jewish students or believers from any other tradition. Most often they had not. I shared with them the story of a Muslim father I had interviewed in Medan, North Sumatra, Indonesia. He told me about the terror he had experienced in response to a Christian hymn. One of his Christian neighbors hosted a Bible study in his home and the Christians gathered there began their evening by singing, "Onward Christian Soldiers." The Muslim heard the words of that hymn in his own language and through the prism of his culture's tales of Christian violence. As a result, he became so terrified that he woke his young sons to help him barricade the doors and windows of their home to ward off a Christian invasion.

Martin Marty, pre-eminent among American scholars in the study of fundamentalist religions, has provided a definitive reply to the denial of violence in one's own religion. As he wrote in responding to the attack of 9/11, "the killing dimension of religion is an inter-faith phenomenon. It is not something that 'they' do, something that is only in 'their' scriptures."[22] The denial that there is a problem of violence within religion is itself a major part of the problem.

The time has come to abandon the posture of the ostrich. Political and religious leaders, social scientists, historians, and believers share a responsibility for acknowledging religious violence as a significant factor in our world. While we should not exaggerate the threat of such violence, as if our whole civilization were at risk, neither dare we ignore its threat.

The Complexity of Religious Violence

Religious organizations are not self-sufficient agents of violence. Even in medieval Europe, Church resources did not include a standing army

22. Marty, "Is Religion the Problem?" 19.

or the finances to support a war of any duration. The king of an emerging state, Emperor of the Holy Roman Empire, or feudal lord was most often the partner of the Church in religious warfare. In the twenty-first century, such support has often been provided by substate groups, ad hoc organizations like Al Qaeda that cannot be identified with any state or religious organization.[23] In the medieval era or the twenty-first century, religions typically rely upon some partner, such as a nation, an empire, or an ad hoc organization, to provide the means for conducting terrorist attacks or warfare.

Similarly, in episodes of religious violence, religious considerations are not the only motive; political, social and economic factors also play a role. The following chapters illustrate the mix of motives in religious violence. For example, in the sack of Constantinople, Mehmed II promised his forces large economic rewards from looting the city; the imam promised them Paradise for destroying the infidels. Similarly, in the Albigensian Crusade, the knights who volunteered were promised a complete indulgence of their sins; the Kingdom of France gained the previously independent territories in what is now the south of France. A militarily successful religious war offered economic and political rewards for this world as well as religious rewards for the other world. As Professor Louise Richardson has observed in her long career of terrorist research, "religion is never the sole cause of terrorism; rather, religious motivations are interwoven with economic and political factors. Yet religion cannot be reduced to social and economic factors. It is a powerful force in itself.[24] Religious violence is never purely religious in its execution or motivation. Sacred texts, the rhetoric of religious leaders, and the support of religious communities are essential to, but not sufficient for, engendering violence. The denial of religion's role in major terrorist attacks or war is often based upon a confused understanding of the nature of religious violence.

Religious Resources for Violence

While religions need allies for the violence they promote, they offer a unique access to the moral judgment and emotional depths of par-

23. I have borrowed the category "substate groups" from Richardson, *What Terrorists Want*, 5, 50. There are also Jewish and Christian substate groups formed in this century for violent purposes.

24. Ibid., 68–69.

ticipants, giving religion a role of extraordinary power. The transcendent source of religious belief serves a variety of powerful purposes in prompting believers to action. Believers are given divine assurance of the legitimacy of their actions; they kill in the name of God, for the sake of God, however reprehensible their actions might appear to human eyes. The scriptures of the world's major religions provide support for their action: the deity of each of these scriptures commands violent actions of believers and is himself/herself violent.[25] Believers are assured of the eventual triumph of their cause since it is God's cause. Their continued devotion to the cause is not dependent upon short-term victories. In a similar way, religious agents of violence are not constrained by any community of support to limit the casualties of their actions. Religious terrorists find their source of support in God, not any human community; through their eyes of faith, they discern no limits to the casualties they create in the service of the Almighty. For overcoming the doubts and fears that ordinarily inhibit the killing of others, religion offers an invaluable resource.

Religious agents of violence also have several organizational advantages. Religions are trans-national movements. The participants are not confined within the boundaries of one nation-state; they disperse themselves without regard to national boundaries. As a result, it is more difficult to exercise any control over their activities, since restraint of them by one nation only prompts them to move to another. Furthermore, because religions are transnational, religious conflicts within one nation easily spread to its neighbors: The Thirty Years' War (1618–1648), for example, engulfed the nations of central Europe and Scandinavia in battles marked by a shared religious conflict and a variety of issues specific to the particular nations involved.

In addition to their transnational characteristic, many religious organizations do not restrict their leadership positions to persons officially licensed by the organization. Self-appointed religious entrepreneurs exercise their leadership solely by their charismatic gifts. They are able to awaken in their followers experiences of humiliation and disrespect to be avenged by killing. This informal leadership model makes any official religious organization immune from counter-attack.

---

25. For violence in Jewish, Christian, and Islamic scriptures, see Nelson-Pallmeyer, *Is Religion Killing Us?*; for violence in Hindu, Buddhist, and Sikh scriptures, see Palmer-Fernandez, *Encyclopedia of Religion and War.*

Religious terrorists are also more dangerous and difficult to deal with because they are more likely to have a transformational than a temporal goal.[26] Temporal goals, involving territorial claims or the rights of minority groups, can be resolved by negotiations and compromise; neither side gains everything it sought, but no one leaves the table empty-handed. Transformational goals, however, involve an all-or-nothing resolution of conflict. Osama bin Laden's dream of restoring the Islamic *sharia* and caliphate in the whole of the Middle East cannot be attained by incremental changes within existing nations. It requires the abolition of multiple states and their replacement by a single political authority subject to the law of Islam. Finally, religious terrorists have the great advantage of drawing support from the larger religious community they represent: for financial assistance, for recruiting new volunteers, and for concealment when needed.

For all these reasons, religious terrorists are the most dangerous. They cannot be destroyed by counter-terrorist military action; typically such efforts only serve to increase their supply of recruits and the conviction of their supporting community that they alone are able to counter the hostility of the perceived enemy.[27] They are not amenable to a termination of violence by means of negotiations and compromise. Their transnational character makes perpetrators difficult to police and religious conflicts likely to spread from one nation to others. They are not responsive to the threat of deterrence since they do not identify their interests with the survival of any nation-state, or even with their own personal survival. They regard the military reaction of their perceived enemy to an attack as simply another resource for their own cause. In the words of Professor Richardson,

> religiously motivated terrorist groups, therefore, tend to be more fanatical, more willing to inflict mass casualties, and better able to enact unassailable commitment from their adherents. As such, they are much less susceptible to conventional responses such as deterrence or negotiation. So while religion is a cause of terrorism only in combination with other social and politi-

26. For the distinction between the temporal and transformational, see Richardson, *What Terrorists Want,* 13, 61.

27. Ibid., xix.

cal factors, religion does make terrorist groups more absolutist, more transnational, and more dangerous.[28]

In brief, religions escalate the danger in conflicts over territory, political power, and economic goods.

Signs of the Increasing Frequency of Religious Violence

During the past few decades, there has been a significant increase in the number of violent episodes involving one religion or another. A partial list of such events, organized by decade, suggests their frequency and the variety of religious groups engaged in violence. I expect that the following list of events will be out of date by the time this page is printed. That does not matter; I intend it to be suggestive, not exhaustive.

In the 1970s began:

- The Protestant-Catholic "Troubles" in Northern Ireland.[29]

- The Singhalese Buddhist-Tamil Hindu civil war in Sri Lanka.

- The systematic slaughter of Palestinian Muslims by Maronite Christians in Lebanon.[30]

In the 1980s

- Christian-Muslim wars erupted in a series of African nations; by 2007, Sudan had suffered 2 million casualties.

Beginning in the 1990s,

- Islamists plunged Algeria into a civil war with over 150,000 casualties.

- Anti-Hindu terrorist activity erupted in Kashmir followed by recurrent Pakistani-Indian conflicts.

---

28. Ibid., 68–69.

29. For a brief account of the role played by clergy in the Irish Troubles, see McTernan, *Violence in God's Name* 29, 88f.

30. A journalist in Lebanon at this time has described Maronite monks "carrying heavy boxes of ammunition across [the monastery grounds]" and Christian day-school students who persuaded their school bus-driver to stop on morning trips to school "at a certain ravine so that the they [the young students] could look at the new crop of mangled corpses thrown into it every night" (Cobban, "Religion and Violence," 1124).

- Suicide bombers of the first intifada killed Jewish civilians followed by Israeli "surgical strikes" on Palestinians followed by more of the same in the intifada of 2000.

- Islamists attempted to destroy the World Trade Towers with a load of bombs delivered to the basement-parking garage.

- Ache Islamists in northern Sumatra revolted against the Indonesian government.

The 2000s were marked by a series of terrorist attacks:

- The 2001 attack on the World Trade Towers and the Pentagon.

- The 2002 anti-Israeli attacks at the Kenyan resort of Mombassa.

- The 2002 triple bombings in Bali.

- The 2004 bombing in Jeddah, Saudi Arabia.

- The 2004 bombing of commuter trains in Madrid.

- The 2005 bombing in Bali.

- The 2005 bombing of subway trains and a double-decker bus in London.

- The 2007 attempted car bombings in London and Glasgow Airport

While Islamist radicals were the most frequent agents of violence in this partial list, I need to note that all of the world's major religions—Islam, Judaism, Christianity, Buddhism, and Hinduism—were represented in violent actions of one sort or another. No religion has a monopoly on inspiring and legitimating organized killing.[31]

The table below suggests the growing prominence of religion in terrorist activities from the late twentieth to the early twenty-first century.

31. For information on the role of violence in specific religions, see the relevant articles in Palmer-Fernandez, *Encyclopedia of Religion and War.*

Year	Number of Known Terrorist Groups	Number of Such Groups with a Religious Identity
1968	11	0
1990's	50	12
2004	77	40[32]

The role of religion in the violent projects of terrorism has been growing. Regrettably, the counter-violence of the American government's response to the attack of 9/11/2001, initiating wars in both Afghanistan and Iraq, has significantly augmented the terrorists' resources: increasing the number of terrorist recruits and the number and geographical dispersion of Al Qaeda cells, strengthening the terrorist position in the larger Muslim community, and enhancing their financial support.[33]

Jesus's Peace Mandate[34]

The writings of the five theologians in this book are concerned with a peaceful alternative to religious violence. It may have been a crusade against an "enemy religion," as Islam was then perceived, or a war to destroy a form of the Christian religion offensive to an established Church. The thirteenth-century Albigensian Crusade and the post-Reformation wars of the sixteenth and seventeenth centuries were in large part fueled by such intra-Christian hostilities.

These five theologians, however, did not initiate the Christian concern for peaceful resolutions. That had its origins in the person of Jesus, his life and teaching as recounted in writings of the New Testament.[35]

32. Richardson, *What Terrorists Want*, 81. Professor Richardson identifies the United States State Department as the source for her 2004 data.

33. Ibid., xix–xxii.

34. I use the term "mandate" to indicate a command that orders relationships within a community and between a community and those outside of it. Negatively it excludes violence and other violations of others. Positively it enjoins respect for others, especially those least likely to command respect. I have borrowed the term from Bonhoeffer's *Ethics* and my discussions with Clifford Green on this subject.

35. For the purposes of this book, it is not necessary to establish that the peace mandate of Jesus had its origins in an "historical Jesus" located behind and before the texts of the New Testament. None of the theologians considered in this book had access to the critical historical and literary methods employed by the several quests for the historical Jesus. The only Jesus known to them was mediated through the texts of the

In order to introduce the peace mandate of Jesus I will examine a few sections from the Sermon on the Mount: one of the Beatitudes that introduces that Sermon and three of the Antitheses that provide the conclusion for Matthew's fifth chapter.[36]

Peacemakers in the Sermon on the Mount

> Blessed are the peacemakers, for they shall be called sons of God. (Matt 5:9)

The seventh Beatitude in the Sermon on the Mount uses an unusual concept but expresses a message consistent with the New Testament's accounts of Jesus's teachings. The Greek term for peacemaker is rare in the New Testament. Indeed, the only example of its usage in the whole body of early Christian literature is this one verse in Matthew's Gospel. In Hellenistic literature the term was used frequently, most often as an honorific term of praise for a ruler. Because a ruler had been effective in establishing conditions of peace, he was also given the title, a "son of God." "Peacemaker" was thus a term borrowed from a non-Jewish culture. The word seems especially out of place in Matthew's Sermon on the Mount, which mostly employs Jewish concepts and methods of Torah interpretation.[37]

While the origins of the term seem alien to its Jewish context in the Sermon on the Mount and while the term is not used in other early Christian writings, its meaning is consistent with a large body of Jesus's teachings. As Hans Dieter Betz has written,

---

Bible and subsequent Church traditions. Even Thomas Jefferson, who sought to free the "real Jesus" from the "distortions" of the Gospel writers, had only the negative claims of a Deist worldview to use as his criterion for deleting texts ascribed to Jesus. However, in my discussion of New Testament texts, I will note the judgment of scholars when they identify such texts with the "historical Jesus."

36. The Beatitudes take their name from the first word of each Beatitude: "Blessed." The six Antitheses are so named because of the formal structure of each Antithesis. A written or unwritten traditional interpretation of the Torah is quoted: "You have heard that it was said to the men of old"—to which Jesus replied with a contrary interpretation of the Torah—"But I say to you." I will restrict my discussion to one of the Beatitudes and three of the Antitheses.

37. Betz, *Sermon on the Mount,* 137–39. The Greek word for "peacemaker" is *eirênopoios.*

> [In Jesus's proclamation of God's kingdom,] God is the principal peacemaker and rules accordingly in his kingdom. Consequently, all human peacemaking is done in imitation of God. To the extent that peacemaking is a function of righteousness and the kingdom of God, the work of the disciples as peacemaking agents of God has indeed political implications. The Antitheses are certainly opposed to war and strife.[38]

In the Antitheses, the Jewish-Christian hearers are commanded "to love your enemies." This command is followed by a promise virtually identical with the promise given to "peacemakers": "so that you may be sons of your father who is in heaven" (Matt 5:44–45).

The Political-Societal Context of First Century Palestine

During the first century CE, Palestine was not a free, independent state; it was a small part of the Roman Empire. The faith and culture of Jews, however, did not fit comfortably within the religion and politics of Rome. Rome tried repeatedly to bring the Jewish population into line without success. For example, by cover of night, Pontius Pilate brought into Jerusalem an array of military standards bearing the effigy of Caesar.[39] Since Jewish law did not permit any images to be erected in the city, a large crowd followed Pilate to Caesarea, imploring him to remove the standards. He refused and in response, the Jews staged a five day-and-night "lie-in" around his house.

On the sixth day, Pilate summoned the crowd with the apparent intention of responding to their request. Instead, he commanded his soldiers to surround them and he threatened the protestors with death if they refused to allow the display of Caesar's image in Jerusalem. When his troops drew their swords, the whole crowd fell prostrate, extending their necks and exclaiming that they would die rather than transgress the law. "Overcome with astonishment at such intense religious zeal, Pilate gave orders for the immediate removal of the standards from Jerusalem."[40]

This effective exercise of Jewish nonviolent resistance to the military power of Rome was only one kind of response. During the ministry of Jesus, loosely organized gangs also carried out armed attacks against

---

38. Ibid., 138.

39. Josephus *Jewish War* II:389.

40. Ibid., 391.

representatives of the occupation. A few of these groups invested their leader with a messianic title. While there was no one organization leading an insurrection, the economic and political conditions of life were such as to breed widespread discontent and resentment, especially among the rural poor.[41] Indeed, some New Testament scholars believed that many of Jesus disciples had been recruited from such groups.[42] Even the substantial army of occupation that Rome stationed in Palestine could not completely suppress the festering rebellion. By the year 66 CE, the Jews had begun their armed revolt against Rome, and by the year 70 CE, Rome's military superiority had quashed their revolt.

Jesus carried out his ministry between the successful nonviolent protest of 26 CE that removed military standards from Jerusalem and the failed revolts of 66–70 CE In that ministry, he addressed issues of peace and violence because such issues were part of the political culture of his day. In addition to those supporting guerrilla warfare, those who resisted Roman authority nonviolently, there were also Jews who were the willing accomplices of Rome. Tax collectors were the most prominent representatives of that group to appear in the Gospels. They were often perceived as both personally corrupt and politically disloyal. Nonviolent forms of resistance, armed revolt, compliance, and withdrawal: these were the political options available to the Jews of first-century Palestine.[43]

Jesus addressed the first three of these options. While he did not recommend compliant consent to the indignities and injustice of Roman rule, he did accept in his larger group of followers the tax collectors who

41. Horsley, *Jesus and the Spiral of Violence*. Horsley rejects the identification of any group of Jewish trouble-makers in Palestine by the term Zealot before the emergence of such a self-identified group in the revolt of 66 CE. In the first edition (1972) of *The Politics of Jesus*, Yoder repeatedly used the term Zealot to identify the moral-political option of anti-Roman violence prominent in the world of Jesus which Jesus repeatedly rejected. While Yoder recognized, in the second edition of this book, that his use of Zealot may have been anachronistic, he defended the substance of his argument if not his use of the term "Zealot" (Yoder, *Politics of Jesus*, 57).

42. Oscar Cullman identified Judas Iscariot, Simon the Zealot, Peter, and the sons of Zebedee as active Zealots, former Zealots, or probable Zealots (*State and the New Testament*, 12–17). Judas may have betrayed Jesus in order to create the threat of arrest that would finally precipitate the holy war through which Judas expected the breakthrough of the kingdom of God (Hengel, *Die Zeloten*, 284–92).

43. Recent New Testament studies have called attention to the likely withdrawal of large numbers of the rural poor from any form of politics.

were the despised collaborators of Rome. The oppressive and unstable societal conditions of first century Palestine created conditions that undermined the dignity of ordinary citizens. Jesus repeatedly suggested behavior that allowed persons to assert their own dignity in response to humiliation without recourse to anger, vengeance, or violence.[44] What is most clear in his life and teachings is his radical interpretation of the love-commandment in the Jewish Torah. For Jesus, God had given to the Jewish people the commandment to love their neighbor, and that command of God did not leave room for any exceptions or modifications. The violation of others was always also a violation of God's law. Jesus's interpretation of the love-command was a radical re-interpretation of the Jewish Torah that responded to the conditions of life in first-century Palestine.

The Torah Love-Command in the Antitheses of the Sermon on the Mount

Throughout the New Testament, Jesus presents a series of responses to violence that are not themselves violent. The responses to religious violence of the five theologians considered in this book had its primal origins in the biblical Jesus. For example, in three of the six Antitheses in the Sermon on the Mount, Jesus rejected any response of the injured party that allowed for any violation of the offending party. In the Sermon on the Mount, Jesus rejects traditional interpretations of the Torah as follows. The text reads:

> You have heard that it was said to men of old:
>
> (1) You shall not kill. Everyone, however, who kills shall be answerable to the court (Matt 5:21);
>
> (5) An eye for an eye and a tooth for a tooth (Matt 5:38),
>
> (6) You shall love your neighbor and hate your enemy (Matt 5:43).

I find it helpful to interpret these Antitheses as a unity, assembled together by some redactor now unknown.[45] For example, the rejected

44. See examples of such teaching in my subsequent discussion of the Antitheses in the Sermon on the Mount.

45. "Redactor" is a term used by New Testament scholars. It refers to an author of a text or a portion of a text. For example, the author of the Gospel of Matthew

options in the first, fifth, and sixth Antitheses quoted above share in common a negative relationship to the love of neighbor commandment of the Jewish Torah. Anger is the issue in the first Antithesis, retaliation in the fifth, and hatred in the sixth. All three of these violate, by intent or deed, the command to love one's neighbor. In terms of the Jewish Torah, they all violate Lev 19:18:

> You shall not take vengeance or bear any grudge against the sons of your own people, but you shall love your neighbor as yourself: I am the Lord.

In the Jewish-Christian context of Matthew's Gospel, Jesus is presented as the messianic interpreter of the Torah.[46] He does not give a new law to replace the Law of Moses. However, he did give a radical critique of traditional Torah interpretations, which have compromised and distorted the original intention of the God-given Torah. The first line of these six Antitheses—"You have heard that it was said to the men of old"—clearly identify the context as a debate in which one side has already been rhetorically depicted as a loser. Over against the conventional voice of traditional Torah interpretations, there sounds the authoritative voice of Jesus, the messianic interpreter of the Torah:

> But I say to you:
>
> Anyone who is angry with his brother shall be answerable to the court (Matt 5:21);
>
> But I tell you not to retaliate against the evildoer;[47] (Matt 5:39).

---

is a redactor who assembled differing sources available to him into a continuing and unified narrative. A different redactor put together the materials of the Sermon on the Mount in a particular format as a unified text. Redaction is a process of composition that happens at many stages in the construction of ancient literature. Betz regards the Antitheses as "a very old tradition that, although not coming from Jesus directly word for word very truthfully reflects his concerns and his methods regarding the Jewish Torah" (*Sermon on the Mount*, 212). Indeed, Betz regards the whole of the Sermon on the Mount as reflecting the context and thought of the historical Jesus. "Only the Sermon on the Mount reflects the Jewish environment from which the historical Jesus came. . . . In contrast, those texts that contain only the moral maxim are all Greek and Gentile Christian in orientation. As far as the historical Jesus is concerned, one can conclude that the context of Jewish Torah interpretation is primary. The moral command to love the enemy represents Jesus's interpretation of the command to love the neighbor [Lev 19:18]" (ibid., 299).

46. Johnson, *Writings of the New Testament*, 186–87.

47. Betz's translation from *Sermon on the Mount*, 199 and 280. The NRSV translates this verse: "Do not resist an evildoer." I regard the NRSV admonition of nonresistance

> Love your enemies and pray for those who persecute you (Matt 5:44).

"But I say to you" introduces an authoritative command. Killing is evil, but so is the motive for killing, and that is anger. Like much of the Hellenistic world, both Jewish and Greek, the Jesus of this text presupposes that anger is the cause of murder. To prevent murder, the original intent of Torah, it is not sufficient to prescribe the punishment for killing. Rather, it is necessary to prevent the killing in the first place. That, however, requires learning that anger is not a reliable moral guide for action, that anger, when enacted in a physical attack against another, is an ally of evil, and therefore contrary to the Torah.

In this first Antithesis, Jesus gives a concrete example of a behavior that demonstrates the priority of the love command. He advises his disciples that if they are presenting a gift offering at the altar and then recall something that their brother may have against them, they should leave their gift in front of the altar, go to their brother and first be reconciled with him, and only then return to the altar and offer their gift. (We are not told if this is a brother Jew, a brother in the Church, or a familial brother.) The love-command, for this teacher of the Torah, takes priority over one's other obligations.[48] This is a radical interpretation of the Torah, radical in its claim to get at the root of the law, its original intent, and the root of human behavior, which violates that law.[49]

Similarly, if the law allows the victim of an evildoer to retaliate, causing an equal harm to the perpetrator, as in "an eye for an eye and a tooth for a tooth," the original victim only extends the evil that caused his own wound. To harm the neighbor's body in retaliation is surely not an act of beneficence consistent with the command to love one's neighbor. Here Jesus provides a critique of the literal meaning of a law in order to recover the original intent of that law. This law was known as the *ius talionis* or the law of equal retribution. Its intended use was

---

to evil as a bit of moral counsel that is both masochistic and immoral. It is certainly "incompatible with the rest of early Christian teaching" (ibid. 281). In subsequent discussions of this verse, I will ignore the NRSV translation of *anthistêmi* as resist and rely upon the Betz translation of *anthistêmi* as retaliate.

48. This particular story has a long history in the life of the Christian Church; see chapter five below for some of its variations and embellishments in the Elizabethan Church.

49. Johnson, *Writings of the New Testament,* 187.

to limit or even eliminate the indiscriminate violence of blood revenge. Retribution for a physical injury caused by an evildoer was limited to a comparable injury for the perpetrator of the wrong. If, however, the *ius talionis* was interpreted literally, it would not eliminate evil but multiply it by extending the chain of evil events. As in the first Antithesis, so here the concern is not with punishment but with prevention. Jesus demands that the victim give up his supposed right to cause injury to another: "do not retaliate." Only by desisting from retaliation can the repetition and extension of evil be eliminated. Only by desisting from retaliation may one, perhaps, persuade by example the evildoer to modify his evil ways. Only by desisting from retaliation can the love-command of the Torah be fulfilled.[50]

Instead of retaliation, Jesus tells three stories which suggest alternative responses to violence. The first tells the story of a person given a back-handed slap on the cheek; the second recounts the loss of a garment in payment of a debt; and the third tells of the frequent experience of civilians living in a Roman occupied territory: namely, their coercion to carry a soldier's pack. All three stories depict a total lack of respect for the person who gets slapped, who loses a garment, or gets stuck with a heavy pack to haul. All three stories have the same plot: someone suffers humiliation. And all three stories reflect the kind of experiences that would be common in first century Palestine, especially for the rural poor. Finally all three stories awaken the expectation of retaliation, but that's not the way they end. Instead, the victims in all three stories are sufficiently courageous and imaginative to respond to their abuse in a manner that restores their dignity and could renew the humanity of their oppressor.

The back-handed slap in the first story was intended purely to humiliate a person of lesser status than the person who slapped, perhaps a servant or slave, a woman or a child, someone who "needed to be put in their place," to be reminded of their inferior status. The person slapped did not try to slap back; instead he offered the other cheek. His generous gesture posed a variety of disturbing questions for the person who slapped him. Do you want to slap again? How many times do you need to slap a cheek? Do you really need to exercise that kind of power

---

50. "What is commanded is not nonviolence in general but desistance from retaliation in specific instances" (Betz, *Sermon on the Mount*, 284).

over someone else in order to feel good yourself? What other messages would be communicated through the offer of another cheek?

The second story involves a larger cast of characters and more action. In a court of law, a moneylender has won his claim to the undergarment of a debtor. Apparently the man had used a piece of his own clothing as security for a loan that he could not repay. Instead of trying to steal back the item of clothing that had covered his own body, he gave the moneylender his outer garment, which left him standing there naked. This is not a joke the moneylender appreciates. He is left holding the two garments of the naked man and, according to Jewish law, he has committed a grave offense by causing the nakedness of the debtor. For the moneylender, the situation is embarrassing and not what a man of his position expected. For the debtor, it is perhaps amusing and somewhat satisfying to share his experience of humiliation with the man who caused it.

The third story has a similar plot. Roman soldiers had the authority to claim the services of a farm animal or a civilian of an occupied territory for assistance in transporting heavy loads. The Gospels of Mark and Matthew tell such a story: Roman soldiers compelled a man named Simon of Cyrene to carry the cross of Jesus (Mark 15:21; Matt 27:32). Roman political and military officers, however, did not wish for these temporary burdens to become so oppressive as to kindle revolts. Hence, soldiers could recruit civilians for pack-hauling only within limited distances, like one mile. This civilian, however, offers to carry the pack for a second mile. However, if the soldier accepts that generous offer, he may find himself in serious trouble. He could be fined, demoted or suffer some other punishment. In this story, as with the moneylender, the abused party does not retaliate but offers more than was required of him. Such a response may not only confuse and disturb his abuser, but may open his eyes to the possibility of a similar response to his own experiences of abuse.

The sixth Antithesis offers both a climax and a summation of all six Antitheses. The form of the love command that appears here is most distinctive to the teaching of Jesus in the Gospels and in the whole body of early Christian literature.[51] The biblical Jesus clearly regarded this

---

51. While Jesus's teaching of love for enemies does not have an exact parallel in either Jewish or Greco-Roman sources, it would be historically inaccurate and theologically dangerous to claim an absolute novelty for his position. See Betz, *Sermon on*

teaching as an interpretation of the Torah. Jesus here made explicit the original intent of the Torah command for love of neighbor to embrace all people with whom one had dealings of any kind. The full text of Matt 5:43–44a reads as follows:

> You have heard that it was said, "You shall love your neighbor and hate your enemy." But I say to you, Love your enemy and pray for those who persecute you.

In comparison with other New Testament quotations from the Torah, this text has several unusual features.

First, there is no Old Testament text that links together love of neighbor and hatred of enemies as is suggested by verse 43. Indeed, there is no text of the Old Testament that requires, or even suggests the propriety of, enemy hatred. However, the addition of this clause would strike many people as self-evident. In fact, such a version of this commandment may well have circulated in oral tradition. By adding this clause, Jesus or the unknown Jewish-Christian redactor of these Antitheses would have addressed an unwritten interpretation of the Torah which they could have encountered among their peers.

Second, in Lev 19:18, and in all other New Testament references to the commandment of neighbor love, the texts read "love your neighbor as yourself." However, in Matt 5:43 the phrase, "as yourself," has been eliminated from this quotation. This could be explained as a product of the vagaries of oral tradition. However if that phrase had dropped out in some early stage of oral transmission, we could expect to find other examples in the New Testament of such an abbreviated quotation from Lev 19:18.[52] There are none.

It therefore seems more likely that the omission of the phrase "as yourself" in Matt 5:43 was an intentional act by the unknown redactor of the Sermon on the Mount. The theological position articulated in the Sermon on the Mount as a whole would require the elimination of the phrase "as yourself." For this redactor, it is God who has given the Jewish people the Torah, and it is God's original intent in that Torah that Jesus has recovered. It is therefore important to understand that it is God's

---

the Mount, 309–11, and Schottroff et al., *Essays on the Love Commandment*, 15–20, for examples of both Jewish and Greco-Roman precedents.

52. All of the following have preserved the original version of the Lev 19:18 love of neighbor command: Matt 19:19 and 22:39; Mark 12:31 and 12:33; Luke 10:27; Rom 13:9; Gal 5:14; and Jas 2:8.

love, not human self-love that is the model for the love of neighbor commanded in the Torah. For this redactor, God does not engage in self-love. Instead, God loves the whole of creation and God persists in loving even the humans who ignore God's law and make themselves into God's enemies. Their enmity to God is not able to shut off God's love for them.

Lest the intended audience for the Sermon on the Mount failed to hear and understand who is the model for their love of neighbor, Jesus or the unknown redactor devoted the closing verses of chapter five to make this explicit.

> Your Father who is in heaven makes his sun rise on the evil and on the good, and sends rain on the just and unjust. For if you love those who love you, what reward have you? Do not even the tax collectors do the same? And if you salute only your brethren, what more are you doing than others? Do not even the Gentiles [the pagans] do the same? (Matt 5:45b–47)

If God is our model for loving others, and if God distributes the bounties of nature upon the good and the evil, the just and the unjust, there are then no people excluded by moral failure or human preference from the company of neighbors we are commanded to love. Humans may love themselves well at some times, but not other times; humans may love some parts of themselves and hate other parts. Such vacillations of self-love do not matter. God's Torah would teach us to love our neighbors as God loves us, not as we love ourselves. Therefore, "Love your enemies . . . so that you may be sons of your Father who is in heaven . . . You, therefore, must be perfect [in your love] as your heavenly Father is perfect [in his love]" (Matt 5:45a, 48).

I want to conclude this brief exposition of the peace mandate of Jesus with a suggestion for further reading. Read any of the passion narratives in Matthew, Mark or Luke while this exposition of the Sermon on the Mount is still fresh in your mind. When I did this, I repeatedly found the behavior of Jesus to reflect his teachings in the Sermon on the Mount. In anticipation of his journey to Jerusalem and at the time of his arrest, Jesus did not allow his disciples or followers to defend him by violent means against his captors. When accused and beaten, stripped of clothing and prepared for execution, he did not retaliate. In the language of that time, he also did not call upon a heavenly army of angels to overcome his accusers and guards.

You may find, as I did, that the several passion narratives read as if they had been enacted to embody the peace mandate of Jesus. In subsequent chapters, you will be reading the stories of Christian theologians who lived in worlds far different from our own. They, no less than us, could not ignore the peace message of Jesus, which they met in the narratives of his passion. This is especially evident in the writings of Raymond Lull and Nicholas of Cusa. That is why I did not wish to explore the subject of Jesus's peace mandate without recognizing its prominence in the stories of his passion.

Let me conclude this exposition of the peace mandate of Jesus with a question. Who were the enemies of the Jewish-Christian congregation who were the most likely original hearers of the Sermon on the Mount as now assembled in Christian scriptures? The enemies do not appear to be political figures, although Roman soldiers infested their environment in large numbers. Nor do they seem to be the moneylenders, tax collectors, and large landowners who played such oppressive roles in the economy of rural Palestine. Fortunately, we need think no further, since the text identifies these enemies who are to be loved. And here we come upon an astonishing insight. It is as clear as the text itself.

The enemies are enemies of Jesus's religious teaching; they are not enemies for political or economic reasons. They are the people who are persecuting the Jewish Christians for religious reasons.[53] In the words of Matt 5:44, the enemies whom we are to love are the same enemies for whom we must pray, and they are the ones who persecute us. Like Paul, or Saul as he was known during the time when he persecuted Christians, the persecutors were fellow Jews. Like Paul, they were not nominal Jews, but devout Jews, advanced in their Judaism and extremely zealous for the traditions of their fathers (Gal 1:14). Like Paul, these persecutors perceived their Jewish brethren, who had become followers of the Way, as heretics whose deviant views threatened the authority of their own Jewish faith. As Paul described himself, he "persecuted the Church of God violently and tried to destroy it" (Gal 1:14). Such religious violence could take the form of stoning Christians and killing them, as in the

---

53. For a discussion of the identity of the enemies in the sixth Antithesis, see Schottroff, "Non-Violence and the Love of One's Enemies," 12–13, 18–23. She emphasizes both the relative powerlessness of the Christians in comparison with their persecutors and the irrelevance of the so-called Zealot-Roman conflict for understanding this commandment.

case of the stoning of Stephen (Acts 7:58–8:1). Or it could take the form
of gangs or enraged mobs beating up on Christians or arresting and
imprisoning them without legal warrants. As a result, Roman authorities who had jurisdiction over such matters often defended Christians
against mob tyranny.[54]

The command to love our enemies acquires its social specificity by
locating it in the context of a Jewish struggle against Jewish-Christian
congregations. In relation to the Jewish synagogue, the Christians
were relatively powerless. The social status of their fledgling form of
Christian-Judaism makes this command all the more poignant and
credible. The enemies are blood brothers who have become, because
of their close but conflicting beliefs and practices, blood enemies. The
enmity and the animosity generated by divergent and firmly held religious convictions will be repeated over and over again during the
Constantinian era, when Christians have lost their status as victims and
become the allies of political power. Even then, when the Church had
become the primary agent of religious violence, the peace mandate of
Jesus, and its application to religious enemies, will be remembered, at
least by a few, if not by all.

54. For the role of Roman political, military, and legal officials in protecting Christians against their religious enemies, see the Book of Acts 23:16–34; 18:12–16; and
16:35–39.

2

Christians Orthodox and Heterodox

Thomas Aquinas and the "Manichees"

> During a 1269 banquet with King Louis IX of France, Thomas
> was "rapt out of himself." In the midst of the meal, he struck
> the table and exclaimed, "That settles the Manichees!" He then
> called for his secretary, shouting "Reginald, get up and write."
> Someone finally brought Thomas to his senses. He apologized
> to the king and explained his strange behavior, "I thought I
> was in my study, thinking about the [Manichean] heresy." The
> king provided Thomas with a substitute secretary who would
> write the newly discovered argument that would "settle the
> Manichees."[1]

THIS STORY IS USUALLY TOLD TO ILLUSTRATE THE EXTRAORDINARY IN-
tellectual powers of Thomas Aquinas (1224/25–1274). A man who could
be seated next to the king of France, medieval Europe's most powerful
nation, with no awareness of his social situation, was obviously gifted
with unusual powers of concentration. Equally surprising, however,
is the subject of his mental preoccupation: "the Manichees," medieval
shorthand for the Manichean heresy. In the late thirteenth century, why
should any Christian theologian be concerned with the Manicheans?
Had not that religious movement, so attractive to the young Augustine,
disappeared from the territory of Christendom many centuries ago? In
1269 Thomas was engaged in writing the second part of his *Summa
theologiae*, which, as one biographer has noted, is "Thomas's most
original contribution to theological literature."[2] The *secunda pars* of the
Summa is also the context in which Thomas developed his understanding of religion as a virtue grounded in the created conditions of hu-

1. Cited in Weisheipl, *Friar Thomas*, 236. See also Torrell, *Saint Thomas*, I:288.

2. Weisheipl, *Friar Thomas*, 256.

man nature. In light of such a model of religion—and such theological creativity—why should Thomas be preoccupied with an ancient group of deviant Christians?

I introduce these questions at the outset of this chapter because the thirteenth century religious movement that Thomas called "the Manichees" played such a significant role in shaping his theology. They were the unacknowledged partners in the formation of his theology. While Aristotle's contributions to the theology of Thomas are well known, the thirteenth-century "Manichees" are little known and their role in Thomas's theology is even less well known.[3] Yet they were not an insignificant force in Thomas's world. In fact they were perceived as such a serious threat to the Catholic Church and the unity of Christendom as to provoke a century of religiously sponsored violence. Hence, I begin this chapter not with the writings of Thomas, but with some background, mostly on thirteenth century heresy, with some attention to the translation in the West of new Aristotle texts. For it was the newly translated texts of Aristotle, and not the older Neo-Platonism of Augustine, that provided the antidote for the so-called Manichees of the thirteenth century.

Background

The Rise and Fall of the Cathar Church

During the last quarter of the twelfth century, Christians living in the area now known as southern France were able to choose among several versions of their religion. Some became followers of Peter Waldo in a movement called Waldensians. Many more found their spiritual home with a group of Christians called the Cathari, meaning the pure ones or the purified. This movement of deviant and somewhat disor-

---

3. For example, in Torrell's recent two-volume study, *Saint Thomas Aquinas*, I found four references in footnotes to the Manicheans, one of which was the familiar "legend" of the banquet scene with the King of France. Yet Torrell quite properly noted "one of Thomas's principle contributions to Christian thought is precisely to have taught theologians to distinguish what belongs to the structural order of the nature of things and what arises from the pure gratuitousness of the divine gift. . . . Nowhere does Thomas represent man or the world in the idealist way, as if man had only a life of the spirit and the world represented nothing but matter without any connection to us" (*Saint Thomas*, II:227–28). He did not add that this "contribution to Christian thought" corrected the "idealist" or spiritualized anthropology of the Catharist heresy so prominent in Thomas's world and writings.

ganized Christians came to acquire the name of their more infamous ancestors, the Manicheans or Manichees. In addition to these two new groups, there was the Catholic Church, which had been the church of Waldensians and Cathars before these movements emerged. That Church, which strongly condemned the Cathars, had not yet mobilized any sustained and systematic action against them.[4] In the midst of a prospering society, accompanied by greater luxuries for Catholic bishops and clergy, the ascetic life style of Cathar leadership and the spiritual focus of the Cathar message proved to be very attractive to laity.[5] As a result, this religious movement prospered with many new and devoted followers. In addition, sympathetic local civil authorities provided political protection. Indeed, the Cathar movement grew to such an extent that by the end of the twelfth century they were able to form an organized church with eleven bishops. In Italy and southern France during the late twelfth century, one could say that a facsimile of religious diversity had arrived in Western Europe.

CATHAR BELIEFS

What the Cathars actually believed is a murky subject. Their opponents ascribed to them the systematic belief system of the ancient Manicheans. For Thomas, the Cathars were "the Manichees" who were to be converted by the rational arguments he discovered with the help of Aristotle and once, while dining with the king of France. Similarly, in the inquisitors' manuals, the accused were given the label of Manichean.[6] Reading Thomas Aquinas or the reports of Dominican inquisitors, it would appear as if the Manichean heresy, refuted by Augustine in the fourth cen-

---

4. Catholics did not ignore the Cathars. As early as 1119, the council of Toulouse ordered the civil authorities to assist the Catholic Church in quelling this movement. Action was not taken, however. In the words of Moore, the Church's early response to the Cathar heresy was "piecemeal, ad hoc, and often mild" (*Formation of a Persecuting Society*, 24).

5. In explaining the growth of such alternative forms of Christianity, Tugwell notes "the widespread disillusionment with the official church.... Particularly in the south of France this had led to considerable disaffection with the clergy among the aristocracy and gentry, and this disaffection made them to be sympathetic towards preachers who denounced the worldliness of the clergy and who abandoned their claims to tithes and other such revenues ... the official clergy were on the whole neither setting an inspiring example of evangelical living nor building up the faith of their people by preaching solid doctrine" (Tugwell, *Early Dominicans*, 9).

6. Given, *Inquisition and Medieval Justice*, 46.

tury and last identified in Church records as a heresy at the end of that century, had gone underground only to emerge eight centuries later in the gentry and aristocracy of southern France.[7] It is probable that some of the disparate Cathar communities did bear a family resemblance to the ancient Manicheans, and this was especially likely among those communities influenced by the Bogomils of Bulgaria. However, as R. E. Moore has suggested, it is also likely that the beliefs of many of these Cathar communities were simply a highly spiritualized version of the popular Neo-Platonism mixed with an anti-clerical, anti-sacramental bias and a lively distrust of the local bishop and clergy.[8] The sketch of beliefs below, borrowed from several sources, reflects a Neo-Platonism spiritualized anthropology and the metaphysical dualism of the historical Manicheans that appears to offer the most plausible indicators of Cathar beliefs.[9]

The records of Cathar practices strongly suggest their belief in a purely spiritualized vision of human nature. Human beings are constituted solely by their inner spirit or soul; the body is not part of one's spiritual identity. Instead, the body is simply a prison into which the pure spirit has been sent as a punishment for some primal sin or as a result of an action of the Evil Power. The goal of life for humans is to forge their identity with their inner spirit, so as to be re-united after death with the Ultimate Spirit, the source and destiny of all spiritual beings. The failure to distance one's spirit from the body and its needs results not in the bliss of spiritual reunion but in the sentence of reincarnation. Try again. The ascetic life style of the Cathar leaders exemplified the way to the spiritualization of the person and successful reunion with God. They abstained from sexual relations (including marriage), from the eating of meat, from the enjoyment of luxuries, and from any violent actions.

The cosmological context for this drama of salvation was the absolute dualism of two competing powers: the Good God locked in a never-ending struggle with the Evil One. The Good God is the source of the spiritual life of every human being; the Evil One is the source of the embodied imprisonment of that spirit. Jesus came into this world as

---

7. Moore, *Formation of a Persecuting Society*, 12.

8. Ibid., 24.

9. For medieval sources, see Peters, *Heresy and Authority* 108–37; Nelli, *Écritures Cathares*; Moore, *Birth of Popular Heresy*, especially ch. 6.

a messenger of the Good God, revealing to all who had ears to hear the secret of humanity's spiritual identity.

This combination of beliefs led to some significant negations and revisions in the Christian tradition. First, the Good God is obviously not the Creator of the physical world, and certainly not the Creator of the human body. These were the products of the Evil One. The Genesis account of creation, along with the first line of the Apostle's Creed— "I believe in God the Father, the maker of heaven and earth"—would have to be radically revised. Second, the belief that Jesus Christ was God incarnate also had to be rejected. Mary was not *theotokos*, the mother of God. Nor was Jesus the incarnation of God. Rather, the spirit in Jesus adopted a body-like shadow for temporary use, but there was never any oneness of the spirit Christ with a real human body. The Christological lines of the Apostle's Creed would have to be discarded. Third, the teaching of the crucifixion of Christ was therefore in error. Jesus was a figure more like an angel temporarily visiting the earth, not a body-burdened human being. At some time, the spirit of Jesus departed from the body-likeness of his shadow. However, since the spiritual Christ was never united with a real Jesus body, that Christ could not have suffered crucifixion and death upon the cross. Fourth, Catholic Eucharistic theology was incorrect. Priests could not distribute "the body and blood of Christ" since the physical elements of body and blood had never been assumed by the spirit of Jesus. The Cathar anti-sacramental orientation led them to reject baptism as well as the Eucharist.[10]

I could continue, but this account should suffice to suggest the range of beliefs—both affirmations and negations—characteristic of the Cathar movement.

The Advent of Aristotle in the West

A second movement of a very different kind paralleled the rise and fall of the Cathars: namely, the translation of the full range of Aristotle's writings from Greek or Arabic into Latin. Aristotle's texts on logic had been known throughout the Middle Ages, but his writings on metaphysics, physics, human nature, ethics, and politics were not available

---

10. I do not mean to suggest that Cathar beliefs were constructed in some systematic pattern as I have done, or that any such system was more or less uniform in all Cathar communities.

in the West.[11] Scholars in Constantinople, Spain, and Palermo began translating these unknown texts of Aristotle from Arabic or Greek into Latin during the last half of the twelfth century. By the early 1240s, when Thomas began his studies at the studium of Naples, many of these new Latin translations had become available.

Thomas was fortunate to discover Aristotle when he did, where he did. The studium at Naples, where he first studied, was sponsored by Emperor Frederick and not by the church. It was a secular studium, unlike the University of Paris that was church sponsored. Hence, Aristotle was taught at Naples when Aquinas was a student there, during the time when Aristotle's writings were still under a church ban in Paris. In addition, when Thomas studied Aristotle at Naples, he encountered the mind of Aristotle in the voice of Aristotle. At the studium of Naples, he not only read Aristotle's newly translated texts, but he also had a commentary on Aristotle by Avicenna and, even more important, the guidance of an Aristotelian professor, Peter of Ireland.[12] He did not come to know Aristotle's ideas as filtered through the Neo-Platonism perspective so dominant in the academic and ecclesiastical environments of the mid-thirteenth century.

After Thomas left Naples to study with Albert the Great, he came to know a somewhat different Aristotle, one for whom Neo-Platonism was not so foreign, as it was not that foreign for Albert. Indeed, the difference between the mostly pure Aristotle appropriated by Thomas and the Neo-Platonized Aristotle of Albert was sufficiently great to foster in the fifteenth century an "Albertist" group organized as a correction to the Thomists. For many purposes the difference between these two versions of Aristotle would be irrelevant. For resolving the problems of belief posed by the Cathars, however, it was very important. A Neo-Platonized Aristotle would have been a much less effective vaccine for the Cathar heresy, which was itself often expressed in Neo-Platonism discourse.

11. *The Categories* and *On Interpretation* were the only two works of Aristotle known throughout the Middle Ages.

12. Little is known of Peter of Ireland, except that he was an Aristotelian (Torrell, *Saint Thomas*, I:7–8; Weisheipl, *Friar Thomas*, 18).

Religious Violence in the Thirteenth Century

This twelfth-century experiment with diversity was not destined to survive. The Catholic Church then enjoyed a legal monopoly of religion, one that could be enforced by civil powers if necessary. The Constantinian model of church-government relations required not only the state's enforcement of one religion for all citizens, but the elimination of any theologically incorrect or heretical version of that religion. Hence, this brief experiment in twelfth-century religious diversity led to a century of Christian sponsored violence. The Cathars were not treated as simply another form of Christianity, but were identified as a dangerous heresy that had to be eliminated. Since both Cathars and Catholics were committed to their own form of Christian faith, the process of eradicating the "false" form of faith necessarily became a bloody one.

The Albigensian Crusade

In 1209, Pope Innocent III (1198–1216) called for a crusade to destroy the Cathar heresy.[13] Named the Albigensian Crusade (after the city of Albi, one of the many urban centers of Cathar believers), this crusade was organized by the church in an army manned primarily by French nobles from the north. Those who volunteered for duty in this war against heresy were offered the same kind of indulgence as had been promised to their predecessors who fought in crusades to free the Holy Land from Muslim rule; absolved from all sin they were virtually guaranteed an eternity of blessed communion with God. They were thus inspired to fight with the religious passion of men who were fighting to protect the faith that promised them eternal bliss. Their destruction of the town of Marmande provides one illustration of this passion in action.

Marmande was a modest sized French town on the Garonne River southeast of Bordeaux. In the early thirteenth century it was one of the urban areas with a concentration of Cathar believers. In June 1219 the town was surrounded by a force of crusaders so large as to make any

---

13. Innocent III was in Orvieto, Italy at the time he called for the Albigensian crusade. The Cathars had a strong presence in Orvieto and "perhaps his decision to launch a new crusade from the city during his visit was an effort to counter the [Cathar] perfects and rebuild Catholic piety" (Lansing, *Power and Purity,* 41). The decision to mount a crusade may have also been a response to the killing of a papal legate in the south of France.

resistance an act of folly. Hence, Count Centule and other leaders of Marmande surrendered themselves to the army of crusaders with the hope of thereby averting an attack upon the town itself. However, in negotiations among the crusaders, there emerged a strong disagreement concerning the fate of Count Centule. Church leaders insisted upon his death as punishment for his toleration of heretics. Barons from the north of France demanded his safety, lest they be shamed in all of France for putting to death a surrendered noble. Agreement was finally reached in a pragmatic option: the life of Count Centule would be sparred so that he could later be exchanged for captured nobles held by the other side.[14]

It was this decision, in good part, which prompted the massacre at Marmande. If the blood of Count Centule would not pay for the heresy at Marmande, the blood of the town's citizens would. A contemporary source described the horrors of this scene:

> Clamor and shouting arose, [crusaders] ran into the town with sharpened steel; terror and massacre began. Lords, ladies and their little children, women and men stripped naked, all these [were] slashed and cut to pieces with keen edged swords. Flesh, blood, and brains, trunks, limbs, and faces hacked in two, lungs, livers, and guts torn out and tossed aside lay on the open ground as if they had rained down from the sky. Marshland and good ground, all was red with blood. Not a man or a woman was left alive, neither old nor young, no living creature, unless any had managed to hide. Marmande was razed and set alight.[15]

In this narrative, a collection of well-armored knights entered the defenseless town of Marmande. Their opponents were not other knights—they had already surrendered —but the town's citizens. The narrator then described acts of warfare that were so offensive as to be unbelievable. First, there was no discrimination in the treatment of these citizens: neither social rank, ecclesiastical status, gender, nor age seemed to matter to the crusaders. The local aristocracy—"lords" and "ladies"—were struck down along with children as if they were all equal. (In the wars of this time, members of the aristocracy were not expendable like the common folk, but were valuable for ransom or prisoner exchange.) Then, the narrator notes that all of them had been

14. William of Tudela, *Song of the Cathar Wars,* 187–88.
15. Ibid., 188–89.

divested of their clothing; they were "stripped naked," denied the dignity of clothing before they were killed. Finally, these people were not simply killed, with their bodies left for burial, but their bodies were cut into pieces and strewn about the ground. Even their faces were "hacked in two." The narrator did not add, but we should remember, that in this incident, both the executioners and the executed were Christians. Indeed, many of them were Christians of the same Catholic faith. In this crusade, it was often the case that Catholic believers were slain along with Cathar believers. From the point of view of the righteous crusader, defending his faith against its enemies, all who lived in the territory contaminated by heresy were judged to be equally worthy of death. They left to God's judgment the task of discriminating true believers from Cathar heretics.

Marmande was not the only city that suffered such a massacre during the Albigensian Crusade. Ten years earlier, in 1209, about 20,000 people of Béziers were killed in a similar massacre. A contemporary source sympathetic to the crusaders described it this way:

> And they killed everyone who fled into the [Catholic] Church; no cross or altar or crucifix could save them. They killed the clergy also, and the women and children. I doubt if one person came out alive. Such a slaughter has not been known or consented to, I think, since the time of the Saracens.[16]

Here also the normal norms of medieval warfare were violated. There was no respect for the church as sanctuary: "no cross or altar or crucifix could save them." Nor was there any respect for the clergy, or for women and children —those explicitly identified as victims who were supposed to be exempt from the killing of war. Finally, the narrator compares the "slaughter" to the earlier attacks by Saracens. Christians were not supposed to engage in the indiscriminate violence practiced by their enemies, the Muslims. However, the fact is that Christians frequently did exactly this, in warfare directly sponsored by the Church.

After twenty years of such horrors, the Albigensian Crusade was finally concluded with the Treaty of Paris in 1229. However, the end of the crusade did not mean the disappearance of the Cathars. These believers survived in organized groups and as individuals long after the official peace treaty was signed. Two decades after the Treaty of Paris,

16. Ibid., 21.

Cathar leaders in southern France still found protection in two major fortresses: Montségur, which did not fall until 1244, and Quéribus which lasted until 1255.

While the Albigensian Crusade did not succeed in eliminating the Cathars, it did succeed in expanding the kingdom of France. As a result of the Treaty of Paris, territory which had been independent of French rule—from the Pyrenees in the south almost to Bordeaux in the north and as far west as Béziers   was now absorbed into the kingdom of France. The exercise of military might had its own rewards, even if a thorough spiritual purification of the conquered land was not one of them.

The Inquisition

The second stage in the Church's century-long program to eliminate the Cathars took the form of the Inquisition. In 1231, just two years after the Treaty of Paris, Pope Gregory IX authorized this new arm of the Church specifically to ferret out individual Cathars who had survived the Crusade.[17] Like the crusaders before them, the inquisitors were effective in fostering a climate of mutual violence. Their victims included the unrepentant Cathars condemned to death—and for many of them, death by being burned alive. But the inquisitors themselves also became victims, murdered by local mobs angered by the punishments that were so often unjust.[18] For example, the siege of Montségur was a response to a middle-of-the-night murder of five inquisitors in a nearby town. For church leaders, the violent means of the crusade and the subsequent Inquisition were justified by the goal of preserving the truth of Christian faith. By 1325, there were virtually no Cathars left in Europe to distort the truth of that faith.[19]

17. While the Inquisition was subsequently extended to a variety of different "heresies," it was the initial growth and persistent survival of the Cathar heresy that prompted the church to create the Inquisition.

18. For a list of Inquisition-related riots, murders, and other civil disruptions between 1233 and 1320, see Given, *Inquisition and Medieval Justice*, 113–15.

19. For an account of the final days of the Cathar church, see Weiss, *Yellow Cross*.

Thomas's Non-Violent Response to the Cathars

Thomas Aquinas (born 1224 or 1225) wrote his *Summa theologiae* in the late 1260s and died in 1274. While the Albigensian Crusade was concluded soon after his birth, the struggle of the church with the Cathar heresy lasted well beyond his death.

More important than the chronological convergence of his life with this heresy was his vocation. He was a Dominican, a member of the Order of Friars Preachers that he joined in 1244 while still a student at Naples.[20] The Dominicans had their origins in Dominic's ten-year struggle to win Cathars back to the Catholic faith. Dominic discovered his ministry in 1203 when he persuaded a Cathar proprietor of the inn where he stayed to return to the Catholic faith. The order Dominic founded was an Order of Preachers who, like Dominic, dedicated their learned preaching to persuade Cathar heretics to give up the folly of their ways for a return to Catholic Christianity and their only hope for salvation.

In addition to this preaching ministry the Dominicans were given a second responsibility for Cathar heretics. By the mid 1230s Pope Gregory IX had made the Dominicans responsible for the work of the Papal Inquisition in examining all surviving Cathars. Throughout Thomas's lifetime the Dominicans retained their dual role as preachers and inquisitors, with a special responsibility for Cathar heretics. While Thomas's Dominican vocation did not require him to become a wandering preacher or traveling inquisitor, it did mean that he would devote his intellectual abilities to the task of establishing Catholic truth and Cathar error. This is exactly what he did, especially in his *Summa theologiae*.

From 1150 to 1275 the Cathar movement was planted, grew, and made almost extinct. During this same period the full range of Aristotle's texts became available in Latin. It was Thomas Aquinas who brought together this unlikely combination. He transformed the thought of Aristotle, perceived initially as hostile to faith, into the bulwark of a newly refashioned orthodoxy, one in which the legacy of Aristotle became the antidote to the Cathar heresy. The Aristotelian presupposes the unity of human nature—the soul informing the body—and the unity of the cosmos—there can be only one First Mover. In all respects,

---

20. Weisheipl, *Friar Thomas*, 27.

Aristotelian naturalism was opposed to the spiritualism and cosmological dualism of the Cathars and it had the additional advantage of being supported by careful reasoning.

In his battle with this heresy, reason was Thomas's weapon of choice: not the violent massacres of the Albigensian Crusade and not the torture and executions that accompanied the Inquisition. His theological primer for the instruction of young Dominicans—the *Summa theologiae*—would make explicit the embodied unity of the human being and the oneness of God, the creator and lord of history, so that these Dominicans, in turn, would be equipped to persuade Cathars by rational argument of the truth of Catholic faith. The new translations of Aristotle may have provided Thomas with a vision and arguments for his new Christian naturalism, but it was the Cathar exclusion of nature from God's creation that gave an urgent relevance to his complex intellectual construct.

The role of the Cathars as the unidentified enemy in Thomas's theology has not always been apparent. The large body of literature on Thomas's theology has mostly ignored this religious movement and the violence they generated in thirteenth century Europe. The same cannot be said for Thomas himself. As I will make apparent later in this chapter, the *Summa theologiae* offers lengthy and repeated discussions of "the Manichean heresy," the thirteenth century label for the Cathars. Later in this chapter, I will document Thomas' many and long discussions of the Manichean heresy of the Cathars in his *Summa theologiae*. He cited their "false beliefs" more than ten times as often as he cited the "false beliefs" of any other Christian heresy or religion.

Indeed, Thomas's references to the Manicheans are so frequent as to virtually equal all his references to Judaism, Islam, and paganism combined.[21] This was not a man who took the "Manichean heresy" lightly. He repeatedly went out of his way to specify how much more dangerous this heresy was than the false beliefs and superstitious practices of Judaism, Islam, and paganism. He also explained why the punishment for Manichean heretics had to be more severe than the punishment for

21. Specifically, in all of Thomas's writings, there are 266 references to the Manicheans and 267 references to Judaism, Islam, and pagans combined. For all wordcounts cited in this chapter, I am indebted to the work of Roberto Busa. Father Busa has edited a compact disc edition of all the writings of Thomas Aquinas: *Index Thomisticus*, 1947–1980.

any other form of false belief or practice. Like Saint Dominic, Thomas gave the Cathars a most prominent position in his ministry. He was obviously preoccupied by the "Manichees" at more times than his well-remembered dinner with the king of France.

I might say that the Cathars provoked a spiritual crisis for the church of sufficient urgency to stimulate an intellectual response by a devoted churchman and theological genius, or that the new Aristotle translations provided Thomas with materials for a post-Cathar orthodoxy. In either case, Thomas's *Summa theologiae* offered a non-violent means for resolving the theological issues of the Cathar conflict, though I cannot claim that it did play such a role in history. In part, this is because Thomas's theological legacy did not acquire a normative role in the church until well after the disappearance of the Cathars.[22] Moreover, the Cathar mixture of genuine religious concerns with territorial claims and political power issues made this conflict an unlikely candidate for a resolution that was only theological.[23] Yet the disappearance of the Cathars in Italy did suggest a somewhat different ending to this religious conflict. The Dominican inquisitors here were not simply the efficient police of Languedoc. They provided the kind of learned instruction in the faith that Dominic and Thomas sought so strenuously to further and "the peaceful countermeasures of the Church" in Italy created a different kind of environment.[24] Sometimes in some places, the nonviolent means of reason could play an effective role in resolving religious conflict.

I argue that, seen retrospectively, the Cathars played a constructive—if indirect and unwitting—role in the creation of Thomas's theology. I also acknowledge their role as a distorting factor in Thomas's theology. I will return to this theme after introducing Thomas's theological concept of religion.

22. As Tugwell has noted, "Not until the latter part of the fifteenth century [did Thomas's] *Summa theologiae* begin to be adopted as a theological textbook instead of the *Books of Sentences.* Thomas's attempt to secure a broad theological formation for the [Dominican] friars who were not up to university level courses came to nothing" (Tugwell, *Albert and Thomas,* 242).

23. "For the majority of the southern higher nobility, the Cathars had always been negotiable. The wars had been fought over the control of the south, not over heresy. . . . The Cathars of Languedoc were eliminated primarily by efficient police work" (Lambert, *Medieval Heresy,* 134, 137).

24. Ibid., 140.

Thomas on "Religion"

I turn now from Thomas's historical context to his writings, specifically the second section of the second part of his *Summa theologiae*.[25] Unlike others of his era, Thomas devoted considerable attention to the concept of religion; questions eighty through one hundred of the *Summa theologiae* (or the text equivalent of one book-length volume) are occupied with various aspects of this subject, and it reappears in all other sections of this work. Indeed, over half of Thomas's references to "religion" appear in the *Summa theologiae*, the primary source for the discussion that follows.

In my exposition of Thomas's concept of religion, I will use the Latin term *religio* so that readers will not confuse Thomas's *religio* with the modern concept of religion.[26] As will become evident, Thomas's concept of religion is not the same as ours. We are likely to use the term to identify a particular community of believers, or the tradition that informs the beliefs and practices of such a group. Unlike this usage, Thomas did not apply his concept of *religio* to the several communities of believers known to him. Instead, he applied the concept only to certain aspects of Christian faith and worship. Thus, his concept of *religio* allowed him to distinguish two types of humanity's knowledge of God, two aspects of God's identity, and two dimensions of worshipping that God. It was strictly an intra-Christian concept; it was not a generic concept that identified the Christian church as one species of the genus, religion, along with other species such as Judaism or Islam or even those non-Catholic Christian movements known as heresies. Later Christian theologians will expand this Thomistic concept of *religio* to include other worshipping communities, but that is a second step. Here I am concerned only to explicate Thomas's theology of *religio*.

This first step in the development of subsequent Christian theologies of religion merits attention for several reasons: first, the Thomistic legacy has for too long been ignored, with the result that the Christian concept of religion has been made indistinguishable from the later Enlightenment concepts of religion and second, the later Christian theologies of religion discussed in this book preserve a strong continuity

25. In my exposition of the *Summa theologiae*, further citations will occur in the text.

26. However, in quoting English translations of the *Summa theologiae*, I will retain the English term, "religion."

with, as well as a revision of, the Thomistic theology of *religio*. In addition, Thomas's refusal to recognize his virtue of *religio* as nourished by some non-Catholic, as well as Catholic, communities of worship will lead us back to the Cathars and their role in influencing his theology.

Religio *Defined*

Thomas defined *religio* as a virtue: "*Religio* is a virtue because it pays the debt of honor to God" (*ST* II-II 80, 2).[27] He identified *religio* as one of the several virtues of justice: "The essence of justice consists in fully rending to another the debt owed him" (*ST* II-II 80, 1). Other virtues closely related to *religio* are filial piety and gratitude: filial piety gives to parents what is owed to them and gratitude gives to a friend or benefactor what is owed to her. In my paraphrase of this definition of *religio* I call it an existential-social category of persons who experience their lives as a gift from God and who express their praise and gratitude to God in some communal form of worship. The posture of self-sufficient individualists, who need to acknowledge no power greater than their own and no community of shared values and belief, would be the opposite of the virtue of *religio*. For Thomas, *religio* thus signified an internal attitude expressed in certain actions of persons, and not a social category of groups.[28]

Thomas borrowed much of this definition of *religio* from classical sources, especially Aristotle and Cicero. There was little that was new in his definition as such. What was new was his use of *religio* as a bridging category to integrate the naturalistic model of God-relatedness given in classical sources with the theological understanding given in the Christian Scriptures and tradition.

According to Thomas, all human beings were destined to be religious, that is, to acknowledge God as their creator and the continuing source of their life. To use the distinction common to the whole of his theology, *religio* belonged to the order of the "natural," not the "supernatural." For Thomas the natural belongs to the structure of creation as sustained by God; its fulfillment is not dependent upon that

27. All quotations from the *Summa theologiae* are taken from the Latin-English bilingual edition.

28. In a secondary and derived sense of the term, Thomas could use *religio* as a term applied to a religious community. For examples of his use of *religio christiana*, see n. 34 below.

distinctive grace of God that brings salvation. However, humanity also has a supernatural destiny whose fulfillment is inextricably linked to God's special grace of salvation as mediated through Christ, the Holy Spirit, and the Church. Faith, as the particular relation of Christians with God, is dependent upon the supernatural just as *religio* belongs to the natural order.[29] *Religio* was, therefore, a "moral virtue," not the same as "the supernatural virtue" of faith or a "theological virtue."[30] As a moral virtue, *religio* is theoretically universal, a possibility for all people; it is not grounded in any special revelation of God. *Religio* is God's gift to humanity mediated through the common grace of creation—Cathars, hear this and repent.

Religio and Faith: Points of Identity and Difference

Throughout his discussion of *religio* Thomas offered repeated comparisons between the virtue of *religio* and faith in God mediated by Christ. Sometimes these comparisons were implicit and became apparent only by exploring the materials he consistently excluded from the virtue of *religio*. More often, they were explicit and Thomas specified the characteristics of a faith-relation to God that were not true for the God-relatedness of *religio*. Note well, however, that in these comparisons of *religio* and faith, Thomas was not comparing two objective entities, as if he knew an embodied form of the virtue of *religio* in some religious community other than his own that he could then contrast with his own Christian faith. Rather, in his comparisons of *religio* and faith, he was contrasting two different aspects of humanity's relation to God. On the one hand, there were certain ways of understanding this God-relatedness appropriate to human nature and the created world; on the other hand, there were certain ways of understanding a person's relation to God appropriate to God's gift of grace in Christ. Sometimes, Thomas believed, these two were identical and sometimes they were very different from each other.

29. Thomas's concept of the natural was not the self-sufficient and self-governing natural world of modernity.

30. "Religion is not one of the theological virtues, whose object is the last end, but one of the moral virtues, whose objects are the means to the last end" (*ST* II-II 81, 5); "Religion is not the same as faith, but a confession of faith by outward signs" (*ST* II-II 94, 1).

In the discussion that follows, *religio* and "faith" therefore refer to two different aspects or dimensions of humanity's relation to God. The creative legacy that Thomas left for later theologies of religion appears most clearly in his sketch of the points of identity and difference that unite and differentiate *religio* and faith.

Natural and Supernatural Means of Knowing God

In addition to God's supernatural revelation of himself in Jesus Christ and the inward movement of the Holy Spirit, Thomas also identified at least two distinct natural means through which humanity was prompted to acknowledge, worship, and serve God.

First, human nature includes an "inner instinct" to believe and worship God. Such an instinct led people, before any outward law of worship was given, to improvise the materials of their worship (*ST* III 60, 5; also *ST* II-II 93, 1). This same instinct prompts people to believe in God, unless intentionally thwarted. In Thomas's words, "While faith is not part of human nature . . . it is part of human nature that man's mind should not thwart his inner instinct" (*ST* II-II 10, 1) Later theologians will embellish this inner instinct as an independent and adequate source of human response to God; for Thomas, it is best understood as a limited and no longer intact anticipation of faith.

Second, God has provided in the created world bountiful evidence for a rational mind to discern God's role as creator or first cause. In Thomas's words, "the existence of God and other like truths about God, which can be known by natural reason, are not articles of faith, but are preambles to the articles; for faith presupposes natural knowledge" (*ST* I 2, 2). In distinguishing *religio,* a moral or natural virtue, from the supernatural virtue of faith, Thomas presupposes some combination of natural resources embedded within humanity and the external world for recognizing God as creator and lord of history.

The Impersonal and Personal Identity of God

In both *religio* and faith, humanity is related to the God who is one. These two are both monotheistic, and the oneness of God reappears as a norm throughout Thomas's discussion of *religio*. As a result, the Cathar belief in two competing gods, a polytheistic belief in many gods, and the practice of idol worship would automatically exclude such communities from their capacity for nurturing the virtue of *religio*. However, there were communities of believers that were contemporaries of Thomas who believed in, and worshiped, one God, such as, Judaism and Islam. According to this norm of *religio*—to pay reverence to one God—both of these groups could be *religio*-fostering bodies of believers, though Thomas never made such a suggestion.

While God's oneness is thus acknowledged in both the virtue of *religio* and Christian faith, the full identity of this one God is not known equally in *religio* and in faith. In *religio*, this one God is honored in "one aspect" only: namely, as creator and lord of history or "the first principle of creation and government for all things" (*ST* II-II 81, 3). Christian faith, in contrast, knows God in the form of the three persons of the Trinity: God the Father, God the Son, and God the Holy Spirit. In his discussions of *religio*, Thomas consistently avoided attributing any aspect of God's Trinitarian identity to God as known in *religio*.[31]

This somewhat impersonal and limited identity of God known in *religio* led Thomas to locate the natural virtue of *religio* one step below the supernatural virtue of faith. To be sure, *religio* was a virtue higher than filial piety or gratitude. However, the generic God-relation of *religio* was of less value than the particular God-relation of faith.

> To show reverence to God as creator, which is the act of the virtue of religion, is nobler than to show reverence to an earthly father, the act of the virtue of piety. But to offer reverence to God as Father is nobler still than to offer this to God as creator and lord. As a consequence, religion surpasses the virtue of [filial] piety, but Piety the Gift [of the Holy Spirit that inspires in us that we have a special filial attitude towards God] exceeds religion. (*ST* II-II 121, 1)

What is striking in this contrast is not the lesser status of *religio* in comparison with faith. One would expect a theoretical possibility of nature to be less valued than faith received as a gift of God. What is striking is the close proximity of the virtue of *religio* to a faith in God known in Christ, especially coming from the advocate of such a faith. According to Thomas, the God known in *religio* may not be the fullness of God known in Christ, but it is the same God. Indeed, throughout his

---

31. In his discussion of religion, Thomas only once alluded to God as triune, and that was in response to the objection that religion could not be one virtue because "in God there are three persons" (*ST* II-II 81, 3).

several points of comparison between *religio* and faith, Thomas is clear about this major issue: in the differing aspects of *religio* and faith, it is the same "one God" who is the object of honor and reverence, though in the virtue of *religio*, this God is apprehended in a more general and limited manner than in faith.

Characteristics of Worship in *Religio* and in Faith

In both *religio* and faith, believers are prompted to express their reverence and honor for God in worship. The worship of God is understood as necessary from both points of view. As a virtue, *religio,* like faith, is primarily an internal quality of the person. However, this internal quality requires the nourishment of external worship activities in order to be strengthened and become a firm "acquired virtue." "God ought to be worshipped by external as well as internal actions" (*ST* II-II 81, 7). The reason such worship is necessary is not for God's sake, "but for our own sake, because when we do so our mind is subjected to him and in this our perfection consists" (*ST* II-II 81, 7). The activity of worship is therefore necessary both for the virtue of *religio* and for a Christ-oriented faith in God. And for both, external materials and activities are essential as a means to arouse the mind to pay honor to God.

> Hence, in divine worship the use of corporeal things is necessary so that by using signs, man's mind may be aroused to the spiritual acts that join him to God. Therefore, the internal acts of religion are principal and essential, while the exterior acts are secondary and subordinate to the internal acts. (*ST* II-II 121, 1; also 81, 7)

The "corporeal things" of this world, so blithely rejected by the Cathars, belong to all people in their worship of God.

In all these respects—the object of worship, the necessity of worship, and the necessity of external materials/activities in worship—*religio* and faith are in agreement. However, in worship, Thomas identifies a strong difference between the God-relationship of *religio* and the God-relationship of faith:

> Religion offers fitting worship to God. Hence, two things must be considered in religion; first, that which religion offers to God, namely, worship, which is the matter or object of religion; secondly, the person to whom worship is offered, namely, God. [In religion] acts that worship God do not contact God directly, as

> do acts of faith, for example, when by believing God we reach
> him. For this reason, God is the object of faith not only because
> we believe in God but because we believe God. Fitting worship
> [of religion] attains God only in the sense that acts which wor-
> ship God, such as sacrifice, are performed out of reverence for
> God. Hence, it is clear that God is related to the virtue of reli-
> gion not as its object or matter, but its end. (*ST* II-II 81, 5)

In *religio*, believers have a direct relation with the external materials of
worship and only an indirect relation with the God who is the end of
their worship.

> Hence, it is clear that God is related to the virtue of religion not
> as matter or object, but as its end. Consequently, religion is not
> one of the theological virtues whose object is the last end, but
> one of the moral virtues, whose objects are the means to the last
> end. (*ST* II-II 81, 5)

In faith, believers have a direct relation to God as the object of their
worship. In the acts of worship believers "know God" and not merely
the materials and activities of their worship.

In discussing worship, Thomas is consistent in distinguishing the
worship of the virtue of *religio* from the worship of those bounded
by a common faith in Christ. The thick veil of theological anonymity,
so prominent in his discussion of God's identity in *religio*, is equally
prominent in his discussion of God-relatedness in worship. The resources of nature, adequate to lead people to pay homage to God, are
no substitute for the gift of God's grace given in Christ. Thomas did
not allow these two interpretations of God-relatedness to be confused.
This careful differentiation of *religio* from faith laid the groundwork for
later theologies of religion that both borrow from and modify Thomas's
understanding of *religio*.

From his theological definition of *religio*, it would seem as if
Thomas could have embraced both Judaism and Islam as legitimate—if
incomplete and partially erroneous—sources of *religio*. Like Christianity,
both of these communities acknowledged one God, and since Thomas

used the "worship of one God" as a criterion for recognizing *religio* in contrast with every sect and superstition, both Judaism and Islam would appear to have qualified as communities that nurture the virtue of *religio*.[32] Like Catholic Christianity (and unlike the Cathars) both of these communities recognized the earth and its many forms of life as the creation of God.[33] Like Christianity, both Judaism and Islam provided ample opportunities for public worship, with prayers and scripture readings, giving thanks and praising that "one aspect of God" of concern to Thomas in *religio*. Like Christianity, both of these communities employed a variety of physical objects in their exercise of worship, stimulating the minds and turning the hearts of their believers to God. In all these respects, Thomas's definition of *religio* could have embraced Judaism and Islam because of their monotheistic worship of God as creator and Lord.

Perhaps the same claim could even be extended to the pagans, both those from the ancient world and those who were the contemporaries of Thomas. In their worship of the sun or a variety of different gods, did they not intend to express the moral virtue of *religio*—honoring God—albeit in a confused manner? However wrong or inadequate their immediate object of devotion may have been, did not their intention express that moral virtue of justice by which Thomas defined *religio*?

Such possibilities, of course, are hypothetical, and contrary to Thomas's position. Thomas frequently modified *religio* with the adjective *christiana*, but he never linked *religio* with Judaism, Islam, any Christian heresy, or any form of paganism.[34] While *religio* may appear to be a virtue nourished in many communities of believers, in fact for Thomas, *religio* is realized in only one group, the Christian congregations in fellowship with the Pope.[35] While in Thomas's view, *religio* belonged to the natural order and faith to the supernatural, so that the two remained

32. "Now the worship of one God belongs to religion. Therefore superstition is contrary to religion" (*ST* II-II 92, 1). "True religion professes faith in one God" (*ST* II-II 81, 3).

33. Thomas did not deny that Muslims and Jews believed in God as creator, though he refuted as erroneous certain forms of that belief held by Muslim philosophers.

34. For examples of *religio christiana*, see the Foreword to the *Summa theologiae* and *ST* II-II 30, 4; 32, 8; 93, 1; 157, 4; 188, 5; *ST* III 60, 3; 62, 5; 63, 2; 63, 3; 65, 1 and *Summa Contra Gentiles* I 5, 2 and IV 34, 3.

35. This exclusion does not apply to the Eastern Orthodox Church. See n. 42 below.

theoretically distinct from each other, in practice, for Thomas the natural virtue of *religio* was dependent upon the healing gift of supernatural grace mediated by the Church. Later I suggest some reasons for the gap between this theoretically open concept and its limited application.

Thomas's Theology of Other Believers/Other Worship

I have coined the category of "other believers/other worship" to include the different faith communities known to Thomas, specifically Christian heresies, Judaism, Islam, and paganism. After developing the categories Thomas applied to these communities, I offer an interpretation of the conceptual dichotomy that characterizes his total discussion of religion: on the one hand, the virtue of *religio* is realized only among Catholics while other communities of believers are identified as sects or heresies and their worship as superstition.

Other Believers as Sect or Heresy

If Thomas's theology of *religio* is grounded in his baptism of Aristotle's naturalism, his conceptual framework for locating communities of other believers is rooted in his preoccupation with the Cathars. This is especially apparent in his definition of sect that functions as one of his two primary categories for identifying communities of other believers.[36]

Sect had two basic uses in the writings of Thomas. First, a sect was an historical category referring to diverse schools of thought in classical philosophy (Platonic, Aristotelian, Stoic, and Epicurean) or groups holding differing beliefs in first century Judaism (Pharisees, Sadducees, and Essenes). Second, a sect was a theological category applied to groups of other believers in his own era. Only the second use is relevant to his theology of other believers/other worship.

As applied to communities of believers that were his contemporaries, Thomas used sect to identify a group holding a belief or teaching judged to be erroneous in light of Christian norms. A sect was a heresy, as Thomas claimed in an etymological argument, and in this somewhat strange definition, we meet once again Thomas's preoccupation with

---

36. Superstition is the other term Thomas used to designate groups of other believers. Like sect, superstition was defined in opposition to *religio*. However, sect and superstition differed in their primary reference. Sect identified a false form of belief or teaching, while superstition designated a false form of worship. Heresy is a species of disbelief, but idolatry is a species of superstition (*ST* II-II 94, 1).

heresy. In Thomas's words, "heresy takes its name from choosing and sect takes its name from cutting, as Isidore notes. A heresy and a sect are the same" (*ST* II-II 11, 1).

This use of sect is peculiar to Thomas, and differs from its usage in late medieval literature.[37] In the late thirteenth century, the use of sect was not confined to groups with deviant beliefs or practices. Rather, sect functioned as a generic category encompassing all known religions, the Christian religion as well as others. Sect was thus not a pejorative concept, as is heresy, but a theologically neutral category that encompassed all known religions; it was a generic category used much as religion is used in our own time.

For example, more than a century before Thomas wrote the *Summa theologiae*, Peter Abelard (1079–1142) used sect as a generic category equally applicable to the religions of a Jew, a Christian, and a pagan philosopher.[38] A few years before and after Thomas completed the *Summa theologiae*, sect was used with this same meaning by a disparate group of late thirteenth century authors: Roger Bacon, Raymon Lull, and Marco Polo.[39] These three writers surveyed a variety of "sects" considerably larger than Abelard's sample of Jew, Christian, and pagan, since they all included newly acquired knowledge of Asian religions. Medieval theologians and writers of travel literature needed one term that could embrace Christianity and the religions of the Mongol Empire, China, and Central Asia. For many authors of this era *secta,* together with *lex* or law, provided neutral generic categories for all known religions.

Thomas's definition of sect was therefore unusual.[40] By defining sect as heresy, he made this proto-sociological category of the late thir-

37. For examples of the medieval usage of *secta* as a proto-generic category including many religions and Christianity, see chapter 3.

38. "We are men belonging to different religious schools of thought (*secta fidei*) . . . One of us is a pagan from those they call philosophers . . . one is called a Jew, the other a Christian" (Abelard, *Dialogue of a Philosopher*, 19). In this edition, Pierre Payer consistently translates *secta* as "school of thought" and *secta fidei* as "religious school of thought" (Ibid., 20 n. 3). For the complete Latin text, see Abelard, *Dialogus inter Philosophum.*

39. Examples of such a use by these authors appears in chapter three.

40. Thomas had at least one precedent for his identification of sect with heresy. In 1142, Peter the Venerable had used "sect" and "heresy" as interchangeable. Kritzeck, in explaining his translations from this text, notes that he consistently renders *secta* as "sectarian" (*Peter the Venerable and Islam,* 32). Thomas's use of *secta* is thus consistent with that of Peter the Venerable, but not with his near contemporaries from the last decades of the thirteenth century.

teenth century into a polemical concept of theology. His concept of sect as heresy, therefore, reflected not the limits of the Latin language available to him, but his own preoccupation with the Cathar heresy. He simply extended the application of sect as heresy from Cathar Christians to all non-Catholic communities.

Thomas also explained the identity of sect and heresy, and their difference from *religio*, in terms I would describe as quasi-psychological.

> A heresy and a sect are the same. Each is a work of the flesh, on account, not of the act itself of unbelief in respect to its proximate object, but of its cause, which is either the desire for an improper end, arising from pride or covetousness, as we have mentioned, or even some illusion of the imagination, which according to Aristotle is a source of error. The imagination somehow belongs to the flesh in that it acts with a bodily organ. (*ST* II-II 11, 1)

It may be instructive to note here that Thomas's characterization of sect resembles Freud's later concept of religion. For Thomas, as for Freud, humanity often fell victim to excessive desires of "pride or covetousness." For Thomas, as for Freud, such excessive and unrealistic desires often found expression in the beliefs of a religion (Freud) or sect (Thomas). For Freud, the Christian belief in God the Father was a projection born of such psychic need; for Thomas, the beliefs of a sect were "works of the flesh . . . by reason of their cause" or source in some excessive desire or illusion. Catholic Christianity thus fostered humanity's virtue of religion, according to Thomas, while other believers bore witness only to the folly of their own psyches.

In his application of sect to other groups, the concept was most often linked with heresy, but Thomas did not limit the application of this category to Christian heretics. For instance, he also referred to Islam and pagan groups as sects. Thus, he wrote about the barbarians who worshipped idols in their "sects" and "Mohammed [who] founded [a] sect committed to erroneous doctrines."[41] From Thomas's point of view, it made perfect sense to extrapolate his category of sect as heresy to pre-Christian barbarians and post-Christian Muslims.

---

41. For barbarians, see *Boethius on the Trinity*, II 3, 3; for Mohammed, see *Summa Contra Gentiles*, I 6.

Other Worship as Superstition

Superstition was the other term Thomas used to designate groups of other believers. Like sect, superstition was defined in opposition to *religio*. However, sect and superstition differed in their primary reference. Sect identified a false form of belief or teaching, while superstition designated a false form of worship.

> Just as religion is not the same as faith, but a confession of faith by outward signs, so superstition is a profession of unbelief by outward forms of worship. We call it idolatry, and not heresy, for this signifies a false opinion. Heresy is a species of disbelief, but idolatry is a species of superstition. (*ST* II-II 94, 1)

In his discussion of other believers/other worship, Thomas most often named Christian heresies and Islam as forms of a sect; both were species of unbelief. Judaism and paganism, in contrast, were most often categorized as forms of superstition. However, since there was considerable overlap in his use of sect and superstition, any of the four types of other believers—Christian heretics, Jews, pagans, and Muslims—might be classified as sect, superstition, or both.

Thomas identified three forms of superstition, or that form of worship "contrary to *religio*": 1) idolatry, or any form of worship which "gives divine honor to a creature"; 2) "divination" which involves the consultation of demons and predictions of future events; and 3) "certain observances" in which rituals of purely human origins are used under the guise of *religio* (*ST* II-II 92, 2).

In Thomas's judgment, three groups of other believers engaged in various forms of superstition: pagans, Jews, and Christian heretics. Paganism was a form of superstition because of its idolatry and its use of rituals to foretell the future. Judaism was a form of superstition because its ritual observances were no longer divinely sanctioned. In Jewish worship, "the term "counterfeit religion" means the name of religion applied to purely human institutions. Consequently, this counterfeit religion is nothing other than the worship of the true God performed in an unbalanced way. An example of this is worshipping God according to the Mosaic law now that the new law of Christ has come" (*ST* II-II 92, 2;

also *ST* II-II 93, 1). Or, as Thomas made the same point in another context, "to observe the Mosaic Law in the age of grace does not, as a class of sin, amount to idolatry; it is almost equal, because both are forms of the plague of superstition" (*ST* II-II 94, 3). Finally, Thomas identified Christian heresies as a form of superstition since, in the worship of congregations such as the Cathars, "ministers impersonate the whole Church" and thus contaminate that worship with falsehood, promising what they have not been entrusted to deliver (*ST* II-II 93, 1).

In summary, Thomas discerned not only the absence of *religio* in all non-Catholic communities, but the presence of something divisive and irrational.[42] The beliefs of these other believers were false and self-serving, and their worship was, at best, nothing but a human invention, and at worst, idolatry. Groups with such beliefs and practices had nothing in common with *religio*. They did not and could not nurture the virtue of *religio*. That happened in only one body of believers: the Catholic Church. Thomas thus constructed an impassable gulf that divided the Christian nurture of *religio* from the irrational beliefs and foolish practices of all other believers. As a result, his theology of religion, when considered as a whole, is surprisingly dualistic. On the one hand is *religio*; on the other, are sects and superstition. On the one hand is the Church; on the other, are heresies. On the one hand is Aristotle's newly baptized naturalism; on the other, his critique of Cathar beliefs extended to embrace all other believing communities known to him.

Thomas's Dualistic Theology of Religion

If we join together Thomas's explication of *religio* with his definition of sect and superstition, and their application to communities of other believers/other worship, the dualism of his incipient theology of religion becomes apparent.

Thomas identified *religio* with a moral virtue that is a form of justice. He believed that all people were indebted to God as their cre-

42. This statement does not apply to the Eastern Orthodox Church. Throughout this discussion, I have bracketed out Thomas's view of Eastern Orthodoxy. In his works on Christian doctrine in general and in his specialized writings on issues mostly debated in the East (*De Rationibus Fidei; Contra Saracenos; Graecos et Armenos;* and *Contra Errores Graecorum*), Thomas does not seem to have raised the question of *religio. Religio* was not as issue for Thomas in his discussion of those he considered schismatics (as different from heretics). I am indebted to Professor Louis Roy, of Boston College, for this clarification.

ator and Lord and that they paid this debt by giving honor to God in worship. *Religio,* therefore, was never only a matter of belief, but always entailed the action of worship. Because *religio* was a moral virtue, he deliberately analyzed its components in terms appropriate to a virtue of nature. The God of *religio* was only the "one aspect of God" related to creation and providence, not the Father, Son, and Holy Spirit of the Christian Trinity. The knowledge of God characteristic of *religio* was grounded in the created conditions of human life, specifically an inner instinct and natural reason, not the revelation of God given in Jesus Christ. The God-relationship of believers in *religio* was less intimate than the God-relationship of faith, since the presence of the Holy Spirit, uniting believers with God, was not a part of *religio*. In this account of *religio*, Thomas is heavily indebted to his classical sources.

From this account of religion, it might appear as if believers could meet their obligation to God, and thus come to acquire the virtue of *religio* in any number of communities who acknowledged God as Lord and creator. In practice, however, Thomas's theology of religion came to the opposite conclusion. When he wrote about the other communities of belief known to him, he described their teachings as heretical and their worship as superstition. Only in the Christian Church could believers fulfill their obligation to God, and thus realize the virtue of religion. What might seem to be a universal possibility in theory was in actuality a possibility only in one single religion. Why such a bifurcation between the theory of religion and its practical application? There are several sources that can be identified for the dualism we find in Thomas's theology, including his Augustinian influence, his vocation as a Dominican, the church's ongoing conflict with the Cathars, and the "Constantinian" link between civil government and the Church that existed in his era. All of these factors merit analysis.

Augustinian Theology

The first is Thomas's theological source: namely, Augustine and especially his doctrine of original sin and grace. While Thomas may have borrowed much of his philosophy from Aristotle, in his theology he was an Augustinian. Augustine's understanding of original sin and grace was especially decisive in setting limits to the Aristotelian naturalism that informed his theoretical model of *religio*.

For Thomas, as for Augustine, God's grace flowed in an endless stream of gifts that both theologians grouped together in two types. First, there was the grace of creation that people experienced as a natural love of the good. The several natural virtues identified by Thomas were thus not the product of a self-sufficient human nature, but they were, in part, a gift from God and a witness to God's grace of creation, working through and with human needs and choices. As a natural virtue, *religio* is one of the many virtues made possible by the continuous interaction of human choice and divine grace that, together, make human life human. In describing the virtue of *religio*, Thomas therefore described it as if it were a universal possibility for all humanity, dependent solely on the grace of creation, as if the created order had not been perverted by sin.

However, for Thomas and Augustine, the latter "as if" condition is counter-factual. According to Augustinian theology, human beings live in the condition of original sin that has dramatically distorted the original condition of creation. To illustrate Augustine's doctrine of original sin, it may be helpful to imagine someone who had been unusually strong and energetic, but now suffers from some debilitating illness. Such a person is no longer able to do with much exertion what she or he had previously done with ease. As a result of sin, humanity's condition is like that of such a sick person. Without the healing medicine of grace, people living in the diseased condition of sin are not able to realize those virtues that, in the integrity of their created nature, had come naturally to them.

That is my paraphrase of Thomas's position. He puts it as follows:

> Man's nature can be considered in two ways: firstly, in its intactness, as it was in our first progenitor before sin; secondly, as it is spoiled in us after the sin of our first progenitor. Now in either state, in order to do or to will any good at all, human nature needs divine assistance, as primary mover, as was said above. But in the state of intact nature, in respect of the sufficiency of his capacity to perform actions, man could by his natural endowments will and perform the good which was proportionate to his own nature, which is to say the good of acquired virtue; but he could not will or perform the transcendent good, which is to say the good of infused virtue.
>
> But in the state of spoiled nature man falls short even of what he is capable of according to his nature, such that he cannot fulfill the whole of this kind of good by his natural endow-

ments. Yet since human nature is not wholly spoiled by sin so as to be deprived of the whole good proper to nature, man can indeed, even in the state of spoiled nature, perform some particular good actions by his natural powers, such as building houses, planting vines and the like. He cannot however perform the whole good that is connatural to him, so as to fall short in nothing. So a sick man is capable of some movement by himself, yet he cannot move perfectly with the movement of a healthy man unless he is healed by the aid of medicine. (*ST* I-II 109, 2)

For Thomas, *religio* is a "good of acquired virtue" which humanity, in its original integrity, could achieve with merely the assistance of God's grace as mediated through creation. However, people actually live in "the state of spoiled nature." While they can still achieve some goods, such as the physical acts of building houses or planting vines, they no longer can achieve the spiritual good for which they were destined. To do this, they first need to be healed of their spiritual illness. This miracle—the healing of human nature—happens only through the grace of Christ as mediated by his Church. The communities of other believers lack the divine grace to heal the distorted desires of the heart. Hence, the best these communities can offer is the self-serving illusion of a sect and the magic of superstition. Augustine's narrative of God's grace overcoming sin thus explains, in part, why Thomas's concept of *religio* as a seemingly universal possibility for all humanity becomes an actuality only in the Catholic Church.

The nature of humanity's knowledge of God, as envisioned by Augustine and Thomas, further illumines his dualistic theology of religion. For Augustine and Thomas, a person's knowledge of God includes the love of God. In Augustine's language, people come to know God only as they find "the love of God shed abroad in their heart." The knowledge of God therefore includes both the right cognition and the right love. For Thomas, only those Christian churches in union with the Supreme Pontiff communicate the right cognition of God; by definition, the Cathars and other heresies communicate false doctrine and hence people are not directed to God, but are "severed from him" (*ST* II-II 10, 3). In Thomas's judgment, the false doctrines of a heresy do not lead heretical believers to God but away from God: "nor can it be that he who has a false opinion of God knows him in a way, for what he thinks is God is not really God" (*ST* II-II 10, 3).

Similarly, only the miracle of grace, healing and restoring fallen human nature could turn humanity from its vain desires to the love of God. The right cognition of God and the right love of God were not, in the condition of sin, universal possibilities; they required God's healing grace of salvation and that, for Thomas, was mediated only through the Catholic Church.

I can summarize the two types of God-knowledge proposed by Thomas, along with an absent third possibility more prevalent in the modern era, by borrowing a paraphrase of Thomas's theology. First, there is "the natural cognition of God which occurs with fiducial faith in the context of justice, piety, gratitude, and finally the infused grace of charity."[43] Second, there is "the defective use of the natural cognition of God which occurs without faith in the context of injustice, impiety, ingratitude, and finally the direction of the will away from God." In terms of Thomas's theology, the first type of natural knowledge of God corresponds with the virtue of *religio*, a universal possibility only actualized within the grace-sustained community of Christ; the second corresponds with those communities of other believers who are turned "away from God" while still bound by the chains of selfish desire and illusion. What Thomas did not offer in his discussion of religion was a third possibility of "the Enlightenment [which] imagines neutral human beings, neither delivered up to injustice, impiety, and ingratitude, nor religious enthusiasts."[44] Thomas's theology of religion is thus a consistent expression of his Augustinian heritage, at least within the limits of the church's mid-thirteenth century struggle with heresy. If only the Church provided access to the healing powers of grace—and that means the Church "whose head is Christ and whose vice-regent is the Supreme Pontiff,"not any congregation which may choose to call itself Christian—then only the Church provided the context within which the virtue of religion may be realized (*ST* II-II 39,1; also II-II 1, 10).

From Thomas's point of view, his theological insistence upon the actualization of *religio* only within Catholic Christianity was not an invention of himself or his Church. It was simply a reflection of God's rescue mission to fallen humanity. It was God who chose his Son, Jesus Christ, to provide the only means of humanity's salvation. It was Christ

43. I have borrowed the language for these three types of God-knowledge from Rogers, *Thomas Aquinas and Karl Barth*, 157.

44. Ibid.

who chose Peter and his successors to have the sole authority in determining matters of doctrine and faith. In Thomas's view, the conditions of religious monopoly were established by God's initiative, not merely the legal codes of the Holy Roman Empire. Thomas only defined *religio* as a virtue and explained the reasons for its absence in non-Catholic and non-Christian communities. In Thomas's view, it was God, not Thomas, who set the limits and conditions of his healing grace that alone converted the warped heart of believers to make *religio* possible. And it was the universal condition of sin—not some minor moral defect, but Augustine's original sin—that emptied the theological category of *religio* of all candidates but one.

By itself, however, Thomas's Augustinian theological heritage is not sufficient to explain his position. There are, after all, a variety of Augustinian theologies that explicitly identify a variety of non-Christian religions as means of God's healing grace. Karl Rahner, and others who have adopted his "inclusivist" theology of religion, did not have to reject traditional doctrines of sin and grace in order to expand the sphere of God's healing grace to include non-Christian communities of believers. Nor can one explain the single-religion focus of Thomas's theology merely by locating it in the late thirteenth century. As will appear in the next chapter, several different theologians explicitly acknowledged a plurality of religions within a few years after Thomas had written his *Summa theologicae*.

While Augustinian theology plays an essential role in Thomas's theology of religion, it does not provide an adequate explanation of it. For a full explanation, I return to "the Manichees" and Thomas's vocation as a Dominican.

Thomas's Dominican Vocation and the Manichees

By 1269, the Church had been in the business of eliminating the Manichees for about one century. As early as 1119, efforts were already underway to recruit local political authorities to take action to suppress the growing Cathar groups on their territory.[45] While these efforts were not successful, in their intention they were consistent with the military actions of the Albigensian Crusade and the subsequent Inquisition.

---

45. The Council of Toulouse; see n. 4 above.

Thomas's theology was itself one more manifestation of the Church's century long struggle to "settle the Manichees."

However, the Manichean (Cathar) heresy is not a frequent subject of attention in the exposition of Thomas's theology. It would seem as if this human tragedy, perceived as a threat to Catholic truth and the unity of all Europe, had never touched the mind and heart of Thomas. It would also seem as if his Dominican vows were irrelevant to his intellectual labors. Yet, Thomas was quite explicit in identifying the purposes of his *Summa theologiae*: it was to be a theological primer for beginning students, especially for young Dominicans—the same Dominicans who would later serve the Church as inquisitors and preachers whose learning would equip them to convert Cathars back to the Catholic faith.[46] In light of his known devotion to his Order and his faith, it does not seem reasonable to interpret Thomas as if he were a rootless intellectual whose only responsibility was to extend the flow of new ideas to an audience of academics detached from the history in which they live. Thomas wrote for those who would promulgate the Christ whom he loved and who would therefore be enabled to deal with the social disruptions in theological truth and religious unity. Heresies in general and the Cathars in particular were very much a part of his thought. Since, however, this is not usually taken to be the case, I will provide further evidence from his writings.

In his discussion of other believers, the focus of his writing is not Judaism or Islam, but Christian heresies in general, and the Manicheans in particular.[47] For example, a simple word count discloses the dominance of the category of heresy over any of the alternative groups of believers known by Thomas. In all of his writings, his references to the varied religious groups have this frequency:

Judaism	35	(including only *Iudaismus*)[48]
Islam	41	(including Saracens, Moors, and Mahomet)
Pagans	191	(including *paganos* and *gentilitas*)
Heresies	1,972	(including heresy and heretic)[49]

46. "Since the teacher of Catholic truth has not only to build up those who are advanced, but also to shape those who are beginning, the purpose we have set before us in this work is to convey the things that belong to the Christian religion in a style serviceable for the training of beginners" (*Summa theologiae Prologus*/Foreward).

47. Thomas did not use the historical category of Cathars, but consistently identified this heresy as Manichean. I will follow his usage in discussing his critique of this heresy.

The difference in these numbers range from fifty-to-one to ten-to-one. Clearly, it was the urgent historical problem of Christian heresy, not a theoretical consideration of other religions (in the modern sense of that word) that drove Thomas's theology of religion. The task of dealing with heresies in general and the Cathars in particular is one that fell to Thomas in large part because of his role as a Dominican.

Consistent with his preoccupation with heresies, Thomas articulated a double standard for policies directed towards members of sects engaged in some form of superstition. In a general statement concerning the appropriate form of punishment for false forms of worship, Thomas echoed the views of his day:

> We find that in every country the people are wont to show the sovereign ruler some special sign of honor, and that if this be shown to anyone else, it is a crime of high treason. Therefore, in the Divine law, the death punishment is assigned to those who offer Divine honor to another than God. (*ST* II-II 85, 2)

Since all communities of other believers known to Thomas shared some form of false belief or worship, and since such contamination automatically excluded them from the possibility of knowing or worshipping God, all Saracens or Moors, Jews, pagans, and Christian heretics would, in theory, be equally liable to the death penalty for offering "Divine honor to another than God."[50]

In fact, however, Thomas advocated the most severe punishment only for heretics, suggesting a sliding scale of toleration for others engaged in false worship. For example, the rituals of the Jews "may be tolerated [because] their rites foreshadowed the truth of the faith which we hold" (*ST* II-II 10, 11). As for heretics, however, they deserve only excommunication from the Church and death from the temporal authorities.

> [Because of the sin of heretics], they deserve not only to be separated from the Church by excommunication, but also to be

48. Thomas referred to "Jew" and "Jewish" more than 5,200 times, but virtually all of these were references to the Old Testament or the interpretation of its texts.

49. Busa, *Index Thomisticus*.

50. "By false knowledge of God, man does not approach Him, but is severed from Him. Nor is it possible for one who has a false opinion of God, to know Him in any way at all, because the object of his opinion is not God" (*ST* II-II 10, 3).

severed from the world by death. For it is a much graver matter to corrupt the faith that quickens the soul, than to forge money, which supports temporal life. Wherefore if forgers of money and other evil-doers are forthwith condemned to death by the secular authority, much more reason is there for heretics, as soon as they are convicted of heresy, to be not only excommunicated but even put to death.

[While the Church may have mercy for the repentance of one in error], if he is yet stubborn, the Church no longer hoping for his conversion, looks to the salvation of others, by excommunicating him and separating him from the Church, and furthermore delivers him to the secular tribunal to be exterminated thereby from the world by death. (*ST* II-II 11, 3)[51]

Thomas here echoed a papal bull of 1231 that established the guidelines for the secular punishment of heretics: life imprisonment for those who repent; death for those who do not.

This same kind of double standard applied to the use of physical torture for unbelievers. Those who

have never received the faith, such as the heathens and the Jews . . . are by no means to be compelled to the faith. [But as for heretics and apostates, they] should be submitted even to bodily compulsion, that they may fulfill what they have promised, and hold what they, at one time, received.[52]

Heretics thus may be subjected to physical torture, but not members of non-Christian communities. Here also Thomas echoed a papal decision; in 1252 Innocent IV declared that the rector or podesta of a city would be required to use torture to force heretics to confess.[53] Thomas simply confirmed the legitimacy of torture as a means to obtain a true confession of deviant faith from a suspected heretic.

Finally, among the heresies, all are not equally prominent, or equally bad, in the writings of Thomas. Only the Manichean heresy—the

51. Here and elsewhere, Thomas appears to have viewed heresy as a kind of social disease; it was contagious and could undermine the faith of others. Therefore, exclusion from the Church (excommunication) was not sufficient to protect the faithful, if heretics were allowed to mingle with faithful Christians in society.

52. *ST* II-II 10, 8. "The unbelief of heretics, who confess their belief in the Gospel, and resist that faith by corrupting it, is a more grievous sin than that of the Jews [or] that of the heathens, because the latter have not accepted the Gospel faith in any way at all" (*ST* II-II 10, 6).

53. *New Catholic Encyclopedia*, 7:538.

Cathars—was raised as an issue in each of the articles of faith developed in the *Summa theologiae*, from the Being of God through the doctrine of Creation to the Incarnation and Crucifixion.[54] In fact, in all the writings of Thomas, there are as many references to the Manicheans as there are to the combination of Judaism, Islam, and paganism.[55] Furthermore, among all forms of unbelief, the Manicheans were the worst:

> Since heathens err on more points than Jews, and these in more points than heretics, the unbelief of heathens is more grievous than the unbelief of the Jews, and that of the Jews more grievous than that of the heretics, except in such cases as that of the Manichees who, in matters of faith, err even more than heathens do (*ST* II-II 10, 6).
>
> The Manichean heresy is more grievous than the sin of other idolaters, because it is more derogatory to the divine honor, since they set up two gods in opposition to one another, and hold many vain and fabulous fancies about God. It is different with other heretics, who confess their belief in one God and worship Him alone. (*ST* II-II 94, 3)

In contrast with the abundant information about Manichean teachings, readers of Thomas learn relatively little about the practices and beliefs of either Judaism or Islam. For example, the *Summa contra gentiles* restricted its information on the doctrines and rituals of Islam to a recitation of the standard stereotypes circulating in late medieval culture.

1) Mohammed, in his doctrine, his personal life, and the behavior of his followers, was determined by pleasures of the flesh.

> He [Mohammed] seduced the people by promises of carnal pleasure ... and he gave free rein to carnal pleasure ... [and] he was obeyed by carnal men.

2) Islam was intellectually deficient, as were its believers, and its truths were mixed with make-believe. As for proofs of the truth of [Mohammed's] doctrine, he brought forward

> only such as could be grasped by the natural ability of anyone with a very modest wisdom. Indeed, the truths that he taught

54. *ST* I 8, 3; I 63, 5; II-II 25, 5; II-II 94, 3; III 14, 1; III 16, 1; III 37, 1.

55. Specifically, there are 266 references to the Manicheans and 267 for Judaism, Islam, and paganism combined (Busa, *Index Thomisticus*).

he mingled with many fables and with doctrines of the greatest falsity. No wise men, men trained in things divine and human, believed in him from the beginning. Those who believed in him were brutal men and desert wanderers, utterly ignorant of all divine teaching.

3) Mohammed did not vindicate his teachings by miracles but only by force of arms.

He did not bring forth any signs produced in a supernatural way, which alone fittingly gives witness to divine inspiration; for a visible action that can be only divine reveals an invisibly in-spired teacher of truth. On the contrary, Mohammed said that he was sent in the power of his arms—which are signs not lack-ing even to robbers and tyrants . . . [and he used these ignorant believers to] force others to become his followers by the vio-lence of his arms.[56]

4) No prophet of the past foretold the coming of Mohammed.

5) The materials which he borrowed from the Christian Scriptures were distorted by him.

In this litany of accusations, Christian readers of the late thirteenth century would not learn anything new about the religion of Islam; these charges had provided standard fare in Christian polemics since the mid-twelfth century. Yet, on this one page of the *Summa Contra Gentiles*, Thomas provided his most substantive discussion of the reli-gious beliefs and practices of Islam.[57]

The absence of such materials in the *Summa Contra Gentiles* is all the more striking since this text has consistently been viewed as if it had been written for the use of Christian missionaries engaged with a Muslim population in the newly re-conquered territories of Spain.[58]

---

56. *Summa Contra Gentiles*, I 2, 73.

57. Ibid.

58. Tugwell has provided a balanced response to the legend that Thomas wrote the *Summa Contra Gentiles* as an aid to Dominican missionaries working with the Muslim population of newly re-conquered Spain. On the one hand, he rejects the traditional view that Thomas wrote the *Summa Contra Gentiles* for missionary purposes in Spain: "It used to be maintained, on the basis of a fourteenth-century life of Raymund of Peñafort, that the *Summa Contra Gentiles* was commissioned by Raymund to be a text-book for missionaries, but this legend has now been decisively refuted as incoherent and unhistorical." On the other hand, Tugwell allows for the possibility that Thomas wrote the book in response to a request from the Master of the Dominican Order for "a

The only reason this legend could have been taken seriously for so long is because Thomas did discuss, repeatedly and at some length, the philosophical-theological arguments of Averroes, Avicenna, and other Muslim philosophers. From the point of view of a missionary engaged with ordinary Muslims, whose popular forms of belief and worship bore little resemblance to the philosophical issues of interest to Thomas, the *Summa Contra Gentiles* would most definitely not have been a user-friendly text.

As a Dominican, Thomas was far more preoccupied with the Cathar heresy than with Islam or Judaism. These two traditions fell under the strictures of his anti-heretical theology only because, in his view, they also failed to provide that divine grace which alone enabled people to give God the honor that is his due.

Thomas's dualistic theology of religion was thus firmly grounded in his Augustinian theology of the divine-human relationship and his role as a Dominican with responsibility for heretical movements. Without the Cathar threat to Catholic truth, without the obligation of Thomas as a Dominican to respond to that threat, he might have followed the Aristotelian sources for his theology in a quite different direction. It was the combination of a thirteenth century Dominican ministry with an Augustinian theology that, together, shaped Thomas's incipient theology of religion.

Christian theologians who formulated theologies of religion after Thomas will ignore his dualism. They are not interested in heresy within Christendom, but in the expanding world of religions outside Christendom. During the mid-thirteenth century, the religious demographics of the world known to Europeans changed dramatically. In part, this was a result of the Mongol invasion of Europe in 1241–1242 and the subsequent contacts between Europe and Asia. Christendom and the world of Islam, when combined, were suddenly dwarfed in territory and population by the Mongol Empire that at one time extended from the Pacific to the Adriatic. In light of this changed situation, Europeans had to begin the process of rethinking the role of their faith among the newly discovered people and religions of the East.

In part, the religious demographics of Europe changed because of the re-conquest of Spain from Muslim rule. Especially in Aragon–

---

supply of treatises against the errors of unbelievers, heretics and schismatics" (Tugwell, *Albert and Thomas*, 252).

Catalonia, Christian theologians found themselves articulating their faith in a population of which Christians were a minority. Surrounded by Muslim and Jewish neighbors, Christian theologians had to learn, quite literally, a new language if they hoped to share their faith with their non-Christian compatriots. It was in this context of religious diversity in northeastern Spain, its adjacent islands, and in the world at large that a new Christian study of religions was first initiated.

While Thomas lived and wrote after the re conquest of Spain and in the midst of an on-going diplomatic and religious exchange between the Popes and Kings of Europe, on the one hand, and the several Khans of Asia, on the other, these events beyond the borders of Christendom played virtually no role in his theoretical constructs. Thomas wrote from the perspective of his origins in Italy, his service in the Papal court, and his university post in Paris: that is, he was a spokesman for Christendom and the ecclesiastical unity that bound it together. When he appropriated Islamic and Jewish philosophical sources, it was for the purpose of strengthening the intellectual resources of Catholic Christianity against its heretical foes, not for understanding the believing communities from which these texts emerged.

Thomas was himself explicit in recognizing the intellectual limits imposed upon him by his social context:

> To proceed against individual errors ... is a difficult business ... it is difficult because the sacrilegious remarks of individual men who have erred are not so well known to us that we may use what they say as the basis of proceeding to a refutation of their errors. This is, indeed, the method that the ancient Doctors of the Church used in the refutation of the gentiles, for they could know the positions taken by the Gentiles, or at least had lived among the Gentiles and had been instructed in their teaching.[59]

Thomas had not lived among the Saracens or Moors, the Jews, and pagans against whose arguments he wrote in his *Summa contra gentiles*. He could contend with their philosophical arguments, available to him through texts, but he did not have the social experience of living among Muslims and Jews and so had no experiential basis for an understanding of the faith and worship of these communities. The dualistic theology of religion that he constructed reflected his social location

---

59. *Summa contra gentiles*, I 2, 62.

in the Church and the academy, as well as his theological vision and Dominican ministry.

Thomas's Ambivalent Response to Violence

Throughout this chapter, I have focused on Thomas's peacemaking response to the Cathar crisis of thirteenth century Europe. I have consistently interpreted his *Summa theologiae* as a "beginning theology" written for his Dominican brothers responsible for the re-conversion of Cathar heretics to the Catholic faith.[60] Rational persuasion was Thomas's alternative to the methods of organized warfare or physical coercion. In part, my interpretation of Thomas' theology is an effort to correct the all too frequent ahistorical reduction of the *Summa theologiae* to a body of timeless truths. In part, my interpretation reflects my reading of Thomas in the twenty-first century.

The American "war on terror" that initiated this century resembled in some respects the Albigensian war against the Cathars. The murder of an innocent papal legate in the south of France provoked a papal decision to launch the Albigensian Crusade, just as the killing of several thousand civilian workers in New York and Washington set off the "war on terror." In addition, the growing power of the alien Cathar movement posed an increasing threat to the beliefs and values of the Christian tradition, as did the upsurge of Islam in the Middle East, Asia, and Africa. I therefore understood Thomas's theology as offering a Christian alternative to violence. Wars need not be the only or preferred means for resolving such conflicts.

Thomas, however, was not a consistent advocate of nonviolence. He never repudiated the violent means employed by the collusion of Church and government in the Albigensian Crusade.[61] Indeed, he explicitly supported the use of torture by Church inquisitors when required to elicit a confession of heresy. He also defended the obligation

---

60. *ST* Prologue.

61. The differing goals of church and civil authorities in war efforts could lead to undesirable consequences for both parties. For example, French knights from the north were often more interested in expanding the territorial boundaries of French rule than in eliminating the Cathar heresy. Thus, the 1225 Treaty of Paris greatly expanded the territory ruled by France but left intact several significant communities of Cathar believers. Similarly, the king of Aragon who was a fervent Catholic himself and no protector of Cathars was killed by knights from the north while leading a defense of the sovereignty of his rule.

of civil authorities to execute non-repentant Cathari (*ST* II-II 10, 8; *ST* II-II 11, 1). This is why I describe Thomas's response to violence as ambivalent.

Noting Thomas's ambivalence on violence, however, does not provide a twenty-first century reader with a license for dismissing his position. Indeed, I find it difficult to imagine any public Christian response to violence from the Constantinian era that would not be ambivalent. Interpreting Thomas's theology as a nonviolent response to the Cathar crisis also entails a recognition of the multiple constraints of that era.

3

Christians among Other God-Fearers[1]

Ramon Lull's Dialogue of a Christian, Jew, and Muslim

King Louis IX, Thomas's banquet host noted in chapter 2, was best known as a saint and crusader. He led two failed crusades against Egypt. Ramon Lull posed a theological critique of these crusades, "Why do the papacy and Christian princes use force of arms to conquer and convert—thus imitating Muhammad—rather than preaching and martyrdom, the arms by which Christ and the apostles converted the world."[2]

RAMON LULL WAS BORN ABOUT EIGHT YEARS AFTER THOMAS AQUINAS. He and Thomas shared an intense piety and commitment to reason. Shortly after Thomas had completed the second half of the second part of the *Summa theologiae* (1272), Ramon wrote the *Book of the Gentile and Three Wise Men* (1274–1276).[3] The prior chapter of this book focused on Thomas's discussion of *religio* in the second half of the second part of the *Summa*. This chapter focuses on the *Book of the Gentile*,[4]

---

1. I borrow the category of God-fearing from the New Testament (Acts 10:22). It is an inclusive category embracing all those who worship God without sharing a common ethnic or religious identity.

2. Hillgarth, *Kingdoms,* 1:158.

3. For Thomas, see Torrell, *Saint Thomas,* 14; for Lull, see the Bonner volume (below) 1:99–100.

4. Lull, *Selected Works of Ramon Llull.* (In the late twentieth century, Lull scholars, like Anthony Bonner, changed the spelling of Lull's last name from Lull to Llull. In my text I used the older spelling, which at the time of my research I found more useful for identifying translations and studies of Lull's works. However, for the sake of accuracy, I preserved the Llull spelling in all book titles in which it appeared.)

All English quotations from *Book of the Gentile and Three Wise Men* will be from Bonner's critical edition and translation, 1:110–304; page citations will appear in parentheses in the text.

which will give us the opportunity to encounter the quite different minds of these two Christian theologians in works written within a few years of each other and in response to similar issues of religious violence and diversity.

Like Thomas, Lull sought to persuade others of the truth of Christ by a new method of reasoning. Like Thomas, he lived in an era of violence, triggered or exacerbated by religious conflicts. Unlike Thomas, Lull was a literary hero of his island. His huge statue in the harbor still welcomes visitors to Majorca. His many writings, including his popular novels, established Catalan as a written language. He was a man of many talents and much energy.

Lull's father was an officer in the army of King James I whose forces captured the island of Majorca from the Muslim Almohad Dynasty. Lull was born on Majorca where he lived for the first half of his life. While Muslims, Christians, and Jews preserved their identities in separate religious communities under the rule of James, the three groups did not coexist peacefully. Shortly after the conquest of the island, the King had to restrain attacks by Christians on Muslims; he also had to put down a Muslim rebellion.[5] Similarly, while James authorized Christian clergy to preach in special services for Jews or Muslims, such events could not be held in the churches of Christian neighborhoods; such locations proved to be too dangerous for the non-Christian participants.[6]

Early in his career, Lull had a painful personal experience of such religious hostility. After nine years of instruction in Arabic and Islamic texts by a Saracen slave, Lull and his tutor got in an argument. Lull was

---

Copies of *Book of the Gentile* have been preserved in manuscripts of three languages: Catalan, Latin, and medieval French. The Prologue in all three of these, and the Epilogue in the French version, claim that Lull wrote the book first in Arabic and then translated it into Catalan. No Arabic manuscript has survived and there is no agreement among Lull scholars as to whether any ever existed. Bonner based his English translation on the Catalan family of manuscripts; in his judgment, Lull wrote the book in Catalan. He has edited a critical edition of the Catalan text: *Obres Selectes de Ramon Llull* (1:107–272).

One of Lull's followers in Paris translated *Book of the Gentile* into Latin during Lull's lifetime; it is now available in a reprint edition: *Raymundi Llulli Opera omni*, 2:21–114. In order to relate Lull's concepts of religion to Thomas's Latin, I will occasionally cite the Latin text as well as the Catalan in a footnote. For further information on texts and sources, see Bonner's "Introduction" to *Book of the Gentile* (1:100–103).

5. Hillgarth, *Kingdoms*, 1:163.

6. Ibid., 1:166.

told that the unnamed Saracen had blasphemed Christ; in response, Lull struck the man several times. Angered by Lull's abuse of him, the Saracen later smuggled in a sword and attempted to kill Lull. While he wounded Lull in the stomach, in the struggle that followed Lull somehow prevailed and had the man arrested. While imprisoned, the Saracen hung himself. This tragic escalation of violence came to symbolize for Lull the religious situation of Majorca.

Shortly after these events, Lull wrote *Book of the Gentile and Three Wise Men.* The Prologue introduces the religious violence that is a central theme of that book. Lull wrote of "the rancor or ill will among men, who hate each other because of diversity and contrariness of beliefs and of sects" (1:116). This problem of mutual hostility generated by religious conflict is identified again in the epilogue where Lull calls attention to "the difference or contrariety that causes us to be enemies with one another and to be at war, killing one another, and falling captive to one another" (1:301). In *Book of the Gentile,* Lull not only pursued this theme of inter-religious violence, but proposed a means for resolving the conflicts created by religious differences.

Background

While Ramon and Thomas were contemporaries, they lived in different worlds. Thomas lived in the midst of European Christendom and its intra-Christian conflicts. Lull was born and self-educated on Majorca, an island on the frontier of Christendom, where Muslims, Christians, and Jews worshiped in their respective mosques, synagogues, and churches. Thomas was a Dominican, an ordained priest and professor of theology and philosophy. Lull was a Christian layman with a very limited education in philosophy and theology. Because neither Ramon Lull nor his medieval Majorcan setting are well known, I will offer some background on his political-religious context and two decisive turning points in his life.

Majorcan Politics and Religion

From the eighth through the early thirteenth century, the western Mediterranean had been "a Muslim lake" and the Iberian Peninsula had been politically joined to, or dominated by, North Africa.[7] During this

---

7. Lull, *Illuminatus,* 2.

time, Christian kingdoms on the peninsula, such as Aragon, had been investing their foreign energies in protecting or expanding their territory north of the Pyrenees. For example, Peter I, the father of James I of Aragon, allied himself and his forces with the nobility of southern France fighting against Albigensian Crusaders; in 1213 he was killed in battle against the Crusaders from the north.[8] No one questioned the theological orthodoxy of Peter, but he opposed the intrusion of northern French forces into "territory over parts of which he was suzerain."[9] However, the church's hunt for heretics coincided with the kingdom of France's hunt for territory. The 1225 Treaty of Paris that concluded the Albigensian Crusade against the Cathars also delivered territories north of the Pyrenees into the hands of France. About the same time, the Almohad Dynasty that had been ruling much of what is now Spain began to collapse. By 1229, a mere four years after the war against the Cathars had ended, the Aragonese army had refocused its attention from the north to the south where they surrounded the City of Majorca (present-day Palma). By 1248, the tiny kingdom of Granada was the only remnant of the Muslim empire left in Spain.

Even after the Christian conquest of Majorca, however, the island retained its ties with the Muslim world of the western Mediterranean. On the island itself, Christians constituted only a bare majority of the population; 30% to 40% of the population was Muslims; another 5% to 10% were Jews prominent in government, finance, and medicine.[10] In addition, the prosperity of the island depended, in good part, upon its trade with North Africa. Under the rule of James, Majorca was a growing economic hub between Christendom and the Islamic world of North Africa. In its foreign relations, the island was bound by treaties to its trading partners in North Africa.[11] Majorca and the kingdom of Aragon had agreed to defend Egypt and Tlemcen (another North

---

8. Runciman, *Medieval Manichees,* 142.

9. Ibid., 141.

10. If Muslims surrendered their city peacefully to the Christian army of James I, he guaranteed them their safety, property, laws, and religious practices (James I, *Chronicles,* 2:540–41). The importance of their economic roles, especially in managing irrigation and the production of textiles, also established their value for James' growing kingdom (Hillgarth, *Kingdoms,* 1:171–82). As a result, every territory conquered and ruled by James retained a large Muslim population. For religious demographics, see Lull, *Selected Works,* 1:9.

11. Hillgarth, *Kingdoms,* 1:155–56.

African state) if attacked by a Christian crusade. North African states, in return, offered hospitality to the consulates of Majorca, employed the island's soldiers as mercenaries, and trans-shipped the goods arriving by camel caravan from the East to Majorca for forwarding to Europe. Both Majorca and North African states agreed to protect the trading fleet of the other.[12] Ramon thus lived on the edge of Christendom in a world that was, in many ways, more Muslim than Christian.

Lull's "Conversion" and Illumination

As the son of an officer in the army that conquered the City of Majorca in 1229–1230, Ramon's family were minor aristocrats. Lull identified himself as a knight. As a young adult, he married, fathered two children, served as household manager for James II, and engaged in "licentious activities" and the composition of love poems. This was his life until age 32.

While working on one of his love poems, the crucified Christ appeared to Lull, not once but during four or five nights in a row. He successfully ignored most of these visions except for the last. Then he finally realized that "God wanted him, Ramon, to leave the world and dedicate himself totally to the service of Christ"[13] (1:13–15). Lull identified this event as a "conversion to penitence." As in the case of St. Paul, Lull's conversion brought with it a specific missionary charge: namely, "the task of converting to His worship and service the Saracens who in such numbers surrounded the Christians on all sides[14] (1:15). Later, Lull became clear that his newly acquired missionary vocation included three specific components.

> 1. To accept dying for Christ [martyrdom] in converting the unbelievers.
>
> 2. To write the best book in the world against the errors of unbelievers.

---

12. Ibid., 1:159.

13. All citations to Lull's autobiography, *Vita coaetanea* or *Contemporary Life,* refer to Bonner's translation, Lull, *Selected Works,* 1:13–48 and are provided in parenthesis in the text, not footnotes.

14. *Contemporary Life* also appears in Lull, *Doctor Illuminatus,* 11–41. "Saracen" originally referred to a group of desert peoples living between Saudi Arabia and Syria. For medieval Christians, it referred to all Muslims regardless of their ethnic identity or origins. As in Lull's quote, the term was also a political-military category: "the Saracens who in such numbers surrounded the Christians on all sides."

> 3. To procure the establishment of monasteries where the languages of Saracens and other unbelievers could be learned so that, from among those properly instructed, the right people would be ready to be sent out to preach and demonstrate to the Saracens the truth of the Catholic faith in their own tongue (1:13–16).

In the five decades between his conversion in 1263 and the writing of his autobiography in 1311, Lull did manage to achieve, in good part, these three goals. To achieve his third goal, he made repeated journeys throughout Christendom—to Paris, Rome, Genoa, and Pisa—urging popes, bishops, universities, monastic orders, city councils, and wealthy Christian laymen to sponsor centers for the linguistic training of missionaries. He did persuade James II to establish Miramar, a seminary on Majorca that provided instruction in the Arabic language as well as other subjects. In 1311 he played a similar role at the Council of Vienne, which adopted his proposal for a lavish set of university positions in Arabic and other languages.

For his first goal, he made repeated journeys to proclaim Christ in several cities in North Africa, in spite of his intense fear of the dangers in such a venture. He expected to be killed by acting so boldly, and once he was so immobilized by fear that he could not board the boat to Africa. His commitment to risk his own life in preaching and debate with Saracens, and his repudiation of killing others, was a significant part of his Christian identity. As noted in the epigram of this chapter, Lull imagined

> the Sultan of Egypt sending a mission to the pope to remark how strange it was that the pope and Christian princes used force to conquer the Holy Land—thus imitating Muhammad—rather than preaching and martyrdom, the arms by which Christ and the apostles converted the world.[15]

According to legend, on the last of his many journeys to North Africa, when he was in his eighties, he was stoned to death in Bougie (in present Algeria), but it now appears that he was only evicted. By this time, the expanding empire of Aragon-Catalonia-Majorca had enough mercenary troops, merchants, and consulates scattered throughout the North African cities in which Lull carried out his missionary activities to make expulsion a more prudent policy than killing the empire's

15. Hillgarth, *Kingdoms*, 1:158.

best known author. He apparently died on the voyage home. He was not quite a martyr, but he was certain that Christians shared their faith by a willingness to die and not by the killing of others.

It was the second task that proved to be the most puzzling, for Lull and for the scholars who have studied Lull's writings. Ramon wondered how he could write the "best book in the world against the errors of unbelievers" since "he had scarcely learned more than a bare minimum of grammar and since he could conceive neither the form nor manner of writing such a book" (1:15). After Lull's conversion experience and before his European travels, writing, and missionary journeys around the Mediterranean, he engaged in a nine-year program of self-education, almost all of which occurred on Majorca. As a center for higher education in Christian and Islamic studies, Majorca suffered from some serious deficiencies, even when judged by the standards of that time: it had no university, no seminary, no monastery with a house of theological studies (such as the Dominican houses in Italy where Thomas taught theology), and very limited library resources.[16] Ramon's resources for "writing the best book ever written" were limited not only by his own education but also by the educational resources of Majorca.

In his autobiography, Lull recounted the solution God provided for his limited education and resources on Majorca:

> Ramon went up to a certain mountain [Mount Randa] … where it happened that one day while he was gazing intently heavenward the Lord suddenly illuminated his mind, giving him the form and method for writing the aforementioned book against the errors of the unbelievers. (1:22)

Lull immediately left the mountain and went to an abbey "where he began to plan and write the book in question." This divine illumination happened approximately nine years after the "conversion to penitence," or about 1274 when Lull would have been 42 years old.

While Lull developed his "Great Universal *Art* [Technique or Method] for Finding Truth" in many of his writings after 1274, he never provided any hint as to the written source or sources that might have informed his construction of this new method. Through most of the

---

16. The Cistercian monastery on the island included some *magistri* as early as the 1230s, but no theological students until after Lull had completed his self-education (see Johnston, "Introduction," in *Evangelical Rhetoric of Ramon Llull*). Its library included many condensed versions of theological and philosophical literature.

intervening centuries, the identity of a written source for Lull's new way of thinking remained a mystery, lost in his nine-year transition from conversion to illumination. Later I will return to the question of Lull's unidentified source(s).

Book of the Gentile and Three Wise Men

Book of the Gentile is a complex piece of writing, surely one of the most unusual forms of Christian theology ever created. At one level, it reads like a novel, as if it were written in the magical realism style of modern Latin American literature. Lull was, in fact, not only a philosopher and theologian, but an author whose novels played a significant role in establishing Catalan as a written language.[17] At another level, *Book of the Gentile* offers an account of an inter-religious dialogue among a Jew, a Christian, and a Muslim. Lull identifies these three as "wise men" and each of them is an intellectual representative of his particular religion. Lull's new philosophical method is another dimension of his book.

In addition, the *Book of the Gentile* offers a mostly accurate account of thirteenth century Islam in the Western Mediterranean. Lull may be one of the first non-Muslim Islamicists who sought to educate a broad readership about that religion. Finally, the book is also an example of Christian apologetics addressed primarily to Muslim readers. Indeed, many of Lull's arguments for his Christian faith may be especially alien to readers of the twenty-first century precisely because they were constructed to appeal to Muslim readers of the thirteenth century.

Through each of these dimensions—narrative, dialogue, philosophical method, Islamic studies, and Christian apologetics—Lull is laying the foundation for a new Christian understanding of Judaism and Islam as religions similar to, and different from, Christianity. He repeatedly presents his new method of understanding these religions as an alternative to the violent rhetoric and inter-religious conflict characteristic of his own society.

I will examine Lull's new approach to religions by exploring each of these five dimensions of his book.

---

17. *Felix* and *Blanquera* are two of his better-known novels; for English translations of these novels, see the bibliography.

Narrative Framework

Extending from the Prologue through the Epilogue, and embracing four books of philosophical-theological arguments in between, a narrative provides the literary framework for *Book of the Gentile*. It also sets forth Lull's ideal of inter-religious relationships.

THE PROLOGUE

The story begins in the Prologue that introduces its varied characters and plot. The main characters are the Gentile and a Jew, a Christian, and a Saracen, Lull's three wise men. None of these four have proper names; they are all representatives of different constituencies in Lull's world. The identity of the Jew, Christian, and Saracen is somewhat obvious. Each of them represents one of the religious communities of Majorca. Unlike Thomas, who limited the application of his category of *religio* to the Christian community, Lull identified all three of these God-fearing communities as religions, but only these three.[18] Communities that did not worship God, for example the Tartars whose beliefs were both polytheistic and idolatrous, did not count as a religion for Lull.

The identity of the Gentile is not as obvious. His geographical and cultural origins are the best clues that Lull provides. The Gentile comes from a distant land where no one knows anything about God or a resurrection; that means, the Gentile is a pagan whose home is within neither Christendom nor the world of Islam. From Lull's other writings, we can infer that this Gentile is a Mongol, or in the medieval vocabulary of Lull, a "Tartar."[19] Since Lull consistently described the Tartars as the

18. Lull used the concepts of law (*lex* in Latin; *lig* in Catalan) and sect (*secta* in Latin; *secte* in Catalan) as generic categories of religion. See footnotes for examples of Lull's use of *lex/lig* and *secta/secte* in Latin and Catalan editions of *Book of the Gentile*.

19. The Gentile, who came from a distant land without knowledge of God or a resurrection, represented for Lull the vast populations of Asia ruled by the Mongol Empire: "for every Christian there are a hundred or more that are not Christian" ("*Petitio Raymundi*," 2:174–75). The "Tartars," as Lull called them, always had a special place in his missionary vision because there were so many of them and because they "had no religion" ("Tartari non habent legem") and were open to receiving Christian missionaries, and because if they did not become Christian, they would become Muslim and pose new threats to Christendom ("*Petitio Raymundi*," 2:174–75). Their presence in his writings spanned the whole of his career, and he traveled as far as Cyprus on a missionary expedition to the Tartars after he learned (falsely) that they had conquered the whole of the Kingdom of Jerusalem. In *Doctrina pueril*, he described the Tartars as "a people without religion (*lex*), who have no knowledge of God . . . some of whom wor-

most numerous people on the earth, this demographic fact is not irrelevant to his narrative:"their emperors have lands of more than twice
the extent of those of Christian and Saracen rulers together."[20]

In his distant home, the Gentile became depressed when he thought
about his future: as he aged, his bodily pleasures would diminish, his
illnesses would increase, and he would have to live with the certainty
of his own death. To escape from such apprehensions, he decided to
travel to distant lands, seeking some distraction of beauty or grandeur
that could free his mind, at least temporarily, from his anxiety for his
future. But alas, while he discovered many new sights and wonders of
the world, none relieved him of his despair. By the time he met the three
wise men, his inner condition had become etched into his bodily appearance: he is emaciated, with unkempt hair on face and head, and
eyes sick from incessant weeping.

Each of the three wise men had gone alone for a walk in the woods.
They meet by chance and have a joyful reunion since they are friends
who enjoy each other's company and who enjoy discussing their favorite subject, religion. One is a Jew, one a Christian, and one a Saracen.

Lull creates a fantasy context for the characters and plot of his
story. The Gentile and the three wise men meet each other by chance
in a grove of five flowering trees. Each of the flowers is inscribed with

ship idols, others the sun, moon, and stars, others birds and beast, others the elements"
(cited in Lull, *Selected Works*, 1:111). In *Book of Contemplation* (1272), written in the
same period as *Book of the Gentile*, he described the religious practice of the Tartars
in these same terms: Tartars know nothing of God but "adore the sun and beasts and
serpents" (cited in Peers, *Ramon Llull*, 71). In *Book of the Tartar and the Christian*, the
Tartar also knows nothing of God or any life beyond the death of the body (*Opera omni*
4:367). Like the Gentile in *Book of the Gentile,* this Tartar initiated his religious quest in
response to the terrifying prospect of death. Like this Gentile, Lull gave him the same
professional identity: a man "wise and learned in philosophy" (*sapiens & eruditus in
Philosophia*) (Ibid.).

Anthony Bonner rejected any identification of Lull's Gentile with the "more or less
primitive peoples" of the Mongol Empire (Lull, *Selected Works*, 1:111 n. 7) because
Lull portrayed the Gentile as "very learned in philosophy" (1:111) and "a master of
philosophy" (1:197). However, that is the same role Lull assigned to the Tartar in *Book
of the Tartar and the Christian* (1:285–86). Lull could cast his Tartars as philosophers
whenever it suited his literary purposes, and in *Book of the Gentile* the philosophical
element of the Gentile's identity is a necessary fiction because, by Book IV, the Gentile
becomes engaged in a philosophically effective critique of the Saracen's arguments. The
Gentile in *Book of the Gentile* may represent ethnic groups in addition to the Tartars,
but he must be at least a Tartar.

20. *Disputatio Raymundi christiani et Hamar saracenci.*

a pair of words. None of the three wise men have any idea as to what these words mean or their purpose. Fortunately, there is a beautiful lady watering her horse in this grove of five trees. She tells the wise men that her name is Intelligence. She also teaches them how to understand the concepts disclosed in the trees' flowers. The purpose of all the flower-laden words is to teach them how "to love, know, fear, and serve God." Lull thus uses this magical setting as a means of introducing his new philosophical method. All three of the wise men are persuaded by Lady Intelligence to adopt her instruction for understanding the language of the flowers in their conversations concerning the truth of religion. They all express their confidence in the great benefits that would be enjoyed by all people willing to think through issues of religious truth by this new method.

> "Ah! What a great good fortune it would be if, by means of these trees, we could all—every man on earth—be under one religion and belief, so that there would be no more rancor or ill will among men, who hate each other because of diversity and contrariness of beliefs and of sects![21] And just as there is one God, Father, Creator, and Lord of everything that exists, so all peoples could unite and become one people, and that people be on the path to salvation, under one faith and one religion, giving glory and praise to our Lord God."
>
> "Think Gentlemen," the wise man said to his companions, "of the harm that comes from men not belonging to a single sect, and of the good that would come from everyone being beneath one faith and one religion. This being the case, do you not think it would be a good idea for us to sit beneath these trees, beside this lovely fountain, and discuss what we believe, according to what the flowers and conditions of these trees signify? And since we cannot agree by means of authorities, let us try to come to some agreement by means of demonstrative and necessary reasons."
>
> The other two agreed to what this wise man had said . . . and they decided to hold their discussion according to the manner the lady indicated to them. (1:116)

---

21. "Under one religion and belief" appears in Catalan as "en una lig e en una creeça" and in Latin as "in una lege & in una fide." "Because of diversity and contrariness of beliefs and sects" reads in Catalan "per desvariació e per contrarietat de creences e de sects" and in Latin "propter diversas fides & contraries leges diversorum populorum" (*Obres Selectes* 1:113 and *Opera omni* 1:225).

In the remainder of the Prologue, the three wise men meet the despairing Gentile and agree to prove for him the existence of God and a resurrection, using the flowers on the trees and instructions from Lady Intelligence.

Before proceeding with this narrative, I want to note some of its unusual features.

1. The friendship of the Jew, Christian, and Saracen. Their mutual respect and appreciation of each other were, for Lull, the opposite of the mutual inter-religious animosity that he deplored. Lull's version of personal relations across religious boundaries on Majorca, while idealized, was based upon the extensive interactions among members of differing religious communities. The government of King James did not enforce a variety of church laws, including a ban against the practice of non-Christian religions, required differences in dress, and restrictions in business, professional, and social relations.[22] As a result, forming friendships across religious boundaries was not impossible.

2. The new method of thinking about religious differences was not presented as a product of any particular religion. To the contrary, none of the three wise men had any clue as to the meaning or use of the word-inscribed flowers. All three wise men were depicted as the passive pupils of Lady Intelligence. It is the authority of the new method she introduced to them that would govern their future debates on religion. Lull is here introducing the role of reason as a norm for religious truth that is distinct from every particular religion.

3. In the words of the wise men, Lull discloses his preoccupation with the necessity for one religion. This is the only way Lull can imagine a cure for the problems of religious conflict. Like Thomas, Lull lived in an age of religious monopoly, not only as a desired condition but one that would be enforced by political authority, when necessary. In the case of Majorca it is clear from the writings of King James I and the island's subsequent history, that the

22. Hillgarth, *Kingdoms*, 1:167–73. Lull's fictional inter-religious dialogue had its analog in social reality. In 1266, Alfonso X of Castile founded a college in the newly conquered territory of Murcia for the purpose of brining together scholars of the three religions (Urvoy, "The 'Ulama' of al-Andalus." 874).

Constantinian principle of one state, one religion was normative there also.[23] After the Christian conquest of Spanish territory, James and his successors expected Muslims and Jews to convert to Christianity in large numbers. To hasten this process of conversion, in 1299 James authorized Lull to preach in the synagogues of the Jews on Saturdays and Sundays and in the mosques of the Saracens on Friday and Sundays.[24] The religious diversity of the late thirteenth century was accepted only as a temporary condition. When it had not disappeared two centuries later, the political expulsion of Jews and Muslims became the solution to the problem of religious diversity. Majorca, along with all of Spain, eventually did achieve Lull's desired goal of one religion, not by the peaceful recognition of reason that he proposed, but by the coerced exclusion of all non-Christians.

Book I

The three wise men proceed to develop their arguments proving the existence of God and the reality of a resurrection. Some of their proofs concerning the existence of God would be familiar to Thomas.[25] During the whole of Book I, as in the Prologue, Lull does not differentiate the three wise men from each other. Their differing identities as Jew, Christian, and Saracen are subsumed into a common identity as exponents of the new rational method of Lady Intelligence. They take turns in developing arguments to prove the existence of God and a resurrection.

As expected, their joint efforts are successful. Near the end of Book I, the Gentile has been transformed:

23. James's response to a Saracen rebellion in his newly acquired territories suggested the limits of his support for the continuing religious practice of Muslims. "It pleases me much, for if, on account of the treaties made with the Saracens I did not drive them out of this country, should they now have done anything owing to which I should be justified in driving them out, I would be delighted to be the means of destroying them entirely and their accursed sect, and that those temples where the name of Mohammed has long been proclaimed and invoked should be retrieved for the faith of Christ" (*Chronicles*, 2:475–76).

24. See Bonner's "Introduction," in Lull, *Selected Works*, 1:38 n. 42.

25. For example, the first proof focused on differing degrees of size, goodness, being, etc. which corresponded with Thomas's proof by gradations (the fourth of Thomas's five proofs for the existence of God) (1:120).

> . . . a divine radiance illuminated his understanding. He felt his
> soul unburdened of the torments and sorrow which error and
> lack of faith had so long and grievously tormented him. Who
> could recount the joy and happiness the Gentile felt, or tell you
> of the blessing he bestowed on the three wise men? (1:147)

The Gentile is so overcome with gratitude to God for the illumination of his mind that he decides to share his joy with family and friends
in his homeland, where people know nothing of God or a resurrection.
He therefore begs the three wise men to teach him their doctrine, which
each offers to do, but alas! Their doctrine is not the same.

> "What?" cried the Gentile. "Are the three of you not of a sin-
> gle religion and belief?" "No, for one of us is a Jew, the other a
> Christian, and the other a Saracen." "And which of you," asked
> the Gentile, "has the better religion, and which of these religions
> is true?" (1:148)

For the latter questions, each wise man replied in a differing way and
they began to argue, "speaking one against the other" (1:148).

By the end of Book I the Gentile has recovered from his shock and
the wise men have regained their composure. They agreed to a debate
for the Gentile so that he and they might determine "which of them was
on the true path and which in error."

At this point, the narrative has set the stage for the inter-religious
dialogue that follows. Each of the three wise men will now present
the salient beliefs of his religion and, following the directions of Lady
Intelligence, each will develop arguments to support those beliefs: the
Jew in Book II, the Christian in Book III, and the Saracen in Book IV.

Before proceeding through these beliefs and arguments to the
inconclusive conclusion of the Epilogue, let me call attention to some
changes in Christian reflection on religions suggested by the plot developments of Book I.

1. The Gentile has been converted and his life transformed, but to
   what religion? Not Christianity, Judaism, or Islam for the three
   wise men did not introduce the particularities of any of their faiths.
   They spoke in Book I only of matters they shared in common.

2. Nevertheless, the results of their common presentation are quite
   impressive, especially since the Gentile appears to be a represen-

tative of the largest known population of religionless humanity.[26] Even though the Mongol Empire was a long distance from Majorca, Lull wrote extensively on the need for a unified Christian missionary approach to the Tartars.

3. The ability of these three representatives of differing religions to convert the Gentile also discloses the similarity of these religions. They are not only different from each other; they are also alike each other. While all this happens in a fictional narrative with no known historical antecedents, it does signal a significant turn in the Christian understanding of religions. In the writings of Thomas, any comparison of the Christian religion with other believing communities only establishes their total and profound differences, such as the superstitious practices or heretical beliefs of non-Christians. In contrast, Lull's narrative implies a common religious core, shared by the three God-fearing religions of Majorca, to which the Gentile is converted.

Epilogue

The Epilogue begins with the Gentile once again in prayers of thanksgiving, repentance, and rejoicing. After he completes his lengthy prayers, he tells the three wise men that he is ready "to select and choose that religion which, by the grace of God and by your words, seems to me to be true" (1:300). But just then, he is distracted by the appearance of two of his countrymen, and he begins to share the news of his new religion with them. The three wise men take the opportunity of this distraction to depart. They do not wish to know the Gentile's decision. Instead, they wish to leave open the question of which of these three religions he judged to be true.

> We should debate and see which of us is in truth and which in error. For just as we have one God, one Creator, one Lord, we should also have one faith, one religion, one sect,[27] one manner of loving and honoring God, and we should love and help one another, and make it so that between us there be no difference or contrariety of faith or customs which difference and contra-

26. See n. 19 above.

27. Catalan and Latin of this phrase are as follows: one faith (una fe; unam fidem), one religion (una lig; unam legem), one sect (una secta) (*Obres Selectes* 1:269; *Opera omnia*, 2:931). The Latin translation dropped "one sect." Lull, *Selected Works*, 1:301.

> riety cause us to be enemies with one another and to be at war,
> killing one another and falling captive to one another. And this
> war, death, and servitude prevent us from giving the praise, rev-
> erence and honor we owe God every day of our life. (1:302)

They then make plans to return to the grove of five trees and word-inscribed flowers in order to discuss matters of religious truth according to the manner that Lady Intelligence showed them.

Lull concludes his narrative with the three wise men's words of farewell to each other.

> They took leave of one another most amiably and politely, and
> each asked forgiveness of the other for any disrespectful word
> he might have spoken against [the other's] religion. Each for-
> gave the other. (1:303)

This is not the typical ending of religious dialogues in the ancient and medieval worlds. None of the wise men give up their religion for the sake of another religion in the course of the dialogue. The Gentile is the only convert in the group, and by the end Lull even refrains from telling his readers which religion he chose as true. None of the religions were caricatured and made an object of ridicule. Each of the three wise men—the Jew, the Christian and the Saracen—asked for the forgiveness of the others in case he had offended their religion.

Inter-Religious Dialogue

In the inter-religious dialogue depicted in *Book of the Gentile*, Ramon Lull has his three fictional participants agree to exclude from consideration any appeal to "community-specific self-guaranteeing authorities."[28] Instead of appealing to one of the textual authorities of any religion, they agreed to seek the truth only by means of "demonstrative and necessary reasons" (1:116), as instructed by Lady Intelligence.

Later in *Book of the Gentile*, Lull illustrated the kind of confusion created for inter-religious conversation by assuming a normative role for the scriptures or doctrines of any one religion. For example, the Jew spoke of the misunderstanding created by the texts of the Torah in the

---

28. In his 1991 book on the necessary role of apologetics in interreligious dialogue, Paul Griffiths proposed a series of rules for such activity. One of these rules required participants to exclude from their dialogue any appeal to "community-specific self-guaranteeing authorities" (Griffiths, *Apology for Apologetics,* 82–83).

Hebrew Bible, even though all three religions appeared to accept the Law of Moses.

> We and the Christians agree on the text of the law, but we disagree in interpretation and commentaries, where we reach contrary conclusions. Therefore, we cannot reach agreement based on authorities and must seek necessary arguments by which we can agree. The Saracens agree with us partly over the text, and partly not; this is why they say we have changed the text of the law, and we say they use a text contrary to ours. (1:170)

As another example, the Christian identified his religion's doctrines of the Trinity and Incarnation as sources of confusion and misunderstanding for both Saracens and Jews.

> The Jews and Saracens do not understand the Trinity in which we believe, and they think we believe in another trinity different from the one we really believe in, one that does not exist in God, and this is why we cannot agree with them, nor they with us. (1:217)

> We [Christians] do not believe that Incarnation which [the Jews and Saracens] think we believe, and our belief in the Incarnation of the Son of God is different from what they imagine, and as a result we cannot agree and are opposed because of differing opinions. (1:233)

In these examples, it is apparent that the scripture or doctrine of any one religion provided no basis for agreement on issues of truth across religious boundaries, but instead contributed to the division among religions. As a result, before beginning their dialogue in *Book of the Gentile*, Lull's three wise men agreed to exclude the authoritative claims of their differing scriptures and doctrines for the purposes of their inter-religious conversation.

> Since we cannot agree by means of authorities, let us try to come to some agreement by means of demonstrative and necessary reasons. The other two [unidentified wise men] agreed to what this wise man had said. And they sat down and began to study [the new method of reasoning to which they had just been introduced] and they decided to hold their discussion according to [this] manner. (1:116)

Lull's introduction of the five magical trees and Lady Intelligence re-enforces the exclusion of any particular scripture and doctrine from a normative role in inter-religious dialogue. Unlike the three wise men, Lady Intelligence does not represent any religious community or its self-guaranteeing authorities.

The three wise men also adopted two other rules for their dialogue. When one of the wise men is explaining or defending the beliefs of his community, none of the other two wise men will "raise objection to what he said, nor contradict the other, since contradiction brings ill will to the human heart and ill will clouds the mind's ability to understand" (1:149). As a result, their dialogue does not take the form of an exchange between them but is more like a series of monologues, interrupted only by the Gentile's questions. Only the Gentile was allowed to question the speaker's arguments, "the better to seek the truth about the true religion."

By themselves, the three wise men could not agree on the order of their presentations. Hence, they all accepted the suggestion of the Gentile that they speak in the historical order of their religion: "which religion [came] first."

Finally, they agreed on a two-stage procedure for their presentations. Each would set forth the major articles of faith in his religion and then, using the word-inscribed flowers of the five trees and the conditions prescribed by Lady Intelligence, each would construct arguments in support of that belief. Lull thus recovered the particular scriptures, doctrines, and mediating figures (Moses, Jesus Christ, and Mohammad) for inclusion in this inter-religious discourse. However, the particularities of each religion are presented as the subject matter whose truth needed to be demonstrated; they were not themselves to function as normative.

Neo-Platonic Philosophical Theology

While the intellectual representatives of Jews, Christians, and Muslims may have bracketed out the normative role of their particular doctrines, scriptures, and founders, they were not left empty-handed. All three religions shared a belief in one God, Creator and Lord of history. They also shared, in somewhat different versions, a belief in a future resurrection. Finally, several thirteenth century forms of these three God-fearing religions shared a Neo-Platonic cosmology that included a distinctive version of God's role as Creator.

According to this Neo-Platonic theology of creation, God sustained and renewed the whole of finite reality by means of several primordial causes or divine agencies. Creation, therefore, is not an event in the distant past, but a continuing activity of each present. The divine agencies active in creation are somewhat like Plato's "Ideas" except they are not merely the pre-existing passive forms of finite entities, but the active source and formative power of such entities.

Furthermore, these primordial causes provide the occasions through which humans come to recognize God. Lull could bracket out the normative authority of all particular revelations of God (Torah, Jesus Christ, Qur'an) because he believed that all people are immersed in an unending flow of events that are potentially revelatory. People need only pay attention to the continuing creative activity of these divine causal agencies in finite forms and wait upon God's grace for a disclosure of God's presence.

Lull's *Book of the Gentile* provides ample illustrations of this Neo-Platonic philosophical structure of his thought. However, readers need to heed the warning that he gives in the Prologue to his book. He has written *Book of the Gentile* for a lay audience. As a result, in this book, he will avoid the technical language required of any science ("obscure words unfamiliar to laymen"), but in a later work, he will use "this same method but with words more appropriate to men of letters, lovers of speculative science." In other words, in *Book of the Gentile*, we will meet only a partial version of Lull's philosophical theological structure as expressed through his narrative.[29]

Thus, in the magical garden of five trees and word-inscribed flowers Lull introduces us to the plural agencies of creation in the flowers of the first tree. He calls these forms of divine energy God's "essential uncreated virtues."[30] They are seven in number and their names are inscribed upon the flowers of the first tree:

29. In later technical explications of his *ART*, Lull articulates an ontology that is directly reflected in his epistemology. The mind thinks in terms of the reality beyond it. He also locates the multiple agencies of creation on a moving wheel in relation to another wheel bearing the four elements of nature.

30. "Uncreated" is a technical term used in Islamic Kalam theology to identify the ontological status of the Qur'an (Chejne, *Ibn Hazm,* 294). Lull intended these "uncreated virtues" to bear a revelatory status similar to that of the Qur'an for Muslims. For

Goodness, Greatness, Eternity, Power, Wisdom, Love, and Perfection[31]

For Lull these divine energies or powers have a dual ontological status. On the one hand, they are the active forces sustaining and creating the world in which we live. For that reason, they are not distant from the human mind, even if their proximity is not always recognized. On the other hand, they exist in the mind of God, in the Divine Logos. They are therefore as essential to God's existence as to the world's existence. As one of Lull's wise men noted,

> By the above-mentioned six [word-inscribed] flowers we have shown and proved God's existence, and by proving God's existence, we have proved in Him the existence of the above-mentioned flowers [the seven uncreated virtues], without which God could not have existence. Now since He exists, it necessarily follows that the flowers, that is to say, His virtues exist. (1:123)

While Lull's wise men set out to prove only two articles of faith (God's existence and a resurrection), in fact they proved three: the existence of God's "essential uncreated virtues" as well as the existence of God and a resurrection. For these active uncreated virtues are embedded in both the finite beings of the world that they sustain and in the mind of God.

Before following the Gentile on his path of divine revelation and transformation, I need to note briefly the Lull research of the past fifty years that informs my interpretation of his philosophical-theological framework. In my prior discussion of Lull's experiences of conversion and illumination, I noted an unanswered question in Lull studies: namely, what were the written sources that shaped the structure of Lull's thought? While it seemed obvious that the combination of Lull's limited education and the limited library resources of Majorca did not equip him to construct single-handedly the complex system he called the "Great Universal *Art* [Technique or Method] for Finding Truth," the identity of such sources remained a mystery until the last half of the twentieth century. Then in 1960, Dame Frances Yates established Lull's continuity with the ninth-century philosophical theology of

---

the doctrine of an uncreated Qur'an, see the article "Kalam," *Encyclopedia of Islam,* 4:469.

31. In later writings, Lull changes the name of these creative agencies from "essential uncreated virtues" to "Divine Dignities" and increases their number from seven to nine or sometimes, an unspecified number.

John Scotus Eriugena as developed in his book *Periphyseon* or *De divisione naturae.*[32] But how could Lull on Majorca have gained access to Eriugena's text? It was never widely circulated, it had been written four centuries before Majorca came under Christian rule, and in 1225, Pope Honorius III had condemned the few extant copies of it to be burned.[33] In her essay, Dame Frances suggested that Lull may have discovered this Greek theological version of Neo-Platonism not directly from the writings of Eriugena, but from Honorius Augustudensis' *Clavis physicae,* an abbreviated paraphrase of Books I–IV and literal transcription of Book V of *De divisione naturae.*[34]

Basic to Lull's newly adopted philosophical position is Eriugena's theological Neo-Platonism that he developed from his reading of the Greek Church Fathers, especially Origen, Basil, Maximus the Confessor, and Gregory of Nyssa.[35] This tradition included a fluid cast of divine energies active in the continuing process of God's creation. Eriugena identified these powers of creation by a list of varying names: "what the Greeks call *idéai,* that is, the eternal species or forms or immutable reasons and therefore they were named exemplars . . . and divine volitions . . . and the principles of all things.[36] In addition, "primordial causes" was the name for these powers most frequently used by Eriugena and hence, I have followed this usage in my exposition of Lull's adaptation. These primordial causes are not only the passive model for all finite objects,

32. Yates, "Ramon Lull and John Scotus Erigena."

33. Eriugena's book was condemned because it had become a favorite of heretical groups. The Cathari loved it; indeed, Dame Yates even suggested that the last surviving Cathar leaders (the Perfects) may have brought a copy with them in their 1244 flight from Montségur over the Pyrenees. The court of Majorca and the courts of Languedoc were in frequent contact, including marriage The Almaricians were another heretical group that had adopted Eriugena's text for their cause.

34. Two later publications established the accuracy of Dame Yates' suggestion concerning the means of transmission of Scotist philosophy to Lull. In 1974, Paola Lucentini published an edition of *Clavis physicae;* and in 1989 Jordi Esterlich Gayà used that edition to demonstrate that *Clavis physicae* was indeed the means through which Lull encountered Scotist philosophy (Gayà, "Honori d'Autun i Ramon Llull."). I am indebted to Anthony Bonner for bringing the Gayà article to my attention and sharing an offprint of it with me.

35. In the ninth century, Eriugena was one of the few Latin theologians still reading Greek. His theological NeoPlatonism was rooted not in the writings of Plato, Plotinus, or other philosophers of the ancient world, but in the Greek fathers. He was the translator of Pseudo-Dionysius as well as the author of *Division of Nature.*

36. Eriugena, *Periphyseon,* 228–29.

preformed in the mind of God before any actual objects were created, but they are an active presence in all objects, sustaining them in their existence. These "primordial causes" thus serve as the ontological glue that binds to God all finite forms of being.[37]

Because these primordial causes are now actively engaged in world-building, persons rightly instructed and focused upon certain aspects of the finite world may discern, through the medium of certain finite forms, one or more of these uncreated virtues at work. This is why Lull's magical grove includes an additional four trees that bear flowers inscribed with the names of the seven created virtues (three theological and four classical) and seven vices (seven deadly sins). Here, as elsewhere, Lady Intelligence provides guidance for relating the finite virtues or vices to the uncreated virtues of God. The greater and nobler of the created virtues are those that "most strongly symbolize and demonstrate the uncreated virtues" (1:114). In other words, by contemplating the goodness of a saint, the mind may be opened to perceive the uncreated virtue of God's Goodness. Similarly, "everything which causes the virtues of God to be better represented to the human understanding by means of the vices should be affirmed" (1:115). Even the most despicable expressions of human behavior may become the locus for the disclosure of one of God's uncreated virtues. Perceptions of finite goodness or evil thus provide Lull's three wise men with a new "text" that could disclose God's goodness or other uncreated virtue.

However, such an act of contemplation by itself is never sufficient to apprehend one of God's uncreated virtues. Both Eriugena and Lull presuppose an epistemological limit built into the hierarchical order of being. By our own reason, humans cannot understand those forms of being which are of a higher order than ourselves. In Eriugena's language, "the primordial causes are completely inaccessible to all things of which they are the reasons"; in Lull's language, "the intellect in the thing created [cannot understand] the way in which God makes something out of nothing"(1:165).[38] Knowledge of any of the uncreated virtues, therefore, cannot depend solely upon human initiative and the capacity of reason.

---

37. "All things whatsoever that are perceived or understood whether in the visible or in the invisible creation subsist by participation in [these primordial causes], while they themselves are participations of the one Cause of all things, namely, the most high and holy Trinity" (ibid., 229).

38. Ibid., 30.

However, because God does not wish people to be ignorant of their origins and destiny, God has arranged for the primordial causes of creation, present in all of the visible and invisible creation, to disclose themselves to rational souls. This is the revelatory event that Eriugena named a "theophany" and that Lull identifies as an action of God's grace.[39] At the end of Book I, after the Gentile has heard and understood the many shared arguments of the three wise men, only then "did a divine illumination illuminate his understanding" (1:146–47). In the case of the Gentile, as in the case of Lull himself on Mount Randa, it is only through such a divine intervention of illumination that the human mind could come to recognize one of God's uncreated virtues, These uncreated virtues not only sustain the cosmos and continue God's creative activity into every present, but they also provide the occasions for humanity's knowledge of God that brings with it a new self-understanding. As in the case of the Gentile, the past becomes an occasion for repentance; the future offers new opportunities for praising and honoring God, and instructing others in God's ways. In the epilogue, after the Gentile has heard the differing articles of faith and supporting arguments from each of the three wise men, he is moved to address a long series of passionate prayers to God. While they are mostly prayers of thanksgiving, he does not offer these prayers to God alone, but also to each of God's uncreated virtues that provided the occasions for his recognition of God. These uncreated virtues become personifications of the divine, manifestations of God that need to be recognized and thanked and praised along with God.

I will identify each virtue cited in the Gentile's prayer by printing it in bold type:[40]

> To you holy **Goodness**, O Lord, I give reverence and honor;
> to it I attribute and give thanks for the great happiness I have
> received.

---

39. "And yet anyone who might say that in the intellects of the angels there are certain theophanies of those reasons, that is to say, certain [divine] manifestations which are comprehensible to the intellectual nature, but which are not the reasons, i.e. the primary exemplars themselves, will not, I think, stray from the truth" (Ibid.). Lull did not include Eriugena's category of theophany in any of his writings.

40. The Gentile's prayers fill six pages of text. Some of the Gentile's prayers come directly out of Lull's own life with no basis in the Gentile's story: "May it please you God to let not leaving one's wife, sons, daughters, friends, or worldly possessions . . . banish from my heart the thought of your honor" (1:299).

> Lord God, I adore and bless Your **Greatness** . . .
> Glory and praise be given to Your **Eternity**, O Lord, . . .
> Lord God, that **Power** You possess . . . I worship and fear and honor above all other powers.
> Your **Wisdom** O Lord, I love and worship with all my physical and spiritual strength.
> That **Love** of yours, O Lord, I worship and love, and . . . I give everything, O Lord, to serve and honor and praise Your Love every day of my life.
> Divine **Perfection**, You who are the light and cure of all imperfections . . . to You I turn and to You I ask forgiveness and grace, and counsel and help as to how to serve You and to recover, through You, the days I lost through ignorance and wrongdoing. (1:294–95)

In Lull's version, his newly appropriated Christian philosophy carried within itself the powers of its own piety. Lull presents the new faith of the Gentile as a faith that is open to persons from all traditions and cultures: those who have already learned of God through one religion or another, like the three wise men, and those who know nothing of God, like the Gentile.

By the time the Gentile offers the prayer cited above, he has already decided which of the three religions he will choose. Furthermore, as will shortly be apparent, there are good reasons to presume that the chosen (though not disclosed) religion of the Gentile is Christianity. One would not suspect such a choice from his prayers, however. They are as devoid of any mark of religious particularity as was the first round of instruction by the three wise men, when they proved to him only the existence of God, God's uncreated virtues, and a resurrection. The reader can only conclude that the Gentile has had certain religious experiences that he understands as encounters with one of God's multiple virtues at work in the continuing creation of the world. His prayers do not express the particularity of Christian instruction concerning the trinitarian identity of God or God's incarnation in Jesus Christ.

JEWISH AND SARACEN USES OF NEO-PLATONIC IMAGERY

In the Western Mediterranean of the late thirteenth century, both Judaism and Islam had developed complex theological positions that were as indebted to a Neo-Platonic worldview as was the philosophy of Eriugena and Lull. In particular, the primordial causes of Eriugena or the essential uncreated virtues of Lull played a prominent role in both Cabbalistic Judaism and Islamic Sufism. The *sefiroth* of the Jewish *Zohar* bear sufficient resemblance to Eriugena's primordial causes to have led scholars to suspect some influence of *The Division of Nature* in the construction of the *Zohar*.[41] Lull's new method and the Zohar originated in a common cultural context. The texts for the Zohar of the Jewish Cabbala were first assembled about the same time that Lull wrote *Book of the Gentile* and originated in the small town of Gerona, a major center of Jewish thought in the kingdom of Aragon-Catalonia-Majorca.[42] Early in his career Lull had come in contact with this Jewish movement through his relations with two rabbis in Barcelona.[43] It is not surprising that he would embrace the Christian philosophy of Eriugena as a way of bridging the differences between his own faith and Cabalistic forms of Judaism.

Similarly, many Islamic theologians also employed a Neo-Platonic ontology and epistemology similar to those of Eriugena and Lull. Ibn al-Arabi (1165–1240), one of Islam's greatest Sufi masters, has been identified as a possible source for Lull's new method.[44] Without necessarily accepting that claim, it is apparent that Ibn al-Arabi's theological positions were strikingly similar to those of Eriugena and Lull.[45] God in his essence is unknowable, as in the negative theology of Eriugena and Lull. The Names of God for Ibn al-Arabi function like the primordial causes of Eriugena or the uncreated virtues of Lull. They provide

41. "[Pierre Duhem] was so much struck by the coincidences between the Zohar and Eriugena's doctrine that [in his *System du Monde*] he suggested that the Cabalists who wrote it were familiar with the Scot's work" (Yates, *Lull and Bruno*, 111).

42. "The writings published by the school of Cabbalists whose center was the little Catalan town of Gerona . . . did more than any other contemporary group to unify and consolidate what was pregnant and living in the Cabbalism of Spain" (Scholem, *Major Trends in Jewish Mysticism*, 153 and 170).

43. Hillgarth, *Ramon Lull and Lullism*, 18.

44. "Ibn al-Arabi may have had some influence also on medieval Europe, notably on the Catalan missionary Raymond Lull" (*Encyclopedia of Islam*, 3:711).

45. For Ibn al-Arabi's theology, see Chittick, *Sufi Path of Knowledge*, 33–44.

the ontological bond between the Essence of God and the contingent world. They are also the means through which humans gain knowledge of God. As in Eriugena and Lull, the plurality of these Names (or causes or uncreated virtues) exist only in relation to the knowing mind, not within the Essence of God. Many of these names are identical to those used by Lull.

Without going into too much detail, it would be possible to construct a lengthy list of parallel or identical positions taken from the writings of Lull and Ibn al-Arabi. On the basis of his familiarity with Muslim Sufis, Lull had good reason to believe that the Sufi tradition of Islam would find his new method as congenial to their views of God as would Cabbalistic Jews.

Lull thus envisioned these ontological intermediaries between God and humanity as a new locus of revelation that could be recognized by Jews, Christians, and Saracens. The scriptures and traditions of these three religions would then be validated or repudiated on the basis of this new common norm. In their relative comfort with God's uncreated virtues and the new method of Lady Intelligence, the Jew and Saracen in *Book of the Gentile* were culturally credible as idealized versions of a Cabbalistic Jew and Sufi Muslim.

Islamic Studies

In his study of a religion other than his own, Ramon Lull pursued a series of procedures and disciplines still basic to the study of religions. Language study provided him with the foundation for his studies of Islam. His competency in Arabic allowed him to read the Islamic scriptures, commentaries on such scriptures, and Islamic theology in their original language. He knew enough of the Qur'an by heart to quote some of its texts from memory and he was sufficiently familiar with the basic beliefs of thirteenth century Muslims to construct an accurate exposition and defense of their faith by his Saracen "wise man." To be sure, he was an amateur Islamicist: his opportunity to study with Islamic scholars was either non-existent or very limited. It would therefore be a mistake to idealize Lull as if he were a great scholar of Islam. It would be a more serious mistake to ignore his role in initiating a new tradition of Christian reflection on religion, one that included a disciplined study of a religion other than one's own.

Lull as an Arabist

Lull's only known teacher during his nine-year self-education program was the Saracen slave he purchased to teach him how to read, write, and speak Arabic. Lull, apparently, did not have a comparable tutor in Latin, with the result that he is the only medieval Christian theologian whose mastery of Arabic exceeded his abilities in Latin. While none of Lull's texts written in Arabic have survived in their original language, there seems to be no reason to doubt that all, or large parts of, at least nine of his books were first composed in Arabic, including the lengthy *Compendium on the Logic of al-Ghazzali*.[46]

Apparently, his mastery of written Arabic even extended to calligraphy. In a discussion of one of Lull's later manuscripts, the Sultan of Fez was reported to have praised Lull for the quality of his Arabic writing, as well as his mastery of the language.[47] From indirect evidence, it appears that Lull had learned to think in Arabic. In translating his own writings, he characteristically moved from an Arabic original into a second version in Catalan, not the other way around. In his Catalan or Latin writings, he would sometimes cite and explain Arabic terms, and he once defended his unusual Latin verb-forms as required by the *modus loquendi arabicus*.[48] In every dimension of Arabic, Lull had earned the identity he chose for himself: a *Christianus arabicus*.

---

46. Two of Lull's first three books were written completely or partially in Arabic: *Compendium on the Logic of al-Ghazzali* and *Book of Contemplation* (Lohr, "Christianus arabicus," 60). Bonner lists nine texts written in Arabic (Lull, *Selected Works*, 1:19 n. 74). Lohr identifies an additional three texts written in Arabic (ibid., 60). Lohr also believes that parts of the *Book of the Gentile and Three Wise Men* were written in Arabic, though Anthony Bonner disagrees with this judgment.

The disappearance of Lull's Arabic manuscripts may reflect the linguistic transition from Arabic to Catalan in much of the Western Mediterranean. Except for the territory of Valencia on the Spanish mainland, Catalan had replaced Arabic as the *lingua franca* by the last decades of the thirteenth century.

47. Lohr, "Christianus arabicus," 60.

48. Ibid.

Lull's Version of Islam

The Saracen wise man in *Book of the Gentile* articulates a particular form of Islam that Lull derived from several sources. It is different from the Islam then dominant on the Spanish mainland. A fictional Saracen from that location would have had to be more concerned with matters of Islamic jurisprudence and perhaps with Sufism. Both of these traditions of Islam are noted in the exposition of Lull's Saracen, but only in passing or as a dubious form of the faith. Lull's Saracen represents a combination of rational theology and scriptural orthodoxy. The scriptures of Islam, meaning in the case of this Saracen, both the Qur'an and the Proverbs of Mohammad or the *Hadith,* provide the sources for the twelve "articles of faith" that he teaches the Gentile. The Saracen repeatedly informs the Gentile that his beliefs are derived from these sources: "Since in this discussion we have agreed to talk as briefly as possible, I have therefore told you concisely what our Prophet Mohammed says in the Qur'an and what our wise men say in their commentaries upon our Law (1:274, also 1:287 and 1:292).[49] However, the sacred source of these beliefs is not sufficient to establish their validity in an inter-religious discussion or even within the Islamic community itself. Majorcan Muslims were the beneficiaries of a long theological tradition emphasizing the necessity for rational proof for articles of faith. Since these folks were, in part, Lull's hoped for readers, it is this popular form of Islam dominant on the island of Majorca that Lull's Saracen presents and defends.

Fortunately, the theological heritage of Majorcan Islam has been the subject of sufficient study to identify its primary characteristics and their theological sources. In the eleventh century, Ibn Hazm, the greatest Islamic theologian of the Iberian Peninsula, had spent ten years in Majorca, and a group of his followers continued his teachings to the time of the island's conquest.[50] In the twelfth century, the Almohad religio-political movement became the ruling power in Spain and gained control of Majorca at the beginning of the thirteenth century. Its founder, Ibn Tumart, was also an advocate of theological rationality. Both Ibn Hazm and Ibn Tumart gave a prominent role to Qur'anic

---

49. In writing the phrase "what our Prophet Mohammed says in the Qur'an," Lull commits a theological error of considerable magnitude. From Islam's point of view, such a claim is blasphemy, since it is not Mohammed, but God who speaks in the Qur'an.

50. Urvoy, *Penser l'Islam,* 41–71. Lohr, "Christianus arabicus," 79–82,

studies and the rational discernment of faith.[51] As a result, the core of Majorcan Islam at the time of the island's conquest consisted of studies in the Qur'an and *Hadith* and the rational theology of *Kalam*.[52] Since the Muslims known to Lull had been formed in this tradition, he consistently presupposed this form of Muslim believer: one who expected the articles of faith to be derived from the Qur'an and *Hadith* but established by reason.[53]

In addition to these Islamic theological traditions in Majorca, Lull also had two additional sources that informed his creation of the Saracen wise man. As part of his self-education program, Lull had worked his way through al-Ghazzali's early work, *Maqasid al-falasifa* (*Aims of the Philosophers*)[54] as the source for his own book, *Compendium on the Logic of al-Ghazzali*. In *Aims of the Philosophers*, al-Ghazzali presented an orderly exposition of rational arguments used for establishing religious and metaphysical truths; it was something of a textbook, and contained nothing of al-Ghazzali's critique of these arguments. His repudiation of such rationalist arguments appeared only in a subsequent work, *Tahafut al-falasifah* (*Incoherence of the Philosophers*) (1095). Apparently, Lull never knew *The Incoherence of the Philosophers,* and he therefore presupposed al-Ghazzali's continuing commitment to the construction of proofs for religious and metaphysical claims, as if al-Ghazzali were an advocate of *Kalam* theology.

A second source for Lull's strong commitment to the role of reason in the life of faith was rooted in his Christian commitment to the

51. Ibn Hazm used the category of "necessary demonstrations" (*barahin daruriyya* in Arabic, *rationales necessariae* in Latin) to signify a rational proof for an Islamic doctrine, much like the Qur'anic *burhan* signifying a 'a shining light from God" (Lohr, "Christianus arabicus," 80–81). Urvoy has summarized the Almohad ideology as follows: "It represents a radical attempt to provide a rational basis for belief: the elements of dogma are developed solely according to the dictates of reason" (Urvoy, "The 'Ulama' of al-Andalus," 868). For the theological similarities of Ibn Hazm and Ibn Tumart, see MacDonald, *Muslim Theology*, 245–49.

52. *Kalam* literally means Word of God, but it is also a shorthand phrase for a particular kind of apologetic theology, one that stressed the rationality of religion. The form of *Kalam* is that of a debate in which opposing views are stated, answered, and built upon.

53. Consistent with this model of Islam, the Saracen in *Book of the Gentile* will repeatedly identify his sources as the Qur'an and Hadith, and then proceed to prove by reason the truth of these beliefs.

54. This al-Ghazzali book was known in the medieval West as *Metaphysics* or *Philosophical Tendencies*.

conversion of Saracens. In a half-dozen variations, Lull told the story of Raymon Marti, a Spanish Dominican missionary to the Muslims, who purportedly convinced by reason a ruler in North Africa to abandon the claims of Islam because they were false. In his novel *Felix*, Lull told the story as follows:

> The king then asked the monk to prove to him by necessary reasons that the Christian faith was true, in which case he would convert to Christianity and be baptized, and he would place his country under the dominium of the Holy Church. The monk replied that he could not demonstrate it to be true by necessary reasons. The Saracen was most displeased with the monk's reply, saying that he had done a bad thing in taking him away from the Saracen faith, in which he had always believed, if he could not give him necessary reasons concerning the Roman faith. The king told him that if he could not give him understanding of the Christian faith, he would make him die a cruel death. The monk fled, and the king died in error.[55]

Whether true or false, this story represented for Lull the source of the failure of Christian missions to Saracens. In order to correct the inadequacy of this approach, Lull was committed to proving the truth of all Christian faith claims, including the doctrines of the Trinity and the Incarnation. His method of proof was heavily indebted to the *Kalam* tradition of Islamic theology.

This theologically conservative mix of textual studies and *Kalam* theology did not make Majorca hospitable to Sufism. Sufism was more prevalent in the Spanish mainland, but much less popular on the island. Nevertheless, from the eleventh through the thirteenth century, there was a steady stream of individuals connected to the island by birth or ancestry who had embraced the Sufi way.[56] Lull would have known of the writings and reputations of these Sufi masters, as well as their questionable status among ordinary believers in Majorca. Lull's Saracen seems to acknowledge the ambiguous status of Sufism for typical Muslims of Majorca.[57] While Lull's Saracen recognizes that there are some scholars who do not believe in a literal Paradise, he makes it clear that such views are deviant "Others say that in Paradise there will be no glory of eating

55. Lull, *Selected Works*, 2:693–94.

56. Urvoy, *Penser l'Islam*, 48–50.

57. Lohr "Christianus arabicus" 64.

or of lying with women ... And these men are natural philosophers and great scholars,[58] yet they are men who in some way do not follow too well the dictates of our religion (1:292).[59]

In contrast with his Saracen, Lull was not only sympathetic with the position ascribed to the "natural philosophers" in this text, but also felt a close kinship with the mystical theology, ascetic life style, and disciplined contemplation characteristic of the Sufi movement. For Lull, if not for the majority of Muslims in Majorca, the rationality of *Kalam* and the mysticism of Sufism belonged together in one theology.

Lull's Saracen presents twelve articles of faith derived from the Qur'an and *Hadith*. Lull also introduced his Christian readers to the devotional life of Muslims. Before the Saracen began his exposition of Islamic articles of faith, Lull had him first enact prayers and rites for purifying himself and acknowledging the greatness of the God of whom he would speak:

> When the Saracen saw that the time and hour had come for him to speak, he went to the spring and washed his hands, his face, his ears, his nose, and his mouth, and afterwards he washed his feet and other parts of his body.... Afterwards he spread a cloth on the ground[60] and knelt three times, touching his head to earth and kissing the ground; then, raising his heart, his hands, and his eyes heavenward, he said: "In the name of God the Merciful, the Mercifying, to whom all praise be given, since He is Lord of the world—Him I adore and in Him I trust, for He leads us on the straight path of salvation." And the Saracen spoke many other words, as was the custom in his prayers. (1:258)[61]

In contrast with the derogatory picture of Muslim faith characteristic of medieval Christian theology, Lull frequently presented the Saracen as a model of piety, one to be emulated by Christians. The Saracen's reticence

58. For the identification of the unspecified "natural philosophers and great scholars" with Sufism, see Lohr, "Christianus arabicus," 64.

59. "Dictates of our religion" in Catalan is *manaments de la lei nostra* and in Latin *praecepta nostrae legis* (*Obres* 1:262; *Opera omni* 2:109).

60. The ablutions performed by the Saracen in this ritual of purification constituted a necessary action prefatory to prayer, as prescribed by the Qur'an 5:6. The cloth spread on the ground functioned as a prayer rug and the invocation spoken by the Saracen was a loose version of the *Opening* of the Qur'an that Lull apparently wrote from memory.

61. Lull, not Bonner, translated Allah as *Déu*, the Catalan word for God.

to speak of God without prayerful preparation is, for Lull, an appropriate behavior for all God-fearing believers, Christian or Muslim.

In summary, Lull pursued the study of Islam by first gaining a high level of competency in the Arabic language, as is evident by his writing texts in that language and by reports of his public debates with Muslim opponents. In this process, he gained sufficient familiarity with the Qur'an to quote portions of it from memory, as in the opening prayer of the Saracen. He also learned enough from the *Kalam* theology of his era to borrow some of its methods of reasoning for his own Christian apologetics.

Christian Apologetics

Throughout the several dimensions of *Book of the Gentile*, Lull has been writing as an apologist for the Christian faith. His strategies varied, but his goal was the same: to persuade Jews and Saracens, especially the Saracens, that their faith was, on the one hand, very much like the Christian faith, but on the other hand, had some serious defects which could be corrected by Christian doctrine. Saracens and Jews, in his view, were already almost one with their Christian brothers; this is why the three wise men could convert the Gentile to the unidentified common religious core that these three communities of God-fearing believers shared. Lull's depiction of the similarity of the three religions and the friendly respectful relations of the three wise men provided a model for good civic behavior and, even more important, the inclusive relation of Jews, Christians, and Saracens provided a necessary first step towards the goal of one religion.

Lull's narrative therefore stressed the respectful relations of the three wise men, not only to each other but to the religion of each They were portrayed as engaging in cordial conversation in the beginning, and at the end, Lull had them apologize to each other for any offense that may have inadvertently been spoken against any one of the religions. In the middle of this narrative, Lull's narrator reports the importance of such mutual respect in inter-religious dialogue, and the negative consequences of any religious contradiction or conflict: "it was agreed among the three wise men that none would contradict the other while he was presenting his arguments, since contradiction brings ill will to the human heart, and ill will clouds the mind's ability to understand" (148–49).

Except for the brief squabble near the end of Book I, there was no point at which any of the three wise men contradicted one of his peers. In virtually all of their interactions with each other, the relationships among the three wise men are cordial and respectful as they confidently explore their new method leading to religious unity and truth.

Contemporary readers of Lull need to recognize his Christian purposes in creating such an inter-religious environment. During the reign of James I, Lull, like the King and many of the Franciscans and Dominicans who had newly arrived on the territory of Aragon-Catalonia-Majorca, expected Jews and Muslims to be absorbed gradually into an expanded form of Christianity. While they may have respected the superiority of Arab-Jewish culture as a culture, they had no doubts concerning the saving truth of Christianity. For Lull, like James I, it was only necessary to correct by education the mistaken versions which Jews and Muslims held of Christian doctrine and to point out some of the theological deficiencies of the faith of the Jew and the Saracen; after making such corrections, all would be baptized and become full-fledged Christians and first-class citizens of Aragon-Catalonia-Majorca.

Lull's minimizing of doctrinal divisions and maximizing of common moral concerns resembles in many respects the inter-religious strategy of American Protestants during the nineteenth century. Like them, Lull intended to enlarge Christianity from a position of strength, not by confronting others with teachings peculiar to it, but by appealing to values and cultural symbols shared by all. In brief, Lull served his Christian purposes by highlighting the shared beliefs in One God, a resurrection, a Neo-Platonic worldview, and a set of moral ideals held in common by Jews, Christians, and Muslims in thirteenth century Majorca.

As is apparent, however, Lull's narrative, is only one dimension of this book. The respectful interaction of the three religious scholars may have served one strategy for Christianization, but in this book, Lull also directed a sharp polemic against its primary target, the religion of Islam. The spokesman for this polemic, however, was not the mild-mannered, agreeable Christian wise man, but the Gentile.[62] According to the rules of this inter-religious dialogue, the Gentile was the only one of the four participants who had the right "to answer their arguments

---

62. In his critique of Islam as well as in his account of conversion, the Gentile provided Lull with the most direct expression of his own voice.

as he saw fit" (1:150). By having the Jew and Christian speak first, the Gentile gradually became familiar with their method of argumentation, the word-inscribed flowers of the five trees, and the directions of Lady Intelligence. As a result, by the time the Saracen presented his beliefs, the Gentile philosopher had become a skilled participant in this ecumenical debate. His role of philosophical critic in Book IV was consistently different from his role as eager learner in Books I through III.

For example, the Gentile almost always posed questions of information or clarification to one of his unidentified teachers in Book I, or to the Jew and Christian in Books II and III. In Book IV, however, the Gentile posed philosophical objections to the Saracen's arguments. He had quickly mastered the method of proving one proposition by establishing the "impossibility" or "absurdity" of its opposite. Only in his dialogue with the Saracen did the Gentile use this method to refute the arguments of one of the wise men; in the rest of the book, this method of reaching the truth by establishing the absurdity of its opposite was reserved for the wise men themselves. Only in his dialogue with the Saracen did the Gentile appeal to the word-inscribed flowers of the five trees and the directions of Lady Intelligence; in the previous exchanges between the Gentile and one of his teachers, this was an activity only of the wise man. Only in the dialogue of the Gentile and the Saracen were six of the Gentile's objections left unanswered, leaving the impression that the Saracen had no reply. In contrast with the placid narrative of *Book of the Gentile,* in which all three religions are treated respectfully and as equals, the Gentile in Book IV leaves the reader with the clear impression that the Saracen's religion, when judged by the rational norms of the flowers on the five trees and Lady Intelligence, is most definitely deficient.

While *Book of the Gentile* did not disclose the identity of the victor in the debate of the three wise men. Lull did tell his readers in a later book whose religion seemed to the Gentile to be most true. In *Book of the Lover and Beloved*, written only ten years after *Book of the Gentile,* Lull wrote: "'Say, fool, how do you know the Catholic faith is true and what the Jews and Saracens believe is false and wrong?' He answered: 'from the ten conditions in the *Book of the Gentile and Three Wise Men.*'"[63]

---

63. Lull, *Book of the Lover and the Beloved,* 226.

4

Christians and Other Religions

Nicholas of Cusa's Vision of Global Religious Peace

> Religious rites vary according to place and time.
> Such diversity gives birth to hostility, hatred and
> war.
>
> —The Tartar in *De pace fidei*, 1453

Constantinople: 1453

THE PEOPLE OF CONSTANTINOPLE WERE, FOR THE MOST PART, CONFI-
dent in the security of their city. To be sure, they knew that the Ottoman
Turks had already occupied much of the territory around them. They
also knew that their own city had lost its political influence and was
commercially in the service of their enemy. But it was still a city made
safe by its formidable defenses.

They guarded their harbor with a mammoth chain which, when
extended and supported by wooden floats, prevented any maritime access to the Golden Horn. With this protection, no enemy could enter
the harbor to attack the city by sea. By land, the city was protected by a
fourteen-mile-long complex of two, or in places three, layers of walls.
Within the city, 2,000 Latin forces supplemented 5,000 Greek troops.
Beyond these natural resources, the Christians of Constantinople also
trusted in their supernatural allies: the Mother of God, whose holiest
icon was paraded through the streets in times of crisis; St. Constantine,
founder of the city; and an anonymous angel, scheduled to descend to
the cathedral, Hagia Sophia, to deliver the faithful if the Turks should
ever penetrate their city's defenses.

The Turks invaded Constantinople on the night of May 28, 1453.
The siege had lasted about seven weeks. Mehmed II employed the latest

military technology to conquer the apparently impregnable city. To circumvent the chain across the Golden Horn, he built large oxen-towed carts capable of carrying his ships, one after another, up and down the hills behind the neutral city of Pera. The people of Constantinople had the unnerving experience of watching the masts of a small navy "sailing" over the land. To destroy the walls on the landward side of the city, Mehmed employed the services of a Hungarian gun engineer named Urban. Urban had previously offered his super-cannon to the Byzantine Emperor who had neither funds nor interest sufficient to retain his services. So, the monster cannon went to the Turks: more than twenty-seven feet in length, with a barrel whose walls were eight inches thick, it fired a 1,200-pound boulder more than a mile and with force sufficient to make a hole in the ground six feet deep. It was a new weapon designed for breaking down impregnable walls.

In addition to this technical equipment, Mehmed had an army of more than 80,000 troops who could be rallied for battle by a mix of religious and economic motives. The night before the assault on the city, a group of dervishes and imams traveled from camp to camp, proclaiming the inevitability of Allah's victory over the infidel Christians. Mehmed himself visited these same camps, promising his soldiers freedom to pillage the city. Indeed, the riches from the sacking of Constantinople were so great that long after its conquest, Turks would identify a man of wealth as a descendent from one of those who looted Constantinople.

On the night of May 28, the Divine Liturgy was celebrated in the cathedral to a full house. It was Constantinople's only service in which the advocates of union with the Latin Church (as set forth at the Council of Florence) and their more numerous and vociferous opponents worshiped peaceably together. The cathedral was also the sacred space that seemed to promise safety, the place where the promised angel would descend to deliver the faithful.

The Turks, however, did not know this belief, and merely used their axes to cut open the huge wooden doors. Once inside, each soldier gathered up as many Christians as he could handle, binding them together in pairs, then removing them from the church for safe-keeping as slaves, and coming back for more. In the capture of these individuals, there was no discrimination between nuns and monks, priests and laypeople, scholars and city officials. The cathedral itself was desecrated. The Turks stripped all gold, silver, and jewels from the icons and the altars. The altars themselves became tables for the soldiers to eat upon, and after they were finished, tables for their horses to feed upon. Altars also became beds for raping young women, as well as boys and girls. Those who offered protests were blinded or beheaded. Outside the church, the blood of slain citizens flowed in streams down the streets and a fire burned rare books and manuscripts of both classical and theological literature. As Aeneas Sylvius Piccolomini (the later Pius II) observed, this was "the second death of Homer and Plato."

By the afternoon of May 29, Mehmed arrived in the cathedral and ordered a stop to the destruction of baptismal fonts, altars, and other furnishings. He also ordered an imam to enter the pulpit and pronounce, for all to hear, the Muslim creed: there is no God but Allah, and Mohammed is his prophet. By the first week of June, Mehmed had begun to restore order on the city streets, arrange for its governance, and define the rights and limits of Christians living in a quasi-state within a state. Those who escaped the city by sea, however—mostly some Venetians and Genoese—only knew about events in the first three days, and this is what they reported to their officials back home in Europe.[1] From the responses of European Christians, it is apparent that the messengers were not that interested in the new military technology employed or other aspects of the siege. Rather, they reported the orgy of violence that befell the Christians in the city, along with other violations of their shared faith in Christ. That was the focus of the news that reached Europe. Christians there were preoccupied with a horror that appeared to be the result of hostilities generated by religious differences.

In response to this news, three popes of the late fifteenth century called for a crusade to right the wrongs perpetrated by the Muslim enemies in Constantinople. Their efforts failed, in part because Europeans were exhausted by their own wars against each other, and in part because the newly emergent capitalism made trade a higher priority than faith. By the end of June, just one month after the occupation of Constantinople and one day after the news of its capture reached Venice, the Privy Council of that city had dispatched an ambassador to the new Sultan to establish trading relations.

---

1. Three sources provided information on the fall of Constantinople: Doukas, *Decline and Fall of Byzantium,* provided a contemporary, and often eyewitness, account, along with Runciman, *Constantinople 1453,* and Babinger, *Mehmed the Conqueror.*

In mid-July, soon after the news reached Venice, Nicholas of Cusa learned the fate of Christians in Constantinople. He was then a newly installed bishop in Brixen (now Brixen-Bressanone just north of Bolzano in northern Italy). The first line of his work, *De pace fidei*, reads: "After the brutal deeds recently committed by the Turkish ruler at Constantinople were reported to a certain man ..." (I.1)[2] For a variety of personal and spiritual reasons, these events in far-off Byzantium were especially painful for Nicholas. He knew the city personally. He had traveled there only fifteen years before its capture. He had made friends there among both Latin and Greek Christians. And he had received his "gift from God," the spiritual experience formative for his future thought and faith, while sailing home from Constantinople in the company of Greek Christians. In a classic understatement, he continued the sentence quoted above by identifying himself as a mere tourist, "a certain man, who had once seen the sites of those regions" (I.1).

What Nicholas found most disturbing in the news he heard was the role of religious differences as the cause of such brutalities. "With many sighs he implored the Creator of all things that in his mercy he restrain the persecution, raging more than ever because of different religious rites" (I.1). He prayed so intensely, and for such a long period of time, that "a vision" was finally revealed to him. It was a vision of a heavenly assembly, a global inter-faith gathering under the tutelage of God Almighty, the Word, Peter, and Paul. News of the Constantinople disaster had already reached the heavenly court.

> The King of heaven and earth stated that the sad news of the groans of the oppressed had been brought to him from this world's realm: because of religion many take up arms against each other and by their power either force men to renounce their long practiced tradition or inflict death on them. There were many bearers of these lamentations from all the earth. (I.2)

In the realm of heaven, as in the mind of Nicholas, the brutalities of Constantinople were symptomatic of a problem of even greater import than the suffering of Christians and the loss of Christendom's second capital: namely, the role of religion in inflaming human passions to maim and to kill.

---

2. All quotations from *De Pace Fidei* (*The Peace of Faith*) are from the Biechler-Bond Latin/English edition. Further citations are in the text.

This was, for Nicholas, the meaning of Constantinople. For him, July-August of 1453 was not the time to organize retribution; it was the time to construct a new model of world peace, one that would be based upon the faith of multiple religions. To discern a solution to the problem of religiously inspired violence, it would not be adequate to limit attention to the conflict between Islam and Christianity; such a solution had to take account of all known religions. And this is what Nicholas delivered through the unlikely medium of a heavenly vision, one that begins with tales of suffering Christians and a heavenly interreligious gathering "of a few wise men familiar from their own experience with all such differences which are observed in religions throughout the world" that could establish harmony and "a lasting peace" (I.1).

A Christian Theology of Religion

"Theology of religion" was obviously not a specialized discipline of the fifteenth century; it is a sub-discipline of Christian theology that first flourished in the twentieth century. By linking this kind of reflection with Nicholas, I do not wish to claim that he was a man so far ahead of his age as to be a child of the twentieth century. In identifying some of his writings with a "theology of religion," however, I do claim that the questions he asked, the concepts he used, the religious data he considered, and the methods he pursued are congruent with a theology of religion, especially as articulated in the late twentieth and early twenty-first centuries.

I interpret Nicholas as a transitional theologian, neither medieval nor modern, but both. Accordingly, his thought exemplifies the theme of greatest prominence in his theology: the coincidence of opposites. On the one hand, his thought is consistent with the Christian Neo-Platonism of his medieval past; on the other hand, his theology of religion is congruent with the work of many "modern" contemporaries. Indeed, I would claim Nicholas to be the "founder" of a Christian theology of religion. However, unlike many of his modern successors, Nicholas presented his new theology of religion as a witness to the peace of Christ; it was not a witness to the relative equality of all religions.

The strongest evidence of Nicholas's kinship with contemporary theologians of religion is his use of *religio* as a generic category. As noted in an earlier chapter, Thomas Aquinas used *religio* only in the singular, as in *religio christiana*. Raymon Lull and other medieval theologians used *secta* in the plural, but not *religio*. For example, Roger Bacon compared the *sectae* of the Hebrews, Chaldeans, Egyptians, and Saracens, along with the sect of Christ and the sect of the antichrist.[3] Of necessity, any theology of religion requires some kind of generic category that can include the Christian religion along with whatever other religions were known at the time. By definition, every theology of religion is (at least) post-medieval because an unambiguous generic form of *religio* did not exist in medieval theology.

Nicholas of Cusa was the first post-medieval Christian theologian known to us who used *religio* as an all-inclusive category. For him, each of the God-fearing faiths was "a religion." This group not only included Judaism, Christianity, and Islam, but also "most of the Tartars" (or Mongols) and the "Sissenniis," a community of God-fearing believers of the Roman era (though known to no one but Nicholas).[4] Nor did Nicholas restrict the ascription of "religion" (*secta*) to such God-fearing believers, as had Raymon Lull. Nicholas owned *Liber Tartarorum* (*Book of the Tartars*), Europe's earliest introduction to the mores and religions of the Mongol Empire.[5] He also owned Marco Polo's account of the Yüan Dynasty in China, with its religious demographics for each city that the explorer visited including not only the several kinds of Buddhists ("idolaters") and Muslims, but also the mix of Christianities in Asia: Roman, Eastern Orthodox, Nestorian, and Jacobite.[6] Drawing on these sources, Nicholas unabashedly extended the category of *religio* to all "the polytheists and idolaters" whom he encountered in these sources for Asian religions.

---

3. Bacon, *Opus Majus*, 1:254.

4. "The Tartars, for the most part, believing in one God," *De Pace Fidei*, XVI.54. "[At the time of the ancient Romans,] some, like the Jews and Sissennii, worshipped God in God's most simple unity" (*De Docta Ignorantia*, 25.84).

5. Europeans received their first information about the Mongols from the Franciscan, John of Plano Carpini, *History of the Mongols*. Nicholas owned a copy of John's *Liber Tarartorum* and the text is in his library, Codex Cusanus 203. For an English translation, see "History of the Mongols" in Dawson's *Mongol Mission*.

6. Nicholas's edition of Marco Polo was titled: *De condicionibus et consuetudinibus orientalium regionum*, a 1445 translation by Francisco Pipino. His copy of this text is now housed in the British Library. Introduction and notes to the Biechler-Bond translation of *De Pace Fidei*, xxx and 225 n. 28. Hereafter editorial materials from this book will be identified only as Biechler-Bond.

The notion of a world with many religions requires a second reading, now with the eyes of a fifteenth century reader. All of the claims made above are new. Neither Judaism nor Islam had been identified as *religio*, to say nothing of the practices of Tartars and "Sissennii," people who had not benefited from God's revelation through Adam, Abraham, and their successors. Even a forward-looking thinker about religions such as Ramon Lull drew the line on admitting Tartars to the company of *sectae*. He classified Judaism, Christianity, and Islam as *sectae*, but not polytheists such as the Tartars. And, as we will see, Ramon Lull was the primary influence in shaping Nicholas's thinking about religions. Nicholas, therefore, invented *religio* as an all-inclusive category, or he extended the use of a generic category of *religio* that he found in the *Divine Institutes of Lactantius* (240–320), a theologian with whose works he was familiar.[7] In either case, Nicholas of Cusa appears to be the obvious "founder" of a post-medieval theology of religion.

This, however, is not the way the story of this theological project is usually told. Conventional wisdom now takes it to be self-evident that the generic concept of religion was not a product of Christian theologians but of agnostic philosophers. It did not first appear in the post-medieval West in response to a momentous clash of two civilizations inspired by different religions. Rather, it is assumed that the generic concept of religion appeared in response to the new intellectual freedom and confidence in reason engendered by the Enlightenment. According to the present consensus of scholarship, the construction of a generic category of religion was primarily the work of philosophers and historians of religion; theologians were the last to enter this field of discussion. David Hume's epoch-making book, *The Natural History of Religion*, was merely the superbly crafted version of arguments and data gathered from a host of less skilled writers before him.[8] According to this claim, all of us who today use the generic concept of religion should be indebted to the eighteenth-century philosophers and historians who created this new concept. This, in summary, is generally taken to be the true story of the construction of a generic category of religion.

7. References to the thought of Lactantius appear as early as a 1530 Christmas sermon of Nicholas. See Lohr, "Ramón Lull und Nikolaus von Kues," 227.

8. For this background on Hume's book, I am indebted to my colleague in Lord Herbert studies, David Pailin, of Manchester University.

To illustrate the extent of this wrong-headed claim, I offer a few examples from a variety of fields. The first two are from a pair of English historians, Peter Harrison and Peter Byrne. Both of their comments appear in the opening pages of their books, introducing their historical studies of the concept of religion. According to Peter Harrison, "The concepts 'religion' and 'the religions,' as we presently understand them, emerged quite late in Western thought, during the Enlightenment."[9] Peter Byrne offered a similar judgment: "[in examining] the emergence and development of the concept of religion itself . . . It is easier to see the origins of the modern concept of religion in the European Enlightenment."[10] Specialists in other fields soon adopted this Enlightenment hypothesis as their own. Thus, Talal Asad, an American anthropologist, noted how "the [eighteenth century] idea of Natural Religion was a crucial step in the formation of the modern concept of religious belief."[11] Finally, to give credit where credit is due, the grandfather of this Enlightenment version of "religion and the religions" was Wilfred Cantwell Smith who introduced this history of the concept in 1963.[12] Several of the authors above credited Smith as a source for their own later work.

A reading of *De pace fidei* requires us to reject that Enlightenment hypothesis. The generic category of religion was the product of a Christian theologian writing in response to an inter-religious outburst of violence that was sufficiently brutal to shock fifteenth century Europe. As the title of Nicholas's book suggests, *De pace fide*, his new generic concept of religion served as a necessary element in a Christian witness for religious peace. A commitment to pursue the peace of God's Kingdom, not the rationalism or scientism of the Enlightenment, was the impetus that gave birth to the post-medieval generic concept of religion. Christian theologians have a responsibility to correct the false Enlightenment history of the concept of religion and reclaim the original form of the concept as one element in a contemporary witness to the peace of Christ.

Other reasons for including Nicholas's work within the company of theologies of religion will appear in the explication of his texts. Only one

9. Harrison, *"Religion" and "Religions" in the English Enlightenment*, 1; Harrison, "Science and Religion," 83.

10. Byrne, *Natural Religion,* ix and xi.

11. Asad, *Genealogies of Religion,* 1.

12. W. C. Smith, *Meaning and End of Religion.*

further consideration warrants attention in this context. Like Raymon Lull before him and many of the twentieth century theologies of religion, Nicholas had a soft spot in his heart and mind for the similarities of religions. In his view, the many religions of the world are not as different from each other as they might appear; they are especially not that different from the Christian religion. To be sure, Nicholas did not claim that all religions were in the business of "salvation," as have the so-called religious pluralists who found this purpose served more or less equally well by the several "axial" religions of the world.[13] But if one substitutes Nicholas's language of "Union with God" for the contemporary usage of "salvation," the similarity of positions between this fifteenth century thinker and late twentieth century theologians becomes apparent. Their theologies of religion depend upon a meta-narrative that encompasses and transforms the particular narratives of each faith community, obliterating the different ends or purposes served by each religion.

I find this procedure of Nicholas and his modern successors to be as flawed as is the historical judgment concerning the Enlightenment origins of the generic concept of religion. But this chapter is not the place to develop my critique of their argument from the purported similarities of religions to their essential unity. A variety of "late-moderns" have initiated this critique.[14] In this aside from the fifteenth century, I only wished to claim the theology of religion found in Nicholas of Cusa as the true progenitor of this contemporary discipline.

Biographical Background

Nicholas of Cusa was born in 1401 in the German town of Kues (located on the Moselle River south of Koblenz). His birthplace gave Nicholas his Latin surname, Cusanus, the name by which he was known in most of his adult life and the name by which he will most often be identified in the remainder of this chapter. Kues also provided Nicholas with the site for a combination hospice and library that he founded with funds inherited from his family. The vast majority of manuscripts from his personal library are still available there. They include copies of his books and sermons, the copies made by his own hand of writings by others,

13. Hick, *Christian Theology of Religions,* 13.

14. For a brief review of several "postmodern" theologies of religions, see Knitter, *Introducing Theologies of Religions,* part IV. I first found this position persuasively articulated in Heim, *Salvations.*

and manuscripts copied by the hand of others; most of these include his marginal notes. As a result of this virtually intact library, a great deal is known about the sources of Cusanus's thought. Kues was not only the site of Nicholas's birth; it also provided the sources for much of our understanding of his thought.

What follows is not a biography, but a sketch of major themes in Cusanus's theology of religion, their origins in his life experience and subsequent development.

Academic Studies and the Discovery of Ramon Lull: 1416–1428

Nicholas began his academic studies at the University of Heidelberg in 1416. He did not remain there long, however, and by 1417, he had become a student at the University of Padua. He completed his studies there in 1423, receiving from this university a doctoral degree in canon law (*doctor decretorum*).

Law, however, was not the only subject of Nicholas's studies at Padua. During his years at Padua, he also began reading and copying large portions of manuscripts by Ramon Lull. Nicholas, thus, not only received a doctorate in canon law at the University of Padua, but he also was introduced to the thought of Ramon Lull.[15] It is difficult to determine which of these learnings—in law or Lull—proved to be more decisive in shaping the course of his life and thought.

After receiving his doctorate from the University of Padua, Nicholas went to the University of Cologne (1425–26) where he lectured in canon law and studied theology with his mentor and friend, Heimericus de Campo. De Campo had done his own theological training at the University of Paris, where he had absorbed the thought of Albert the Great and also discovered the ideas of Ramon Lull.[16] Apparently, de Campo had left Paris with enough appreciation for

15. Lohr, "Metaphysics," 545–50. Lohr, "Exzerptensammlung," 373–84. In this article, Lohr identified the first 11 of the 26 selections from Lull's writings in Codex Cusanus 83 as texts that could only have been made from Lull manuscripts in Padua or Rome, not in Paris. Older scholarship did not find credible the claim that Nicholas had any knowledge of Lull before his year at the University of Cologne: for example, Hillgarth, *Lull and Lullism,* 271, and Colomer, *Nikolaus von Kues und Raimund Llull.*

16. Heimericus founded a group of "Albertists" who set the Neo-Platonic elements of Albert over against the more strictly Aristotelian elements of Thomas. See Weisheipl, *Friar Thomas,* 43–44.

Lull to encourage Nicholas to follow in his steps, for by 1428, Nicholas was in Paris, devoting himself primarily to the study of Lull's writings. More accurately, he not only read them, but hand-copied large selections of many of them to add to his growing collection of Lull manuscripts begun while at Padua.

What continues to amaze those who study Cusanus is the extent of his personal collection of Lull's writings. His library includes ten manuscripts with selections from sixty-eight individual writings by Lull, or one-fourth of the two hundred and forty works by Lull then known to exist.[17] As Ludwig Mohler observed long ago, "No other author [than Lull] is represented so completely in the library of the learned Cardinal."[18] And, it is necessary to add, no other author is so consistently denied acknowledgement in the writings of Cusanus. Indeed, Cusanus did not once cite the name of Ramon Lull in any of his writings.

It is not difficult to discern the reason for Lull's absence. By 1442, Cusanus had been publicly accused of heresy.[19] From the late fourteenth century through the end of the fifteenth century, Lull's thought was repeatedly accused of heresy in itself or as associated with heretical movements.[20] Cusanus, writing to defend his own orthodoxy in the middle of the fifteenth century, did not need to associate himself with the heretical suspicions attached to Lull.

The subject of the last chapter, Lull's *Book of the Gentile and the Three Wise Men*, is particularly important for understanding Cusanus's *De pace fidei*. While no copy of this work is included among the 68 titles of Lull's writings in the Cusanus library, there is no question that Cusanus was familiar with it, and that it exercised a strong influence on

---

17. For Lull texts in Nicholas's library, see Marx, *Verzeichnis der Handschriften-sammlung*, 81–90.

18. Mohler, *"Einführung,"* 60.

19. For the charge of heresy, see Hopkins, *Nicholas of Cusa's Debate.*

20. In the late fourteenth century, the Dominican inquisitor in Aragon (Spain) obtained a papal bull prohibiting the teaching of Lull's views. In the early fifteenth century, the Faculty of Theology at the University of Paris initiated a series of prohibitions against the teaching of Lull's thought. See Hillgarth, *Ramon Lull and Lullism,* 269–70. Indeed, the suspect status of Lullism lasted throughout the lifetime of Nicholas and after. Near the end of the fifteenth century, the Dominican inquisitor for Majorca accused an educator-priest on the island of heresy because of his Lullian orientation. Hillgarth, "Unpublished Lullian Sermon," 561.

his composition of *De pace fidei*.[21] Cusanus could hardly have avoided becoming familiar with Ramon Lull's most popular writing. Indeed, he may have had a copy of this work available to him when he wrote *De pace fidei* for it repeats several of the themes from *Book of the Gentile* and in some cases sentences in the two documents are virtually identical. Both documents recount repeatedly the human misery caused by the diversity of religions. Both propose some version of one religion or one faith as a solution to this problem. Both employ the literary genre of dialogue. Both are written in an irenic tone. Neither repeats the hostile stereotypes and polemical arguments against non-Christian religions that were so common in the late medieval world. And, as we shall see, the difference between these two writings about religions discloses with special clarity the distinctive position of Cusanus.

Homo politicus: 1432–1464

From his first professional assignment, before he was even ordained, until the end of his life, Cusanus was engaged in the task of resolving conflicts between contending parties. The council of Basel, to which Nicholas was appointed in February 1432, dealt with a series of controversies whose resolutions shaped the future of the Western church. Nicholas began on the side of the conciliarists, those who would invest the ultimate authority of the church in a council of representatives rather than in a single person, the pope.[22] In 1434, Nicholas wrote a lengthy treatise on ecclesiology, *De concordantia catholica* (The Catholic Concordance) that supported the conciliar position and included Nicholas's arguments for a democratic model of representation and

21. "There can be no doubt that this writing [*The Book of the Gentile and Three Wise Men*] has given Nicholas of Cusa the idea of a similar literary project" (Mohler, "*Einführung*," 61). Also, there can be no doubt that the library of Cusanus at Kues does not include a copy of *The Book of the Gentile and Three Wise Men*, contrary to the claim of Paul E. Sigmund, *Nicholas of Cusa*, 59. In 1995, Jasper Hopkins basically repeated Mohler's earlier assertion: "Lull's *Liber de Gentile et tribus sapientibus* led Nicholas to take seriously the possibility of a universal religion" (Hopkins, "Introduction," *De Pace Fidei*, 4).

22. Councils of the fifteenth century included persons from a variety of positions. For example, the council of Pisa in 1409 had a company of 600 ecclesiastics including 183 bishops, 300 doctors of theology and canon law, and "an innumerable horde of less important clerics." In addition, there were 100 representatives of cathedral chapters and representatives of 13 universities, all of whom had a vote. Hughes, *Church in Crisis*, 325.

decision-making.[23] During the deliberations of this same council, he drafted a proposal for reconciling the Hussites to the Catholic communion, a recommendation for resolving the question of the council presidency, and a plan for reforming the church's calendar. From the beginnings of his career, he was engaged in the task of crafting unity out of dissension.

By 1436, however, Cusanus had given up the conciliar position and aligned himself with the papacy. As a result of this change, a series of popes entrusted him with negotiations vital to the church. In 1437, Pope Eugene IV sent Cusanus and two bishops to Constantinople to win the presence of leaders of the Greek Church in a Council on East-West union. From 1438 to 1449, he was the papal advocate to a series of imperial diets in Germany seeking to win the support of German princes for the authority of the papacy. From 1450 to 1452, Pope Nicholas V appointed him as Cardinal legate to Germany and the Netherlands responsible for dispensing the Jubilee indulgences in these countries. From 1452 to 1460, he served as bishop of Brixen where he was again mired in conflicts. In fact, for two years the civil authority of Brixen did not allow Cusanus to assume his post; on one occasion, soldiers occupied the city and Cusanus himself was imprisoned until he signed a humiliating agreement, which he repudiated as soon as he was free. During the last years of his life, he served as an advisor to his friend, Pope Pius II.

Cusanus was thus a man accustomed to dealing with disagreements and conflicts of many sorts, theological and military. He was not a politically naïve scholar. His task was to win agreement among contending parties and since he was more often successful than not, we must assume that he apparently had the rhetorical and negotiating skills necessary for such work. Yet, in writing *De pace fidei*, he consistently crafted agreements among contending parties that totally lacked any semblance of real politics.

In this way, Cusanus made it obvious that his heavenly dialogues were not a prototype for earthly exchanges among the representatives

23. "For since all [men] are by nature free, every governance ... can only come from the agreement and consent of the subjects, for if by nature all men are equal in power and equally free, the true properly ordered authority of one common ruler who is their equal in power cannot be naturally established except by the election and consent of the others and law is also established by consent" (Cusanus, *Catholic Concordance*, 98). For Nicholas on political theory, see Sigmund, *Nicholas of Cusa*.

of differing religious groups. They were to be taken seriously, as a new understanding of the relation of religions, but not literally, as a guide to Christian negotiations with Muslims.

The Qur'an: 1432–1461

Sometime in 1432, while Cusanus was serving on the council of Basel, he acquired a copy of the Qur'an, or more accurately, he acquired a copy of Robert of Ketton's Latin translation of the Qur'an entitled *Lex Mahumet* or *Lex Saracenorum* as a part of a collection of purportedly Islamic sources known as the *Toledan Collection*.[24] Latin translations of the Qur'an were not common documents in the mid-fifteenth century. Marie-Thérèse d'Alverny was able to identify only fifteen manuscripts from the fifteenth century or earlier that included a translation of the Qur'an; some of these fifteen only included parts of the Qur'an and one of them belonged to Cusanus. As John of Segovia, a Spanish friend of Cusanus observed, "very few Christians have this book [the Qur'an] and it is found in few libraries."[25]

In his study of Islam Cusanus was more limited than Ramon Lull. He was not able to read Arabic, and so his knowledge of Islam was dependent upon Latin translations by Christians. As a result, he found many texts in his Latin translation that apparently gave witness to Jesus Christ as divine—texts that a reader of the Arabic could not find.[26] While in Constantinople, a group of Franciscans showed him an Arabic text of the Qur'an, his brief and only contact with the Arabic original. When he wrote *De Pace Fidei* in 1453, his Latin version of the Qur'an—loaned to John of Segovia while he was in Constantinople—had obviously been returned to him. In this text, he quoted extensively from the Qur'an, especially in those dialogues involving Christian-Muslim differences.

24. In Nicholas's library, the *Toledan Collection* is in Codex Cusanus 108 and includes six other treatises in addition to the Ketton translation of the Qur'an. Codex Cusanus 107 contained two other texts on Islam.

25. D'Alverny reference and Segovia quote from Biechler, "New Face Towards Islam," 185–86.

26. The Ketton translation has been the subject of extensive criticism by modern Islamicists. However, Thomas E. Burman has recently written in defense of the Ketton translation if understood as both a translation and interpretation of the Qur'an in light of Islamic traditions of the twelfth century. See his two articles in *Speculum* (703–32) and *Scripta Mediterranea* (182–97). I am indebted to my Islamicist colleague, Wilfred Rollman, for this reference.

Cusanus also borrowed extensively from the Qur'an in constructing a narrative account of the origins of diverse religions. Needless to say, in 1453 immediately after the "brutalities" of Constantinople, Cusanus did not cite the Qur'an as the source for his story of world religions. His unidentified use of Qur'anic materials, however, does illumine the depth of his own engagement with a religion not his own: he could learn from such a religion something new, something not available from the Christian tradition. In constructing a meta-narrative encompassing the diversity of all religions, he drew upon materials borrowed from a religion other than his own.

His continuing engagement with Islam is shown in his latest writing, *A Sifting of the Koran* (*Cribratio Alkorani*). In 1460–61, just three years before his death, Cusanus yielded to the request of his good friend Pius II and wrote this commentary. On the one hand, this work was consistent with his earlier theology of religion in that he still attempted to identify beliefs common to the faith of Muslims and Christians. On the other hand, however, *A Sifting of the Koran* was a far more hostile work than Cusanus's previous writings. His irenic tone is here replaced by the accusatory language characteristic of the anti-Muslim stereotypes so popular in the late medieval Western world.

While noting these variations in Cusanus's treatment of the Qur'an, we should not lose sight of the fact that he continued to be engaged with the Muslim scriptures from his acquisition of a copy in 1432 to his commentary on it in 1460–61. This was not a typical subject of interest for Christian theologians of the fifteenth century. In his long-standing engagement with the Qur'an, including his responses of both appreciation and critique, Cusanus was an exception.

A New Vision of the God-World Reality: 1437/38–1464

In 1437, Cusanus traveled to Constantinople as a member of a papal delegation to meet with leaders of the Eastern Orthodox Church and persuade them to attend a council of church union in Ferrara (later moved to Florence). As a result of this assignment, Cusanus spent four months in the company of Greek Christians, first in Constantinople and then at sea, en route to Venice. Cusanus was in his mid-thirties then, still a young man for theology, and one who, by his own admission, had not yet found his own theological voice. While he told us virtually nothing about his conversations with the theologians and philosophers he came to know there, he did recount one experience on shipboard that brought him a new understanding of Christian faith, one he pursued for the rest of his life. His account of this divine illumination appeared in a 1440 letter written to his theological mentor that accompanied his book *On Learned Ignorance.*

> Accept now, Reverend Father, what for so long I desired to attain by different paths of learning but previously could not until returning by sea from Greece when by what I believe was a celestial gift from the Father of Lights, from whom comes every perfect gift, I was led to embrace incomprehensibles incomprehensibly in learned ignorance, by transcending those incorruptible truths that can be humanly known. This learned ignorance I have, in the one who is the truth, now set loose in these [enclosed] books.[27]

In light of the social and intellectual context of this experience, it would not be surprising if Cusanus's newly received understanding of theology were to resemble the mystical-Platonic tradition of Eastern Orthodoxy more than the rational-Aristotelian tradition then dominant in Latin Christianity.[28]

In his 1449 work, *A Defense of "Learned Ignorance"* (*Apologia doctae ignorantiae*), Cusanus repeated the claim of 1440: his new understanding of learned ignorance did not come to him "by means of study but rather by the gift of God."[29] After he had returned from Constantinople, however, he did consult some theological sources—not to learn from them, he wrote, but to confirm the orthodoxy of his new insight.[30] In his *Apologia*, he cited the works of (Pseudo-)Dionysius twenty-two times and Meister Eckhart twenty times.[31] For Cusanus, the great teachers

27. Cusanus, "Letter of the Author to Lord Cardinal Julian," in Cusanus, *Nicholas of Cusa*, 205–6.

28. In defending himself against John Wenck's charge of heretical views, Nicholas wrote: "But the Aristotelian sect now prevails. This sect regards as heresy [the method of the coincidence of opposites]. Yet, the endorsement of this [method] is the beginning of the ascent unto mystical theology" (Cusanus, *Apologia*, 46).

29. Ibid., 50.

30. For an analysis of the sources Nicholas had consulted before writing *On Learned Ignorance*, see Cusanus, *Nicholas of Cusa*, 154–58.

31. In a letter of 1454, Cusanus identified Eriugena as the translator of (Pseudo-) Dionysius. Meister Eckhart, like both Lull and Cusanus, was dependent upon the *Clavis physicae* for his knowledge of Eriugena's philosophy. Cusanus' annotations on the *Clavis physicae* have been published by Paolo Lucentini in *Platonismo medievale*. Information in this note is from Moran, *Philosophy of Eriugena*, 279.

of mysticism were the "true theologians," those who had anticipated a learned ignorance in theological matters.

While the name of Ramon Lull was absent from Cusanus's references to many "true theologians," Lull's sources were cited: John Scotus Eriugena's *Periphyseon* and Honorius Augustodunensis' *Clavis physicae*.[32] These Latin versions of a Greek vision of God and humanity, so peripheral to Latin theology, were the sources that shaped the mind of Lull, though he, in his time, did not dare cite them because of thirteenth century suspicions concerning their orthodoxy. By the fifteenth century, Cusanus could claim these Western sources of Greek theology and the Greek context for his mystical experience.

The intellectual results of that experience first appeared in Cusanus's 1440 book, *On Learned Ignorance*. We have no reason to doubt that some kind of crystallization and focus happened during the fall and winter of 1437–1438. We also have no reason to doubt that the materials of this new vision reflected the prior study and intellectual development of Cusanus, including his borrowings from Lull, as well as his interaction with Greek theologians and philosophers. The God who gave Cusanus this gift of light was so thoroughly interwoven with this world that we should not be surprised that the stuff of social contexts and prior learning was divinely refashioned into a new insight.

Cusanus's New Theology of Learned Ignorance

Religions within the God-World Reality

Although the vision that Cusanus received during his voyage from Constantinople to Venice may neither seem new in the history of religions, nor have been new in the mystical theological tradition from Eriugena to Lull, it was new for Cusanus. This is apparent from the theology he constructed shortly after his return to Italy in 1438. Later, in the summer of 1453, he was able to compose *De pace fidei* within the

---

32. In the library of Cusanus, Eriugena is identified as John Scotus or John Scotus Erigena (Cusanus, *Apologia* 56 and 61); Honorius is identified as Theodorus (Ibid., 61). Nicholas did not own a copy of Eriugena's *Periphyseon*, but there is ample evidence for his familiarity with Book I of this text in the marginal notes he made in a Codex now owned by the British Museum. He obtained his knowledge of the *Periphyseon* Books II through V through the excerpts in *Clavis physicae*, the same intermediary that Lull used (Codex Cusanus 202). For a detailed discussion of the evidence linking Nicholas with the writings of Eriugena, see Beierwaltes, "Cusanus and Eriugena," 115–52.

span of merely two months only because he had already formulated the intellectual framework for such a theology of religion. It was a product of God's gift to him someplace on the waters of the Mediterranean or Adriatic.

The literary corpus that began to appear soon after this revelatory event consists of three texts: *On Learned Ignorance* (*De docta ignorantia*: DDI); *On Conjectures* (*De coniecturis*: DC); and *A Defense of Learned Ignorance* (*Apologia doctae ignorantiae*). The mystical and theological vision appears most fully in *On Learned Ignorance* (1440). *On Conjectures* (1442) fills out the implications of this vision for Cusanus's theory of knowledge concerning God and this-worldly realities.[33] Finally, *A Defense of Learned Ignorance* (1449) restates and clarifies issues developed in the prior two texts.

Religions are not the subject of a focused discussion in any of these three writings, and yet they are not ignored. In these early works Cusanus already understood 'religion' as a generic concept and used the term not only in its plural form but also as a singular collective category embracing all religions.[34] While he understood the Christian religion to be one among the many religions included in this generic concept, he also believed that Christ had a unique and decisive role in all religions, serving the "desired end of peace." As he wrote, "you see that there is no perfect religion, leading to the final and most desired end of peace, that does not embrace Christ as mediator and savior, God and human, the way, the truth, and the life (DDI III 8.229). In brief, the position he explicated in some detail in *De pace fidei* (1453) is, in these earlier writings, anticipated if not fully developed.

---

33. Subsequent citations to these works are abbreviated in the text. All citations (book, chapter, and paragraph number) are to the Latin edition.

34. For examples of the plural use of *religio*, see *Learned Ignorance* III 1.184 and *On Conjectures* II 15.150. For an example of a singular use of *religio* with a generic meaning, see *Learned Ignorance* I 26 where Nicholas observed that all religion (*omnia religio*) used affirmative theologies in their worship. For a similar use, see *Learned Ignorance*, III 8. In *On Conjectures*, Nicholas used *religio* seven times as a singular generic term in discussing the ways in which religions varied: according to cognitive orientation of believers (intellective, rational, or sensible), according to the strength of spiritual or temporal concerns, and according to different parts of the world (DC II 15.147–50).

Cusanus's Vision of God

Cusanus introduced his new "method of reasoning in theological matters" with his somewhat new concept of God. Echoing Anselm, Cusanus proposed that God was most properly understood as the maximum "than beyond which there can be nothing greater" (DDI I 2.5). This maximum, in turn, is not some isolated abstraction of the human intellect, but is the being of all the different objects of our universe.

> Clearly, then, God ought in no respect to be conceived to have being in the manner in which something singular—which is different and distinct—is conceived to be. Nor [ought He to be conceived to have being] in the manner in which a universal or a genus or a species is conceived to be. Rather, [he ought to be thought to exist] beyond the coincidence of the singular and universal. (ADI 9)

Since God is more than the whole of the universe, Cusanus distinguished between the maximum as absolute (or God) and the maximum as limited or contracted (or the universe). He expressed the relationship between these two forms of the maximum in terms of his concepts of enfolding and unfolding. The multitude of worldly objects, in their plurality of forms, is enfolded within the unity of God; conversely, the diverse forms of worldly objects are unfolded in the concrete existences of our world. In a short and relatively simple version of this theological position, Cusanus wrote, "God is the enfolding of all in the sense that all are in God, and God is the unfolding of all in the sense that God is in all" (DDI II 3.107). A somewhat longer version may shed further light on the mystery of unity and diversity that lies at the heart of the maximum.

> No one understands how God, whose unity of being does not exist by the intellect's abstracting from things nor as united to or as immersed in things, is unfolded through the number of things. If you consider things apart from God, they are nothing ... If you consider God apart from things, God exists and they are nothing. (DDI II 3.110)

Cusanus moved back and forth between the unfolding of diversity in the constitution of our cosmos and the enfolding of this same diversity in the unity of God. In brief, the concepts of unity and diversity, which were to be so prominent in Cusanus's theology of religion, provided the structure for his theology and cosmology.

For Cusanus, this sense of God's reality led him to an understanding of religion somewhat distinctive for his era. He understood the truth of religion to have been first constituted or made manifest independently of the biblical tradition. The ubiquitous God of his theology could not be concealed from all humanity in order to be disclosed to one particular people at one particular time. Instead, Cusanus presumed some sort of primordial revelation of this one maximum to all humanity from the beginning of time. For example, he wrote that "this maximum, which also the indubitable faith of all nations believes to be God" (DDI I 2.5). He repeatedly insisted upon the universality of this faith:" there never was a people who did not worship God and believe that God was the absolutely maximum" (DDI I 7.18). In every place and every time, including "[the time of ancient Rome], all believed God to be the one maximum, than which there cannot be a greater" (DDI I 25.84). The universality of faith in one God and worship of one God is a conviction running through all of Cusanus's writings on religion.

While he claims that this maximum was always acknowledged by the faith of all nations, all people in these nations did not always correctly understand it. Cusanus offered several discussions of the pagan religions of ancient Rome to illustrate the kind of confusion that could happen in humanity 's response to the maximum. Basically, the problem with the pagans is that they incorrectly worshipped God in God's unfoldings rather than in God's simple unity. A long quotation from *On Learned Ignorance* illustrates the way in which Cusanus connected his theology of the maximum with humanity's worship of one maximum and its confused form of idolatry.

> The ancient pagans used to ridicule the Jews, who worshipped the one, infinite God whom they did not know, while the pagans themselves were worshipping God in God's unfoldings, that is, they were worshipping God wherever they beheld God's divine works. At this time all believed God to be the one maximum, than which there cannot be a greater, but there was this difference between all human beings: Some, like the Jews and the Sissennii, worshipped God in God's most simple unity, as the enfolding of all things, but others worshipped God in the things where they found the unfolding of God's divinity by taking what they sensibly perceived as a guide to the Cause and Principle. In

this last way the simple folk were led astray, for they did not take what was unfolded as an image but as the truth. As a consequence, idolatry was introduced among the common folk, while the wise, for the most part, correctly believed in the unity of God, as can be ascertained by anyone who will carefully examine Cicero's *On the Nature of the Gods* and the ancient philosophers. (DDI I.25.84)[35]

In the beginning of this passage, Cusanus appears to explain idolatry in terms of the difference between pagans and Jews. Jews worshipped God in God's simple unity; pagans worshipped God in the multiple unfoldings in the objects of our world. Both peoples worshipped the same God, but they worshipped this God in different ways. By the end of that paragraph, however, he has changed the focus of his explanation. The difference that really matters is not the difference between Jews and pagans but the difference between "the wise" and the "simple folk" or "common folk." All peoples did worship God in God's unity—Jews and Gentiles—as Cicero and the other philosophers had shown. For Cusanus, therefore, the bearers of religious truth will henceforth be identified in terms of their intellectual orientation or their wisdom, not their identification with a particular ethnic group or religious tradition. He thus interprets the Old Testament prophet as one who sees God through the intellect: "[to proclaim maximum unity] the prophet says: 'On that day there will be one God and God's name will be one' And elsewhere: 'Hear O Israel' (i.e., whoever sees God through the intellect) 'for your God is one'" (DDI I. 24.75). For those who see God through the intellect, the deviations of the simple folk in their religious practice could not conceal the truth of God's oneness.

Diversity and Unity in Cusanus's Theology

In his theology and cosmology, Cusanus was a Christian Neo-Platonist. Like Augustine, he rejected the Platonic model of a world-soul filled with life-giving forms of creation and mediating between the world and God. For Cusanus, as for Lull and Eriugena, all universals had their originating domain only within the eternal Logos, not a world-soul. When enfolded, the plurality of such universals was not in contradiction with the simple unity of God, when God's unity was understood in

35. In several places Nicholas referred to the Sissennii. While no one has yet discovered who they were, some have guessed that he may have meant the Essenes.

light of the coincidence of opposites. Like all Neo-Platonist, however, Cusanus did find himself engaged with the distinction between oneness and manyness, unity and diversity. The way in which he related these two different forms of being shaped his cosmology and his theory of knowledge. They deserve our attention here because these same two categories—the one and the many—also inform the conceptual shape of his theology of religion.

For Cusanus, God's oneness is a complex unity that encompasses, and does not exclude, diversity. When Cusanus wrote about unity or oneness, therefore, we need to recognize both the theological location of this oneness and its incorporation of the many. The unity or oneness of which he wrote did not apply to the objects of this world when considered apart from God.

In contrast, the many is a cosmological category that belongs only to mundane entities.

> The unity [of the cosmos] is contracted in plurality, without which it cannot exist. Even though this [limited] maximum embraces all things in its universal unity so that all that are from the absolute maximum are in this maximum, and it is in all things, nevertheless, it does not exist outside the plurality in which it is found, because it does not exist apart from contraction from which it cannot be freed. (DDI I 2.6)

Diversity is therefore as essential to the structure of the universe as unity is essential to the being of God.

Having noted the theological and cosmological distinctiveness of unity and diversity, we now need to recognize their interpenetration. Cusanus did not exclude plurality and multiplicity from God's unity: "it is not a unity of this [simple numerical] sort that properly applies to God, but the unity to which neither otherness nor plurality nor multiplicity is opposed" (DDI I 24.76). Similarly, since there are no mundane objects that are only mundane but all worldly entities have their being in God, so all such objects disclose their unity in God as well as their diversity in the world.

Cusanus's theology brought with it a range of implications for his understanding of knowledge. In relation to God, Cusanus, like Lull and Eriugena, denied the possibility for any human knowledge of God. He was a believing agnostic, who granted the validity of at least one objection to his teaching of learned ignorance: "when [a critic] says that [the teaching of learned ignorance] destroys the knowledge of God, he speaks the truth. For someone's belief that he knows some thing which cannot be known is not knowledge. With respect to such a thing, knowing is knowing that he cannot know" (ADI 60). The first lesson for any theologian, one that Cusanus discovered on returning from Constantinople, is to recognize God as mystery. In terms of his favorite maxim, "there is no proportion between the finite and the infinite." In God's own being, God is ineffable and God is unnamable. We humans may give God names—Father, Son, and Holy Spirit or pagan names like Jupiter, Saturn, Mars, or Venus. We humans may assign God attributes, such as just or merciful. But for Cusanus, the competent theologian needs to recognize the limited validity of all such language. In God's own being, all such positive attributes or names dissolve in the coincidence of opposites.[36]

While his new theology made God unknowable, it also relativized the so-called rational knowledge of this-worldly objects. For Cusanus, there were four qualitatively distinct noetic agents: the sensible, the rational, the intellective, and the divine.[37] These existed in a hierarchy moving down from the divine to the sensible. The apparent knowledge of each was always in need of correction by the higher level. As an example, he cited the experience of viewing one side of the face of Pope Eugene IV.[38] By itself, the sensible offers only a partial and distorted image of the pope's face: partial in that it is limited by the perspective from which it is seen; distorted in that it offers only a two-dimensional image of a part, not the whole of the face. Reason, therefore, has to correct the sensible data by constructing the image of a whole face.

What is true for the relationship of reason and sense is also true for the relationship of intellect and reason. "If reason rules the senses, it

36. "Coincidence of opposites" is the name for the new theological method Cusanus proposed in *On Learned Ignorance*. A brief description of this method follows: "The coincidence of opposites provides a method that resolves contradictions without violating the integrity of the contrary elements and without diminishing the reality or the force of their contradiction. It is not a question of seeing unity where there is no real contrariety, nor is it a question of forcing harmony by synthesizing resistant parties. Coincidence as a method issues from coincidence as a fact or condition of opposition that is resolved in and by infinity" (Bond, "Introduction," Cusanus, *Nicholas of Cusa*, 22).

37. For the hierarchy of knowledge, see Cusanus, *De Coniecturis*, II Prologue 74, or *Learned Ignorance* I 24.76

38. Cusanus, *De Coniecturis*, II.11.57.

is still necessary that the intellect rule reason" (DDI III 6.217). Reason needed the correction of intellect just as much as the sensible needed the correction of reason. Hence, Cusanus did not call the fruits of reason "knowledge," but "conjecture." By conjecture, Cusanus did not mean a hypothesis to be tested; rather, a conjecture was a form of knowing that was always vague, always approximate, never precise, and always incomplete. To extend the analogy of perceiving the pope's face, we should have to say something like the following. The corrected construct of reason, while an improvement over the sensible alone, is still in need of correction. For reason's whole image of the pope would yield only an individual, one man among many. The intellect, however, by its powers of intuition, could correct for this partiality by abstracting the humanity of this one person from its individual embodiment. For it is the task of the intellective faculty to abstract universals contracted in individual entities. In the words of Cusanus,

> Dogs and other animals of the same species are united because of the common nature of their species that is in them; this nature would have been contracted in them, even if Plato's intellect had not created for itself a species from a comparison of likenesses. . . . Universals, which the intellect makes through comparison, therefore, are a similitude of the universals contracted in things. . . . In understanding, therefore, the intellect unfolds by means of similar marks and signs a certain world of similarities, which is contracted in it. (DDI II.6.126)

Amid the hierarchy of noetic agencies, reason and the intellect appear to have two quite different tasks. Out of the partial representations of the senses, reason constructs whole images of individuals with all their differences. Through the recognition of similarities, the intellect intuits universals that unite the disparate members of the same class of entities. In light of this theory, knowledge which includes the similarities of different entities within the same class—their oneness as contracted universal—along with the differences that divide members of this class from each other will be more adequate than knowledge of particular differentiated entities only.[39]

39. For a contemporary statement of Nicholas's distinction between reason and intellect, I offer a brief summary from Luis Martínez Gómez. "There follows from this . . . the theory with respect to human knowledge, of reason (*ratio*) as an organ perceptive of diversity and opposition, and of understanding (*intellectus*) as an organ perceptive of unity . . . Reason is for us the faculty of perceiving being in all its variety and opposition

This epistemological theory undergirds the dialogues in *De pace fidei*. When one of the "intellectual powers" representing the several families of humanity state some differentiating feature of a religion which appears to make impossible the unity of religions, one of the heavenly tutors—the Word, Peter, or Paul—responds by pointing out the similarity among disparate religions that makes their unity possible. It is as if the representatives of humanity are still only able to think in terms of the analytic categories of reason, recognizing the differences between religions without any sense of their fundamental unity. They need to be instructed by a heavenly tutor in order to develop the capacity of their intellect so as to discern within all the different religions the one religion that finds expression in each.

Diversity and unity, therefore, are not simply the categories prominent in Cusanus's theology of religion; they are also the dominant categories in his explication of his theology, cosmology, and epistemology. The reality of the maximum is itself differentiated according to the manyness of the universe and the oneness of God. Correspondingly, Cusanus's epistemology differentiated human knowledge of worldly phenomena according to the capacities of reason and the intellect, the former equipped to handle plurality and the latter able to discern unity. True knowledge of religions of this world will therefore require the complementary action of both reason and the intellect.

De pace fidei/The Peace of Faith

Preliminary Considerations

First, it is important to consider the title of the treatise itself. Cusanus entitled his treatise *De pace fidei* (The Peace of Faith). "Faith" in this title did not mean "the Christian faith" considered by itself and in distinction from all other faiths. Instead, Cusanus meant a universal faith, a faith common to all the religions known to him, including the faith of Christians. For him, this one faith, manifest in differing ways in each religion, was to provide the grounds for peace. It is this hidden unity of religion that Cusanus articulated in the body of his treatise.

. . . the intellect—a kind of mystical organ for Nicholas—draws nearer to this unity by denying or surpassing the plane of reason. This is done in order to glimpse vaguely or to intuit under a rational obscurity that point of union towards which all things are oriented" (Gómez, "From the Name of God," 88).

In contrast with the spiritual focus of "faith," the "peace" in the title refers to a tangible political and military condition: the absence of any organized or random violence fueled and legitimated by religions. The meaning of this peace grounded in faith becomes apparent by contrasting it with the multiple forms of violation "caused" by the many religions.

"Peace" means the opposite of:

- *War*: "because of religion many take up arms against each other" (I. 2);

- *Persecution*: "the persecution (of Christians in Constantinople) raging more than ever because of different religious rites" (I.1);

- *The enslavement of conquered peoples*: "those reduced to servitude who suffer because of the diversity of religions" (III.9);

- *The mutual animosity and violence that infects the behavior of one religious group against another*: "the sword and the bilious spite of hatred and all evil sufferings" (I.6).

While these examples are all taken from the first few chapters, Cusanus made explicit throughout the treatise his understanding of peace as a condition of the world religio-political order. For example, he dismissed as irrelevant one disagreement concerning an item of faith which, though it appeared insoluble, did not in fact matter because the nation involved was not numerous enough to pose a military threat to the condition of world peace: "They are few and will not be able by arms to disturb the whole world" (XII.41). So the atrocities of Constantinople led Cusanus not to propose a military response, but a world peace based on a new understanding of religious differences.

Second, it is important to consider the intended audience. As a Cardinal of the fifteenth century Church and faithful ally of several popes, Cusanus was in a position to offer a political proposal that might win the attention of the papacy and perhaps, some political leaders of Christian Europe. He was, after all, a *homo politicus* whose doctorate in canon law had opened up a wide range of opportunities for negotiating differences within the church and with civil powers outside the church. Hence, according to his text, he decided to write out the content of his vision, to share it with the religious and political decision-makers of Christendom, so that they would have a new alternative in conceiving of the relations between the religions of their world. As he wrote, "and so in order for this vision eventually to come to the notice of those who have the decisive word in these great matters, he [Cusanus] has written down his vision plainly below, as far as his memory recalled it" (I.1).

This intended audience for his treatise cannot be forgotten in the reading of it. Cusanus wrote for an audience of Christians; he sought to persuade them to adopt a view of other religions as more familiar, less strange. He was not a missionary writing to persuade believers in other religions to give up their faith and become Christians.

Third, we must consider the historical setting of this work. While *De pace fidei* was anchored historically in the 1453 defeat and brutalities in Constantinople, the vision recounted in the text is located far from such painful and conflicted events. Cusanus saw assembled in heaven a council of spiritual and intellectual powers chaired by God Almighty. In addition to God, the Word, Peter and Paul, this heavenly assembly included intellectual representatives of the diverse human families identified by nationality, language, ethnic or religious identity. Like Cusanus, this heavenly council had heard "the sad news of the groans of the oppressed. There were many bearers of these lamentations from all the earth" (I.2). Like Cusanus, the heavenly powers had learned that religious differences played a particularly powerful role in inciting such violence. Like Cusanus, the heavenly powers also knew that it was "because of religion [that] many take up arms against each other and by their power either force men to renounce their long practiced tradition (*sectae*) or inflict death on them" (I.2). Like Cusanus, the heavenly dignitaries resolved to find some solution to this perverse connection between the religions of the world and the cruelties they inflicted. The citizens of earth may have set the agenda, but the representatives of heaven proceeded to resolve the problem in a very peaceful, very heavenly manner.

Fourth, we must keep in mind the cast of characters. A large cast of characters animated his vision. On one side was an illustrious collection of heavenly authorities including an Archangel, God, the Word, and those two pillars of the Church, Peter and Paul. The last three were the primary speakers to answer all questions and objections. On the other side were "the more eminent men of this world" in the guise of "intellectual powers" representing the varied ethnic, linguistic, political, and religious constellations of humanity. They posed the religio-political problems to be resolved. While the substance of these question-answer exchanges concerned religious issues, the speakers representing humanity were consistently identified in terms of their political or ethnic identities. Cusanus named them (without geographical organization) as follows:

Europe	Middle East	Asia
Greek	Arab	Indian
Italian	Chaldean	Tartar
Frenchman	Jew	
Spaniard	Scythian	
German	Persian	
Bohemian	Syrian	
Englishman	Turk	
	Armenian	

In the cast above, Cusanus gave his readers the linguistic groups and emerging nation-states of Europe together with peoples of the Middle East and Asia recently discovered by Europeans.

For Cusanus, the condition of religious diversity could not be separated from all the other forms of diversity in his world. He never regarded religion as a disembodied system of beliefs and practices. For him, religions were always lived out by particular ethnic and linguistic communities. Hence, his speakers are consistently identified by their linguistic or ethnic category, not their religious identity.

Themes in Cusanus's Argument

THE DISTINCTION OF FAITH AND RITES

Basic to the argument of Cusanus is his analysis of religion in terms of the distinct elements of faith and rites. For Cusanus, one faith was common to all religions while rites were different in all religions, and there appeared to be no end to their diversity. As the Tartar (Mongol) observed in the epigraph of this chapter, "I do not grasp how there could be a oneness in these things [rites] which vary according to place and time; and unless it occurs, persecution will not end. For diversity gives birth to division and to hostility, hatred and war" (XVI.54). According to the vision of Cusanus, the heavenly council needed to resolve two issues: first, to recognize the unity of faith in the diversity of world religions; second, to neutralize the diversity of religious rites as potential causes of conflict. In the course of their dialogue, the heavenly council will resolve, to their satisfaction, both of these issues.

The distinction between faith and rites, and their respective role in forming the diversity of religions and the conflict between nations, was not original with Cusanus. He borrowed it from the mouth of Mohammed, or at least a text he assumed represented accurately the view of Mohammed. In one of the texts from the Toledan Collection, Mohammed is quoted as follows: "the religion or the faith of all the [prior prophets] was indeed one, but the rites of the different prophets were actually diverse." In the margin by this text, Cusanus wrote *fides una ritus diversus*.[40] While the above quote is most likely from a Christian interpreter of Mohammed and not the prophet of Islam, it is somewhat amazing that any Christian in the mid-fifteenth century would make a purported teaching of Mohammed fundamental to his argument. Cusanus did. The purpose of his entire essay was to demonstrate to his Christian readers that religious faith is common to humanity and consistent—if not identical—with Christian faith. Insofar as religion is faith, therefore, it could not be the cause of conflict—if, of course, everyone understood the faith of the world's religions as Cusanus did. The villain in world politics, therefore, is not faith but rites. Needless to say, Nicholas did not inform his Christian readers that he had borrowed this understanding of the different roles of faith and rites from a Muslim source.

Armed with this analysis of the problem, Cusanus was able to set forth a solution to the destructive role of religious diversity quite different from that of his spiritual mentor, Ramon Lull. Lull envisioned a world peace conditional upon the conversion of believers from Islam, Judaism, and all other religions—especially those of the Tartars—to Christianity. From the Prologue and Epilogue to Lull's *Book of the Gentile and Three Wise Men*, two speeches by unidentified wise men voice this theme:

> PROLOGUE: What a great good fortune it would be if . . . we could all—every man on earth—be under one religion and belief, so that there would be no more rancor or ill will among

40. Biechler and Cusanus, *Nicholas of Cusa,* 222 n. 12.

men, who hate each other because of diversity and contrariness of beliefs and of sects! And just as there is only one God, Father, Creator, and Lord of everything that exists, so all peoples could unite and become one people,... under one faith and one religion.

Think, gentlemen, of the harm that comes from men not belonging to a single sect, and of the good that would come from everyone being beneath one faith and one religion.[41]

EPILOGUE: Just as we have one God, one Creator, one Lord, we should also have one faith, one religion, one sect, one manner of loving and honoring God ... and make it so that between us there be no difference or contrariety of faith or customs, which difference and contrariety cause us to be enemies with one another and to be at war, killing one another and falling captive to one another.[42]

For Lull, this "one religion," "one belief," "one sect," "one faith" was not merely a spiritual ideal or norm of the present; it was also, and more importantly, a future condition to be realized by the conversion of non-Christians. For Lull, only a situation of religious uniformity could establish peace on earth.

The Archangel in Cusanus's dialogue appears to make the same point as the wise men in Lull's dialogue, only with this difference: the "one religion" of which the Archangel speaks is the hidden reality of all religions in the present:

THE ARCHANGEL: If thus you [God] would deign to do this [to show your face to all people], the sword and the bilious spite of hatred and all evil sufferings will cease; and all will know that there is only one religion in the variety of rites. But if perhaps this difference of rites cannot be removed or if it is not expedient to do so... at any rate, just as you are one, there should be one religion and one veneration of worship. (I.6)

The unity of religion and the diversity of rites belong together; they are not separable from each other. Therefore, the solution to the problem of religiously induced wars required a new understanding of religion, not the reduction of several religions to a single religion.

From his Neo-Platonist perspective, Cusanus knew that there would always be "manyness" in this world. Within the human species,

41. Lull, *Selected Works*, 1:116.
42. Ibid., 1:301–2.

Cusanus recognized a multitude of diversities: political, ethnic, familial, and linguistic. Religion was only one of these diversities and, for reasons to be noted shortly, the human condition and God's action colluded together to foster diverse religions. From his Neo-Platonist perspective, Cusanus also knew that diversity was not the only reality of these worldly entities. They also concealed a unity that became apparent when viewed by the intellect, not the reason. Cusanus thus would teach the decision-makers of Europe to view the plurality of religions from a new perspective, one that would disclose their profound unity. His solution to the problem of religiously sponsored violence required primarily a change in the minds of Europe's leaders, and only secondarily a change in the practice of non-Christian believers. His dialogue ends, having concluded "a peace among religions in the heaven of reason" (XIX.68). It is not a peace of one religion in the singular but a peace of many religions in the plural. His solution presumed a continuing plurality of religions.

The continuity of many religions is consistent with Cusanus's theory concerning the origins of religious diversity: all religions are from God and every religion is an expression of human nature. Both of these claims affirm the singularity of God and the universality of God's prophetic manifestations; both affirm the singularity of the human family and the universality of its religious inclination. Both were borrowed from sources outside the Christian traditions and Scriptures. In order to understand Cusanus's theory of religious diversity, we need to visit the two most important sources from which he borrowed: Robert of Ketton's Latin translation of the Qur'an and Cicero's *On the Nature of the Gods.*

God's Role in Creating Diverse Religions

Cusanus borrowed from the Qur'an one of its distinctive themes: namely, its recurrent claim that God appointed different prophets to all nations to teach each people God's law and rites of worship. The following passages from the Qur'an are examples of this theme.

> For each [nation] We [Allah] have appointed a [different] divine law and traced-out way. Had Allah willed, he could have made you one community (*Surah* 5:48).

Unto every nation have we given sacred rites which they are to perform (*Surah* 22:67).

We sent messengers before thee, among them those of whom We have told thee, and some of whom We have not told thee (*Surah* 40:78).

We have sent thee with the Truth, a bearer of glad tidings and a warner; and there is not a nation but a warner hath passed among them (*Surah* 35:24)

For every nation there is a messenger (*Surah* 10:48).[43]

According to the Qur'an, God sent prophets (messengers or warners) to all nations. God told Mohammed about some of these: the biblical prophets who, for the Qur'an, extended from Adam through Jesus. But God did not tell Mohammed about other prophets. Presumably, these other prophets could include "Indian prophets" such as the Buddha, Lao-Tse, and Confucius. In any case, the Qur'an is specific in extending the action of God through his appointed prophets to all nations of the world. Israel was not the only people for whom God had appointed prophets. God also disclosed his will to the pagans or Gentiles whose religions fell outside the boundaries of the Abrahamic traditions. No nation could claim a monopoly on God's appointed prophets.

The purpose of God's action in fostering these many religions is to stimulate believers to vie with one another in a contest of good works. Which religion leads its adherents to live the most strenuous moral life? Here again is *Surah* 5:48, now with the last verse: "for each [nation] we have appointed a [different] divine law and traced-out way. Had Allah willed, he could have made you one community. So vie with each other in good works."

In his explanation of religious diversity, its origins and benign consequences, Cusanus appropriated the basic claims of these Qur'anic texts. Indeed, in his copy of the Qur'an, Cusanus drew a pointer to this verse (*Surah* 5:48) and wrote in the margin: "*point causam diversitatis sectarum.*"[44] In *De pace fidei*, the Archangel seemed to have studied the

43. All Qur'an quotations are from Pickthall's translation of *The Meaning of the Glorious Koran*. I am indebted to my Islamicist colleague, Professor Louise Marlow, for assistance in working my way into the Qur'an.

44. Cusanus, *Nicholas of Cusa*, 223 n. 13.

Qur'an since he was quite familiar with its view of religious diversity. According to his report to God,

> You [God] appointed for your people different kings and seers, who are called prophets; in carrying out the responsibility of your mission many of them have instituted worship and laws in your name. [The people] accepted these laws as if you, the King of kings, had spoken to them face to face, and they believed they heard not them but you in them. You sent the different nations different prophets and teachers, some at one time and others at another. (I.4)

> Therefore, it is you [God], the giver of life and being, who seem to be sought in the different rites by different ways and are named with different names. (I.5)

In this scenario, the sequence of actions seems quite straightforward. God sends prophets and teachers to the different nations of the world. These prophets establish rites of worship and teachings of law for their people. The people, in turn, believe these teachings "as if the King of kings had spoken to them, face to face." From God through prophets to believing people: this is the way in which the variety of religions in the world was created.

Cusanus also followed the Qur'an in explaining the continuing role of diverse religions: to stimulate people to vie with each other in their service of God. The Qur'an located this rivalry in the sphere of good works. Cusanus recognized that "this rivalry exists for the sake of you [God]" but, for the purposes of his argument, he located it in the sphere of ritual. As he wrote, " [Perhaps] it is not expedient to [remove the differences in rites] in order that the diversity may contribute to devotion, as when any region expends more attentive effort in performing its ceremonies as if they would become more pleasing to you" (I.6).

In constructing his narrative explanation of religious diversity, it is obvious that Cusanus drew primarily on his Islamic sources.[45] To be sure, he never identified the Qur'an as a source for the Archangel's speech. A reader unfamiliar with the sacred text of Islam would have

---

45. Cusanus not only borrowed from the Qur'an, but also complicated its claims. The recipients of God's laws, rites, and teachings were humans, and Nicholas left plenty of room for them to mess things up. God remains a complicit agent in the origins of the different religions, but people play their role too. And there is even a part for the "Prince of Darkness."

no reason to suspect its presence in the writings of a Church Cardinal, especially in a text composed in the summer of 1453. It is the Toledan Collection of Islamic texts, including the Qur'an, and Cusanus's marginal notes on these texts in his library—not the text he wrote for the eyes of his contemporaries—that disclose his appropriation of Islamic sources. There is a familiar aphorism in modern inter-religious dialogue: in dialogue between believers of different religions, the minds of both parties are changed. Cusanus was in conversation with the Qur'an, if not Muslim believers, and it is obvious that his mind was changed.

Human Grounds for Religious Diversity

In addition to the Qur'anic teaching about many prophets, Cusanus offered a second explanation for the proliferation of religions: the classical view of religion as developed by Cicero. For Western authors, it was Cicero who communicated the argument for the validity of religion from the consent of all nations (*ex consensu gentium*). This classical argument began with empirical evidence: everywhere, in all societies, people believe in some kind of power greater than their own. They do not do this because of the influence of one culture upon another. Independently of each other, cultures have adopted the conviction that gods exist. The only explanation for the universality of such a belief is "an innate conviction engraved on their hearts."

> If this realization [concerning the certainty of the existence of God or the gods] was not firmly implanted in our minds, such steadfast belief would not have endured nor been strengthened in the course of time, nor could it have become securely lodged in succeeding generations and ages of mankind.[46]

> So there is general agreement amongst all persons of every nation. All have an innate conviction that gods exist, for it is, so to say, engraved on their hearts. No one denies that they exist, though there is a range of opinions about their nature.[47]

As is apparent from the above quotes, Cicero's version of this argument not only claims to establish the validity of religious belief, but also the diversity of its forms. The difference of opinion about the nature of the gods is as certain as is the certainty of belief in some form of divine

---

46. Cicero, *Nature of the Gods*, II.5.
47. Ibid., II.12.

power. Cicero's argument thus blended together a universal innate conviction with its culturally diverse expression.

Cusanus borrowed both sides of this argument from Cicero: the claim that the universality of religious convictions proved the validity of religion and that the variety of religious convictions was as universal as the innate conviction. As Cusanus wrote in 1450, "the innate sense of religion (*religio connata*) has always appeared diversely in the world. The immortality of our mind is given to us by nature, shown to us by the certain and universal assertion of all men."[48] He made the same point in his earlier (1443) work, *On Conjectures*. Only in that case, he made the content of the universal religion more specific: "there is a specific kind of religion—one which promises an immortal end—that is inherent in all men by nature—as is apparent—and that the inhabitants of this world participate in various ways" (DC II 15.147). For Cusanus, religion was not only innate, engraved on something like DNA, but in its external expression, it always "appeared diversely in various ways." Uniformity in expression was not a characteristic of religion.

The diversity of religions is, therefore, not a condition likely to disappear in the immediate future. God initiated this plurality by the different prophets he sent to the different nations of the world. The universal religious hunger of humanity finds expression not in a single form but in a rich variety shaped by the particular mores and materials of the different regions of the world. In my terms, God and humanity conspire together to preserve religion in both its transcendental unity and its empirical variety.

Cusanus's Argument by Chapters

In this exposition of Cusanus's argument, I will follow the order of his text, for he developed his proposal in several clearly ordered stages. Chapters 1–3 constitute a kind of prologue in which Cusanus introduced the problem of religiously inspired violence along with his alternative diagnosis of the problem and proposed solution. He also developed here his theory of religious diversity, its origins in God and in human nature. Chapters 4 and 5 set forth the philosophical foundations for his argument. The "intellectual representatives" of the Greeks and Italians

48. *Idiota de mente* h. vol. 5 III 15. For English translation, see Cusanus, *Layman on Wisdom*.

quickly recognize the ontological priority of unity to diversity, and the corresponding necessity to discern the unity of diverse phenomena. Chapters 6 and 7 deal with polytheists and idolaters. Cusanus explained how both are engaged in the worship of one God, albeit in a confused manner. Chapters 8–15 focus on a core of purportedly common beliefs shared by Jews, Christians, Muslims, and "most other" religions. In chapters 16 and 17 Cusanus returned to the problem of religion's generation of violence, though now with a focus exclusively on rites. Through Paul's instruction on justification, Cusanus explained why the differences in rites were unimportant since justification and salvation were by faith, not by works. Chapters 18 and19 continued the discussion of rites, now with a focus on Christian sacraments of baptism, Eucharist, ordination, marriage and other Christian rituals. The last half of chapter 19 concludes the treatise, noting that historical research confirms the argument concerning the unity of faith and worship in the diversity of religions.

PROLOGUE: CHAPTERS 1–3

The distinction between faith and rites appears at the very beginning of his treatise: it was "because of different religious rites" that the persecution in Constantinople was "raging more than ever" (I.1). It appears again in the most famous line of this treatise, a veritable Cusanus signature line: "all will know that there is only one religion in the variety of rites" (I.6). The cause of civil and international disturbances, therefore, was not the contents of religion but merely the rites of religion.

PHILOSOPHICAL FOUNDATIONS: CHAPTERS 4–5

The dialogues with representatives of humanity begin with the Greek and Italian, who also speak on behalf of philosophy. The Greek begins by posing a practical difficulty: "How could this unity of religions be introduced by us ... since each nation will accept with difficulty another faith" (IV.10)? The Word's reply states unambiguously the theme to be developed in the remainder of the treatise: "you will find that not another faith but the one and the same faith is presupposed everywhere" (IV.10).

The remainder of the treatise will develop how this one faith is manifest in the worship and beliefs of differing religions just as one wisdom is manifest in differing wise men. The analogy between the unity of wisdom/religion and the many different expressions of wisdom/religion runs throughout these two chapters. The last line blends both: "see how you, the philosophers of the various traditions agree in the religion of one God whom you all presuppose, in that which as lovers of wisdom you profess" (V.15).

The Unity of Religions in Worship: Chapters 6 and 7

In chapters 6 and 7, Cusanus turned his attention to the most apparent differences that appear to divide religions from each other: namely, the worship of many gods and the worship of statues and images. These chapters disclose the plan of persuasion that he followed throughout this treatise. He begins with a Christian norm readily understood by his readers: in these chapters, it is the worship of one God. He will then demonstrate how the worship of polytheists and idolaters is not the gross violation of this norm that it appears to be. Polytheists actually intend to worship one God, but are confused, and idolaters have a misguided veneration of holy figures, which could be perfectly proper if clearly distinguished from the worship of one God. Thus that which appears to be so alien to Christian worship turns out to be not that different from it after all.

In the dialogue of chapter 6, it is the Arab—that zealous advocate of strict monotheism—who poses the question of polytheism: "I ask those who worship more than one god how they can concur with the philosophers in the concept of one God" (VI.17). No polytheist replies to this question—perhaps there were none in heaven. The Word, however, did provide an answer with two arguments.

First, the Word reminded the Arab of the Neo-Platonist model of ontological dependence elaborated in the two prior chapters. One of Cusanus's favorite illustrations of this teaching was the relation between white objects and whiteness. White objects do not possess their whiteness by themselves but only as derived from whiteness itself: "without whiteness existing there are no white things" (VI.17). Similarly, "without divinity existing there are no gods" (VI.17). Therefore, the gods of polytheism while many, derive their "godness" from the one divinity. Those who worship many gods are, in fact and without knowing it, actually worshipping the one God who is the source of the "godness" in the many gods. In light of this, Cusanus did not see a huge gap between the worship of God-fearing Christians and the worship of Asian believers directed apparently to many gods. For Cusanus, it seemed relatively simple for those who worshipped many gods to make explicit in their worship the one God whom they unwittingly worship already.

Second, the Word introduced the biblical doctrine of creation as a belief implicit in the worship of one God. The world, which is one, requires a creator or first cause, who is one. The Word notes that "there was never a people so dull as to believe in plural gods each of which would have been the first cause, source or creator of the universe" (VI 17). After demonstrating that the so-called polytheists were actually confused monotheists, the Word recommended that the polytheists make explicit in their worship what is already implicit and required by ordinary reason: namely the worship of one God, the creator of all.

Chapter 7 established a similar conclusion concerning the worship practices of "idolaters." As previously noted, Cusanus owned and annotated a copy of Marco Polo's account of religious practices in "India," that is, in Asia. So it was an Asian ("an Indian") who posed the question, "What about statues and images?" (VII.19).

The Word provides a two-pronged answer to this question. On the one hand, some images may be helpful to "the worship of one God" and hence to religion. They should have a continuing role in the worship practices of that community. On the other hand, if any image led believers away from "the worship and adoration of the one God, they must be destroyed" (VII 19).

In addition to these considerations, the Word and "the Indian" agree on the desirability of eliminating idolatry in "India" so that "the Indian" people might catch up with the more "advanced" nations of the world. As the Word noted, "the very prudent Romans and Greeks and Arabs have destroyed their idols . . . it is hoped that the Indians as idolaters will act similarly" (VII.20). As Cusanus had noted in his earlier book, *On Learned Ignorance*, among the Romans, only the "simple folk were ever led astray into idolatry; the wise correctly believed in the unity of God" (DDI I.25.84). Cusanus was confident that the Indian people would not wish to remain among the "simple folk" forever.

By this point in his treatise, Cusanus had incorporated all known forms of worshipping communities—worshippers of one God, many gods, and idols—within his encompassing concept of religion. All of them worshipped one God explicitly, implicitly, or potentially. Those that were not yet in full compliance with the norm of worshipping one God could move in that direction easily, by making explicit what they already did, or by joining the post-idolatrous age of enlightened nations. Recognizing the worship of one God as a logical necessity and implicit intention of Asian polytheists and idolaters should not be that difficult for Cusanus's Christian readers, especially those who shared his Neo-Platonist world view. When viewed from the perspective of inner intentions and logic, there is the same goal in the worship of all peoples; only the external expression of that worship differs.

The Unity of Religions in Faith: Chapters 8–15

In these chapters, Cusanus pursued the same strategy as he had in the previous two chapters. He set forth a Christian norm—such as the worship of one God—and then argued that other religions, by intention and/or rational implication from other beliefs and behaviors, also worshipped one God or could easily be led to such worship. However, the focus of these chapters is not worship, but faith in the sense of *fides* or belief. And the other religions are most often not Asian but Western, most often Islam but also Judaism.

In order to identify the consensus of faith, Cusanus set forth a series of normative Christian beliefs: the Trinity, Incarnation, and resurrection; the Virgin Birth, crucifixion, and eternal life or paradise. This litany of beliefs might be described, in the language of Cusanus, as an enfolded version of the Christian faith as unfolded in the Apostles' Creed. In treating all of these beliefs, however, Cusanus intended to stress not their particularity in Christian scriptures and ecumenical creeds, but their universality. These are beliefs. that belong at least to all the Abrahamic religions and, according to Cusanus, some of these beliefs are shared by the believers of all religions.

Belief in a Triune God. In explicating evidence for a universal Trinitarian view of God, Cusanus presupposed a distinction established in his earlier book, *On Learned Ignorance*. All positive names that are attributed to God apply only to God's relation to creatures and not to Godself: "God's proper name is ineffable" (DDI I 24.75). Thus, the proper names for God embedded in Christian doctrine and liturgy—"Father, Son, and Holy Spirit"—are true only for God's relations to creatures (DDI I 24.80). Such names for God may be "appropriate" but more "suitable" categories would be ontological terms, such as "unity, thatness, and identity" (VIII.24) or the tetragrammaton signifying "One and All" or better "All in One" (DDI I 24.75). When Cusanus stated that all people believe in God as triune, he meant that all believe in God as one, but not a static One.

Cusanus then began citing evidence from other religions differentiating distinct elements within God. Jews and Muslims speak of God's soul, or spirit, or wisdom "although most do not notice that they are acknowledging the Trinity" (IX.26). "Pagans also gave names to God according to God's various relations to creatures ... Jupiter ... Saturn ... Mars ..." (DDI I 25.83). He then explained the necessity for such an interior distinction within God in terms of God's "fruitfulness" as creator. In the words of Isa 66:9, the Jews recognized a Trinity implicit in God's fruitfulness: "how could he who has given others the fruitfulness of generation be himself sterile?" (IX.25). The pagans also recognized the necessity for such an inner dynamic: "[Hermes] declared that the cause of all things, God, enfolds in God both masculine and feminine sex, of which Hermes believed that Cupid and Venus were the unfolding" (DDI I 25.83). After providing some examples of implicitly trinitarian discourse in philosophy—such as the Platonic notion of a world soul— Cusanus concluded, "So it is clearly seen that all the wise had touched on something of the Trinity in unity" (IX.27). All religions, and indeed, all the wise, have always understood some interior distinction within God, though they did not recognize the trinitarian implications of their own beliefs. They were not only anonymous theists; they were anonymous trinitarian theists.

Belief in a Resurrection and Incarnation. Cusanus linked together his arguments for the universality of beliefs in a resurrection and the Incarnation. I will explicate first his conviction that the religions of all people hoped for a resurrection, and then turn to the Incarnation, though this reverses the order of Cusanus's explication.

For Cusanus, a belief in a resurrection after death is a central belief of all peoples. It is not limited to Christians, nor is it even restricted to the Abrahamic traditions of Judaism, Christianity, and Islam. In the words of Peter, "does not almost every religion—of the Jews, Christians, Arabs and most other men—hold that the human mortal nature of every man will arise after temporal death to everlasting life?" (XIII.42).

Cusanus knew of some form of resurrection belief in Islam and Judaism; that was not difficult to establish. His conviction that such a belief was also characteristic of the religions of "most other men" was based upon a religious psychological intuition. After discussing this belief as it appeared in Islam and Judaism, the Syrian asked Peter, "What of the other traditions (*sectiis*)?" to which Peter replied:

> The same. For all men desire and expect only eternal life in their human nature, and for this they instituted ceremonies for the purification of souls and sacrifices in order better to fit themselves for eternal life in their nature. Men do not desire happiness, which is eternal life, in any other nature than their own; man does not wish to be anything else but man, not an angel or any other nature; but he wants to be a happy man who would obtain final happiness. Now this happiness is nothing else but the fruition or union of the human life with its source, from which life itself flows, that is, with the divine immortal life. (XIII.44)

The Augustinian argument, from the desire for happiness to the only form of being in which that desire could be fulfilled eternally, is here used by Cusanus to establish the universality of a resurrection hope. In other religions, the rituals of purification and sacrifice thus provided the means of attaining this hope, or so Cusanus understood them.

The Syrian agrees with this teaching of Peter: "the hope of all men is that they can sometime obtain happiness, for this is the end of all religion. And there is no deception in this, for this hope, common to all, is from an innate longing, and to such hope religion, thus likewise innate in all, seeks to attain" (XIII.44). The Syrian then gives expression to one of Cusanus's basic claims concerning world religions: all religions share the same end, goal, or purpose. For Cusanus, that goal is happiness in its final and only adequate form, as union with God. The Syrian does not even need to speak of religions in the plural; he can speak of religion in the singular because he regards the basic script of the many religions to be the same.

While the belief in, and hope for, a resurrection is explicit in the three Abrahamic religions, and implicit in the religions of "most other men," this belief "presupposes" another belief: namely, the actual union of one human with God, one human who could be a representative of all. Peter concludes the lengthy speech quoted above with the following:

> But should this [union with God] be possible for man unless it is conceded that the common nature of all men is elevated to such a union in some person through whom as mediator all men could acquire the ultimate goal of their desires? And this person is the way because he is the man through whom every man has access to God, who is the goal of desires. It is Christ, therefore, who is presupposed by all who hope to obtain final happiness. (XIII.44)

The incarnation of God in Christ therefore establishes the possibility for an eternal union between the divine and the human. Without such a precedent, there would be no grounds for a hope for a resurrection that would unite the human and the divine eternally. The union of God and humanity in Christ therefore provides the necessary precedent for such a union for all people: "therefore if faith holds this [hope for a resurrection], then the human nature is antecedently united with the divine nature in some man, namely in him who is the face of all peoples and the highest Messiah and Christ, as the Arabs and Jews call Christ" (XIII.43). Having established the necessity for an ontological mediator for a resurrection hope, it was only necessary for Cusanus to clarify some confusion in the Jewish and Muslim understanding of the Incarnation. The Persian notes that the Christians in his land reject the incarnation because "the immutable God [cannot] become a man and the creator a creature. Except for a few in Europe, almost all of us deny this" (XI.30). Peter agrees with this denial, and then proceeds to develop a Chalcedonian Christology of two natures.

> Therefore it must be held that in Christ the human nature is so united with the Word or divine nature that the human nature does not pass into the divine but clings in such an indissoluble way that it is not a person separately in itself but in the divine nature; the end then is that the human nature, called to the succession of eternal life with the divine, can obtain immortality in the divine nature. (XI.35)

With that confusion clarified, it is only necessary for Peter to point out the many reasons why the Muslims could recognize the incarnation of God in Christ as consistent with their own teachings: "the Arabs can be brought to accept this belief [in the Incarnation] since through it the unity of God which they most greatly strive to protect, is not violated but preserved" (XII.39). Peter then notes other Muslim beliefs about

Christ that would lead them to recognize the union of his humanity with God.

> The sect of Arabs, which is large, also admits that Christ raised the dead and created birds from clay and many other things which they expressly confess Jesus Christ to have done as one having power; from this belief they can be easily led, since it cannot be denied that he himself did these things in the power of the divine nature to which the human was hypostatically united. (XII.41)

Here, as elsewhere, when the agreement in faith is not yet realized, Cusanus thinks it can be easily attained.

BELIEF IN THE VIRGIN BIRTH, CRUCIFIXION, AND PARADISE. In dealing with these three beliefs, Cusanus temporarily ignored the religions of Asia and ancient Rome, confining his attention to the three Abrahamic religions, especially Christian-Muslim points of disagreement. He began, however, with the Virgin Birth, and on that item, Christians and Muslims agreed: "all who believe that Christ has come [that is, Christians and Muslims] acknowledge that he was born of the virgin" (XIV.46). Only the Jews disagree on this belief and since, as Cusanus stated repeatedly, the Jews are few in number, their disagreement on matters of faith is insignificant since they are not sufficiently numerous or powerful to threaten the peace.

Disagreement between Christians and Muslims concerning the crucifixion was, however, a more difficult matter. Cusanus recognized that the Muslims exempted Christ from a death upon the cross because of their "reverence for Christ." However, if they understood the purpose of Christ's death, they would not deny it. For, as he argued, Christ freely gave up his life in order to show all men that "the life of this world, which is loved so persistently by all, is to be regarded as nothing" (XIV.47). It is the life of the future, the life of the Kingdom of Heaven that matters.

> But no one can enter the Kingdom of Heaven unless he lay aside the kingdom of this world through death. . . . Now if Christ as mortal man had not yet died, he would not yet have laid aside mortality; this would mean he did not enter the Kingdom of Heaven in which no mortal can be. Therefore, if he who is the first fruits and firstborn of all men did not open the heavenly realms, our nature united with God has not yet been introduced into the kingdom. Thus no man could have been in the

> Kingdom of Heaven if human nature united with God had not yet been introduced. (XIV.49)

> Finally, if Christ preached that in the resurrection men will attain immortality after death, how could the world be better assured of this than that he willingly died and was resurrected and appeared alive? (XIV.48)

The cross is the way to humanity's union with God: this is the purpose of Christ's death. It is not atonement for sin. That word is not mentioned in Cusanus's exposition of the crucifixion.

Cusanus resolves the Christian-Muslim difference on Paradise in the same way that Ramon Lull did. First, he dismissed the literal Qur'anic passages which appear to suggest endless sex with beautiful maidens; for Cusanus, the Qur'an's account of sex in Paradise was not likely to arouse the desire of even those men most "given to the vices of the flesh" (XV.51). Next, he gave the heavenly orgy of the Qur'an the best possible interpretation: namely, it was Mohammed's bribe to lure an uneducated populace to give up their idolatry (XV.51–52). Finally, he cited Avicenna's interpretation of these passages as promising "the intellectual happiness of the vision or fruition of God" (XV.52). With this word from Avicenna, he could conclude: "in this matter there will be no difficulty in reconciling all traditions" (XV.52).

THE DIVERSITY OF RITES NEUTRALIZED: CHAPTERS 16–19

The spokesman for the Tartars first appears in chapter 16. Presumably, the prior dialogues have convinced him of the actual or potential unity of religions in matters of faith; at least, he has no questions on such issues. However, he sees no end to religious persecution so long as there is so much diversity in rites—matters such as circumcision, marriage, and sacrifices. The Word calls on Paul to answer the Tartar's concern, and for those of us who live after the Reformation (which Cusanus did not), his first few lines are especially familiar:

> It is necessary that it be shown that salvation of the soul is not granted from works but from faith. For Abraham, father of the faith of all believers, whether Christians or Arabs or Jews, believed in God, and this was credited to him as righteousness: the soul of the just will inherit eternal life. When this is acknowledged these varieties of rites will not be a cause of disturbance. (XVI.55)

Cusanus's Paul then proceeds to explain justification by grace through faith, and even used some technical Reformation language: *pura gratia*, a *solo* qualifying *fides*, and a repudiation of merits. Cusanus then concluded this Pauline lesson on faith in his preferred language of happiness. The divine blessing promised in Christ is the "final goal of desires or the happiness which is called eternal life" (XVI.57).

The Tartar is therefore prepared to share the message with "the simple Tartars" that "it is Christ in whom they can obtain happiness" (XVI.58). But he wonders if "faith suffices." Paul then tells the Tartar that it must be a formed faith. This leads to the recognition of another commonality among all religions: namely, their moral teachings.

> The divine commandments are very brief and well known to all and are common to all nations. Indeed, the light showing them to us was created simultaneously with the rational soul. For God speaks in us that we should love him from whom we have received being and that we should do to another only what we want done to us. Therefore, love is the fulfillment of the law of God, and all laws are brought back to this. (XVI.59)

CHRISTIAN RITES IN PARTICULAR. Cusanus dealt with the problem posed by particular Christian sacraments as a sub-set of the larger problem of diversity in rites. He drew some fine distinctions in this section. On the one hand, Christian sacraments are rites, and therefore, Cusanus cannot exempt them from his prior teaching of justification. Hence, in discussing both baptism and the Eucharist, he acknowledged that neither is necessary for salvation. The Armenian, who has replaced the Tartar, states "It seems necessary to accept this sacrament [baptism] since it is necessary for salvation." To this, Paul replies, "Faith is a necessity for adults, who can be saved without the sacrament when they cannot receive it" (XVII.62). Similarly, the Bohemian (that is, from the party of the Hussites and their concern for communion in both kinds) raises repeated concern regarding the Eucharist to which Paul replies, "If faith is present, this sacrament, as it is in sensible signs, is not thus of such a necessity that without it there is no salvation" (XVIII.66). But having repudiated the necessity for any rite, Cusanus did provide ample arguments as to why Christians should avail themselves of both baptism and the Eucharist—not necessary but obligatory.

Cusanus concluded this discussion of rites with some attention to marriage and ordination. Marriage is a rite practiced in "all nations" and "so, likewise, priesthood is also found in every religion" (XIX.67). For Cusanus, the universality of these two rituals of marriage and ordination will increase the ease of adoption of their Christian forms: "therefore, agreement will be easier in these common things, and also in the judgment of all the others the Christian religion will be proved to observe a more praiseworthy purity in both sacraments" (XIX.67).

Cusanus's judgment here, suggesting conformity to Christian forms in rites, was not typical of him. He more often counseled church leaders to accept a diversity of rites so long as "the peace of faith might not persevere less intact" (XVIII.66). Or, in even stronger language, he warned, "to seek exact conformity in all things is rather to disturb the peace" (XIX.67). On less important rituals, such as "fasting, ecclesiastical duties, abstinence from food and drink, forms of prayers, etc.," Cusanus also advised diversity:

> Where no conformity in manner can be found, nations should be permitted their own devotional practices and ceremonials, provided faith and peace are preserved. A certain diversity will perhaps increase devotion when each nation will strive to make its own rite more splendid through zeal and diligence in order to surpass another and so to obtain greater merit with God and praise in the world. (XIX.67)

While it may not be clear how Paul, who previously proclaimed justification without works, could defend zeal in the conduct of rituals as a path to "greater merit with God," it is clear how Cusanus could make this argument at the end of his treatise: it is the same one he introduced in the beginning, which he had borrowed from the Qur'an.

CONCLUSION: CHAPTER 19

The resources of heaven apparently included some good archives: "very many books of those who wrote on the observances of the ancients were produced and indeed excellent ones in every language" (XIX.68). After examining the writings of these authors, it was discovered that "all the diversity consisted in rites rather than in the worship of one God; from all the writings collected into one it was found that all from the beginning always presupposed and worshipped the one God" (XIX.68). Once this "concord of religions was concluded in the heaven of reason," God commanded the "wise" representatives of humanity "to lead the nations to the unity of true worship and . . . one faith. . .and so establish an everlasting peace" (XIX.68).

Cusanus's treatise did not include any report of the results of this heaven-sent mission to the nations of the world.

Translating Cusanus into Twenty-First Century Discourse

In concluding this discussion of Cusanus's theology of religion, I want to try an experiment. If I transpose Cusanus's theology from his century to ours, what would it look like? What are the negative and positive categories that might provide an accurate description of his position? How might we identify the positive legacy of Cusanus for our present? What would we want to criticize and reject?

Let's begin with some descriptive negations: what his position is not. Of first importance is that, in his theology of religion, Cusanus was not an exclusivist. Had Cusanus wanted an exclusivist doctrinal weapon to hurl at the Muslim enemy in 1453, he had one available, for only eleven years before he wrote *De pace fidei*, the Council of Florence had decreed:

> [The Holy Roman Catholic Church] . . . believes, professes, and preaches that "no one remaining outside the Catholic Church, not only pagans," but also Jews, heretics, and schismatics, can become partakers of eternal life; but they will go to the "eternal fire prepared for the devil and its angels" [Matt 25.41], unless before the end of their life they are joined to it. . . And no one can be saved, no matter how much alms one has given, even if shedding one's blood for the name of Christ, unless one remains in the bosom of the Catholic Church.[49]

Cusanus, however, chose to ignore this completely, even though he was surely aware of the Council's work, for he had personally delivered delegates from the Greek Church to this Council.

In contrast with the position of the Council of Florence, the worship and faith that Nicholas described in *De pace fidei* was not limited by church boundaries. Similarly, the benefit of God's work in Christ was not confined to church members; the hope for a resurrection and eternal life, which he believed was manifest in "most religions," was made

---

49. Quoted in Dupuis, *Theology of Religious Pluralism*, 95–96.

available to all by the reality of God's union with humanity in Christ. An author who advocated "mutual tolerance" (XV.60) in dealing with the diversity of rites in different religions was not about to assign all of humanity outside church boundaries to an eternity apart from God.

Second, in his theology of religion, Cusanus was not a "religious pluralist" as that term was defined in the late twentieth century. John Hick once claimed that Cusanus belonged to his company of "religious pluralists." Hick included Nicholas of Cusa among a group of "pre-modern religious pluralists," and quoted with approval his signature line, "only one religion in the variety of rites."[50] While Hick did not develop his reasons for identifying Nicholas as a pre-modern religious pluralist, Paul Naumann gave an interpretation of "one religion/many rites" that I think Hick would have found convincing. Naumann was a German Cusanus scholar writing in the middle of the past century. I quote him as follows:

> The *complicatio* [enfolding] of the one true religion has become unfolded in the profusion of the empirical religions. . . All religions are only inadequate representations of the one true religion. Each of them in its own way, though only imperfectly, gives expression to the Absolute. . . . The Christian church, however, remains for Nicholas the religious community which comes nearest to the one true religion.[51]

In this version, Cusanus, like Hick, would be a Neo-Kantian. Not only God but also the "one religion" would be thoroughly concealed in the noumenal realm; human beings would only have access to the symbolic unfolding of this noumenal reality in the phenomenal order of this world. All religions (at least all axial religions) would provide equally perfect and imperfect expressions of the one religion.

In light of a close reading of *De pace fidei*, Hick's version of Cusanus has to be rejected. Cusanus never did interpret the relation of one religion and many rites in terms of his *complicatio-explicatio* schema.[52] Indeed, he never completely integrated the slogan of "one religion/many rites" into his own position. For Cusanus, the technically accurate version of this slogan would have to read: one faith/many rites, or one

50. Hick, *Christian Theology of Religions,* 34 and 37.

51. Naumann, *Cribratio Alkoran* as quoted in McTighe, "Nicholas of Cusa's Unity-Metaphysics," 162–63.

52. See the evidence and argument of McTighe above.

worship and faith/many rites. "Religion," for him, was a vague term that includes the more specific elements of "faith" and "rites." Furthermore, any claim to relative parity among different religions runs up against the hard wall of Cusanus's clear statement of faith: one triune God who in the person of Christ unites humanity with divinity and thus gives people "in almost every religion" the hope of resurrection and eternal happiness (XIII.42). This is "the one orthodox faith [to which] all diversity of religions will be led" (III.8). If John Hick had read these passages in *De pace fidei*, I cannot imagine that he would claim Cusanus as a soul mate. For Cusanus to fit the mold of Hick's religious pluralism, he would have had to renounce his carefully crafted statement of faith.

If Cusanus's theology of religion was neither that of an exclusivist nor that of a "religious pluralist," I can imagine him in the company of Catholic inclusivists as represented by the writings of Jacque Dupuis, and hence I find Dupuis to be a more reliable interpreter of Cusanus than Hick. Dupuis makes explicit Cusanus's Christian norms for the universal faith:

> The essential presuppositions upon which the universal religion [of Cusanus] must be based . . . are monotheistic, Trinitarian, and Christological. In these, as Nicholas attempts to show, all are agreed, if not explicitly at least implicitly. If beliefs differ, the ultimate reason is that in himself God remains unknown and is ineffable. All historical religions, then, Christianity included, reflect the transcendent reality only imperfectly; none possess the absolute truth, even if Christianity approaches it most closely with its Trinitarian and Christological faith.[53]

As is apparent from the above quote, Dupuis assigned to Nicholas his own version of Catholic pluralism, what I choose to call a soft form of inclusivism.[54]

As an inclusive pluralist, Nicholas understood all religions to be expressions of a triune christological form of monotheism. This faith was virtually universal. As a soft inclusivist, Nicholas understood

53. Dupuis, *Theology of Religious Pluralism*, 108.

54. Dupuis would not be happy being assigned to any version of the inclusivist position. He intended that his project would overcome the split between Catholic inclusivism and Hick's religious pluralism. I interpret his position as inclusivist because of his commitment to christological and trinitarian norms and because the event of God's union with humanity in Jesus Christ has consequences for all peoples and all religions. Cusanus shared these same commitments.

Christianity to express most clearly the core convictions of this universal faith. However, even the Christian form of this faith was not a finished product; nor was it perfect. And since (according to Cusanus's archangel) God had set this drama of salvation in a theater of religious diversity, these many religions must have their own role to play, their own contributions to make, correcting Christian traditions at some points and extending them in others. This, at least, is my version of a soft inclusivism, as this position is attributed to Nicholas by Jacques Dupuis. I think it is as good a fit as can be made between Nicholas's theology of religion and the conceptual models of the early twenty-first century.

What I value most in Cusanus, and miss in many of my contemporaries, is his grounding of theology of religion in the peace ethic of Jesus. In response to the growing hostility of European Christians to the Muslim Turks who conquered Constantinople, Cusanus invited his fellow Christians to adopt a new view of these religious enemies as people of faith and participants in a "peace of faith" (*De pace fidei*). Like other Christian theologians considered in this book, he extended the "love of neighbor" to include other believers who may be perceived as religious enemies.

Shortly after September 11, 2001, I read stories of Christian responses to Muslim neighbors that reminded me of Cusanus. In Minneapolis and several other cities in the United States, some angry Americans had vandalized the cars of Muslims gathered at their mosques for Friday services. When this news was made public, groups of Christians from neighboring congregations volunteered to patrol parking lots adjacent to mosques during Friday services. In the midst of interreligious hostilities, these people sought to protect those who were perceived as religious enemies—as did Cusanus in the fifteenth century.

While I appreciate Cusanus's continuity with the peace ethic of Jesus, I cannot recommend his version of Catholic inclusivism for the twenty-first century. Cusanus was able to reduce the diverse practices and purposes of the world's religions to nothing but small variations of the Christian religion. He could do this in good conscience because his knowledge of Asian religions was limited to two sources: the *Liber Tartarorum* and Marco Polo. He was therefore free to construe his limited knowledge of other religions in a manner consistent with the Christian story so familiar to him. Christian theologians of the twenty-first century have lost the benefit of such limited sources and gained the burden of reflecting accurately the diversity of practice and purpose among the world's religions.

Cusanus's Significance for the Twenty-first Century

Why does Cusanus matter? Cusanus matters because history matters. While this truism may have become less apparent in our own time, theology cannot forget it. Theology is one of those disciplines that moves forward only by re-discovering and re-engaging with its own traditions. A history of reflection on religious diversity is one of those traditions. This chapter documents the emergence of an inclusive pluralist position within Christian theology back in the days of an intact European Christendom, before the Reformation and before the Enlightenment. Before Nicholas, a theological engagement with other religions extends back to Ramon Lull in the thirteenth century and beyond Nicholas, forward to Thomas Jefferson in the late eighteenth century. These authors are related to each other, to common sources, and, of greatest importance, to a set of common human problems born of religious diversity. I suspect there are countless other voices in this marginal tradition, and I would hope for a coterie of scholars who would unearth their legacies, Jewish and Muslim, as well as Christian. The more voices we can reclaim for each religion, the more resources we will have as we deal with our own current, often hostile, inter-religious situation. History matters because, in theology if nowhere else, traditions matter.

History also matters for the discovery and construction of new knowledge. The sophomores of the world, who take our courses to learn more about the Christian religion, would benefit from an introduction to Cusanus. For all too many of them, the crusades and inquisitions, the persecution of the Jews and other religious minorities, epitomize the relation between Christianity and other believers. Cusanus's mind and spirit could wonderfully complement and modify their somewhat simplistic model of Christianity as a religion of coercion and violence. Similarly, those who construct new theologies of religions could also benefit from some knowledge of their own tradition. Religious pluralists in the last century proclaimed that they at last had crossed the theological Rubicon, shifting from a Christocentric to a theocentric perspective. However, in the early seventeenth century, Lord Herbert had already waded across those waters. Within the Christian religion, he was a pioneer of a theocentric theology. History, in its traditions and our knowledge of them, matters.

Moreover, Cusanus matters because faith matters. In response to the explosion of violent passions in Constantinople, he drafted a proposal of peace. Such a project was not born from pragmatic considerations. As previously noted, he did not compose his text as a realistic guide to negotiations among religions, and the Vatican under three different popes obviously paid little attention to *De pace fidei*. I could only conclude that Cusanus was in this text speaking a word from his faith, not from his political experience. The priority of peace in the Gospels is reflected in his treatise, its title and its argument. In this respect, also, Cusanus is a model for Christians in our own time. He offered an alternative response to the horrors born of religiously inspired passions— not a call for a war without end or a perpetual clash of civilizations, but a call for peace.

5

Wars of Christians against Christians

Herbert of Cherbury's Theological Antidote to Religious Warfare

Father Seguerend, [confessor to the King of France], made a sermon before his Majesty upon the text, "that we should forgive our enemies" (Matthew, 5:43–44). Having said many good things, he at last said, "We were indeed to forgive our enemies, but not the enemies of God, such as were heretics, and particularly those of the [Protestant] religion; and that his Majesty, as the most Christian King, ought to extirpate them wheresoever they could be found."[1]

LIKE RAMON LULL, LORD HERBERT WAS NEITHER A MEMBER OF THE clergy nor was he, by training or career, a professional theologian. In his profession, he served the first two Stuart kings of England as a diplomat and military advisor.[2] He had fought in the Netherlands as a volunteer in the forces of the Prince of Orange (1608 and again in 1614). While

1. Herbert, *Autobiography of Edward, Lord Herbert of Cherbury,* 244–45. Hereafter cited as *Life.* In contrast with the title of this book, Lord Herbert did not conceive of this partial memoir as a genuine autobiography; it ends in 1624 with the termination of his service as English ambassador to France though he lived for another twenty-four years. His text repeatedly states the purpose of this partial memoir as an informal means for passing on advice and wisdom for the next generation: "I pretend no further than to give some few directions to my posterity" (*Life,* 57). Sidney Lee provided "a continuation of the Life" after the end of Lord Herbert's memoir. Any citation after page 250 refers to Lee's "continuation"; all citations before that refer to Herbert's own writing.

2. Lord Herbert was an ambassador to France (1618–1624), a military advisor who drafted a plan for the reorganization of the army (1626), a member of the King's Council of War (1632), and a military historian who wrote an account of a failed English naval blockade (*The Expedition to the Isle of Rhé*). At the King's request, he also authored a paper supporting the role of the king in the life of the church ("On the King's Supremacy in the Church" in Hutcheson, *De religione laici.* Appendix B, 183–86).

in France he attempted to recruit an army of 4,000 Protestants for the Duke of Savoy.[3] Lord Herbert was a Renaissance man whose writings encompassed a variety of genres—poetry, autobiography, history, philosophy, theology, and the study of religions.[4] Although an amateur in all these fields, he was an original and proficient practitioner in many of them. My exploration of his legacy for Christian theology will draw upon a wide range of his writings.

Lord Herbert is seldom presented as a Christian theologian. In many studies, he is identified as the father of deism, the belief that an impersonal God created the world and then left it to run according to its own laws.[5] This absent landlord of the cosmos was not available for interaction with humans nor was he a likely object of religious devotion. Lord Herbert did not know God as impersonal and unavailable. Others claim that Lord Herbert is the founder of Natural Religion, which taught that a new religion of reason had superseded all particular religions. On the contrary, Lord Herbert was preoccupied with the question of determining the truth of the multiple religions of the world; he did not presume their obsolescence.

3. For his military service in the Netherlands, see *Life,* 142–50. For his unsuccessful venture in France, see *Life* 161–69.

4. Citations for his poetry refer to *Poems English and Latin,* edited by Smith. Hereafter cited as *Poems.* His historical writing discussed in this chapter is *The History of England under Henry VIII.* Hereafter cited as *Henry VIII.* His major philosophical work is *De veritate,* first published in 1624. Citations to the 1645 Latin edition refer to a facsimile reprint by Gawlick. Hereafter cited as *DV-L.* Citations for its English translation are from the Carré translation. Hereafter cited as *DV.* Herbert's theological reflections are interspersed in all of his writings, but his most focused discussion of Christian theology appears in two different texts with similar titles: *De religione laici,* edited by Hutcheson and "Lord Herbert of Cherbury's *Religio Laici*" edited by Wright in the *Modern Language Review.* The latter text was written in English, not Latin and addresses issues of faith in the personal style of Herbert's *Life.* Hence, I refer to it as "A Layman's Faith." Lord Herbert's survey of beliefs and practices of non-biblical religions, *De religione gentilium* was first published in Amsterdam, 1663. Page citations for the Latin text refer to the facsimile edition, hereafter cited as *DRG-L.* The English translation, *The Ancient Religion of the Gentiles and Causes of Their Errors,* was published in London, 1705 and is hereafter cited as *DRG.* Lord Herbert may have written *A Dialogue between a Tutor and his Pupil* or it may be the product of one of his early disciples. Herbert scholars are divided on this issue. Within the limits of this chapter, I have chosen to ignore this scholarly debate and the text. It does not add that much to the literature of unambiguous authorship.

5. For claims concerning Lord Herbert's Deism, see Hill, *Edward, Lord Herbert,* 22–28, 94.

The attribution of deism and Natural Religion to Lord Herbert needs to be rejected as post-Enlightenment projections onto an earlier Elizabethan era. Lord Herbert's faith was formed in the Elizabethan Church. His mature theology developed in response to intra-Christian theological disputes and religious wars of the early seventeenth century. His own thought can be correctly understood only when his writings are read in his own historical context. If Lord Herbert were the father of deism and the founder of Natural Religion, he would have had to live during the late seventeenth and early eighteenth century.[6] During this time, some of his disciples did indeed convert selections from his writings into basic texts of deism and Natural Religion. Lord Herbert should not be identified with these later writings by his followers.

In order to correct this confusion, I have devoted a considerable portion of this chapter to a discussion of the different Christian contexts that shaped Lord Herbert's faith and theology. The first is the Elizabethan Church of the late sixteenth century, especially its 1559 *Book of Common Prayer* and the household worship habits of young Herbert's mother, in whose home he lived for most of the first twenty-six years of his life. His mature theological writings disclose a direct continuity with the *Book of Common Prayer*, especially its service of *Morning Prayer*. In his late fifties, Lord Herbert described this early stage in the formation of his faith as follows:

> I bent myself chiefly to the Christian faith contained in the Holy Bible as having in it more exact precepts for teaching a good life and repentance than any other book whatsoever that I could meet with. Besides, I found myself through God's providence born in that Church and instructed even from my infancy in the holy doctrine drawn from thence.[7]

A second church context was quite different from the relatively stable and peaceful Elizabethan Church. Intra-Christian theological disputes and the wars they spawned were the dominant characteristics of this second Christian context. Lord Herbert was an early participant in the Arminian/Calvinist theological disputes in the Church of England;

---

6. For evidence and arguments correcting the claim that Lord Herbert was the father of Deism, see Pailin, "Herbert of Cherbury and the Deists." For evidence and arguments correcting the claim that Lord Herbert was the founder of Natural Religion, see R. Johnson, "Natural Religion."

7. *A Layman's Faith*, 296.

indeed, he formulated the major themes of his mature theology in the anti-Calvinist cause. Later, during his service as the English ambassador to France, he attempted to win political and military support for the position of King James' son in law, Frederick V, then the recently installed ruler of Bohemia. Herbert was not successful in his efforts and Frederick's kingship of Bohemia became one of the first political casualties of the Thirty Years' War. During this same period of time he attempted, without success, to restrain militant French Catholics who were once again engaged in war with French Protestants.

In his later years, he recounted his disappointment in the Church of England as its theological disputes undermined his faith. As a result, he abandoned any particular church as a foundation for faith, and instead "grounded his faith on those points piously assented unto by all Christians."

> I observed many things taught in the said Church which were vehemently opposed by other Christian Churches ... For my final resolution ... of these controversies ... I thought the best grounds for my faith were to be taken from those points which were piously assented unto by all Christians. And to lay aside the disputes and controversies of learned men until they were agreed among themselves and in the meantime to attend a good life and repentance.[8]

Near the end of his life he endured the military siege of his ancestral castle, a period of imprisonment in the Tower of London, and the threatened confiscation of his library as consequences of the English Civil War, fueled in good part by the passions of conflicting Christian partisans. From his personal immersion in Christian worship and his later role in theological disputes and wars, Lord Herbert knew both the resources of Christian faith and the destructive political consequences of doctrinal conflicts in a state-supported religion.

In between the relative stability of the Elizabethan Church and the divisive Calvinist/Arminian conflict was the interlude of Herbert's visit in France. In France young Herbert, the naïve believer, first discovered reasons for suspicion of the clergy in their political role as agents of the state. During his long-term residence in France with a close ally of the French King, Henri IV, Herbert first came to know political policies that fostered peace among Christians.

8. Ibid.

Lord Herbert's most important theological contribution can be summarized in this way.[9] He was a political theologian who sought to separate God's authority from the authority of government. In his view, the clergy were not reliable supporters of political peace. Too often, they pursued the economic and political interests of their constituency or themselves. Their unwillingness to compromise on doctrinal differences made armed conflict too frequently the only means of resolving disputes. He wanted to de-politicize the role of religious communities for the sake of peace. His critique of exclusivist forms of Christian theology (both Calvinist and Catholic) then dominant in Europe was consistent with his political theology. He regarded such theologies as alien to Christi's message and a means to enhance the power of one religion over against another.

Herbert thus denied the claims of any religion to having a monopoly on God's grace. For him God also used non-biblical religions as a means of grace. He accordingly devoted the last years of his life to a quasi-empirical study of world religions. Such a position, I suspect, would make Herbert into a secularist or relativist in the eyes of some Christians today. He was neither. Unlike the secularist, he insisted upon the universal role of religion in human life. For him humanity's engagement with God was not an option, but a practical necessity. The failures of our moral life and our hopes for a fulfillment beyond our finitude required our active engagement with God. In addition Lord Herbert also perceived the necessity of religion to serve as a check upon the excessive claims of reason, just as reason served to restrain the excesses of religious passion. Such a vision of humanity, its limits and possibilities, hardly fits the narrow mold of a secularist.

He was also not a relativist who gave equal value to all religions. God's identity was made known to him in the stories, psalms, hymns, and prayers of Christian worship. For him, God is consistently the One who promises a joyous fulfillment beyond the best satisfactions of the present world. God is the One who renews the human spirit in times of tribulation, who forgives mistakes made and wrongs done, and who gives the penitent a second chance. Such a God is not a synthetic com-

---

9. In 1629, Edward Herbert was given the title "Lord Herbert of Cherbury." Since almost all of his essays and books were written after this date, he is still identified by this title. In this chapter, I will also refer to him as Lord Herbert, while calling attention to the many years of his life that preceded his assumption of this title.

posite of bits and pieces from all religions; it is the God made known in the ministry of Jesus and the worship life of the Christian Church. Without labeling this God as Christian, Lord Herbert simply extended this vision of God's reign into many of the world's religions, but it is the same God who became engraved upon his heart through his experience of Christian worship. *LEAP*

The Elizabethan Church of England: Young Herbert's Formation in Christian Faith

Born in 1582 or 83, about halfway through the forty-five year reign of Elizabeth I, young Herbert grew up during a relatively stable period of the English Reformation. The previous generation had endured a series of extreme changes in England's state religion: from Roman Catholic to a national Catholic Church under Henry VIII (1534–1547), from the Henrician English Catholic Church to the Calvinist Church of Edward VI (1547–1553), and then back to the Roman Catholic Church under Mary (1553–1558). Those who did not follow the changing religious preference of their different rulers faced the prospects of imprisonment, execution, or both. It was not a happy time or place for Christians from any of these three traditions: Roman Catholic, Church of England Catholic, or Church of England Calvinist.

With the crowning of Elizabeth in 1558, however, England adopted a new strategy for building religious consensus. Within the Church of England a policy of patient persuasion replaced the older efforts of religious coercion. A combination of moderate Calvinists and English Catholics created a stable Protestant Church governed by bishops, worshipping according to biblically shaped liturgies, and informed by a theology that was mostly Calvinist. The 1559 *Book of Common Prayer* provided the primary means for the formation of a common faith among the English people. The young Herbert was one of the many Elizabethan Englishmen whose faith was formed by frequent worship from this source.[10] Those who excluded themselves from the Church of

---

10. "By the middle of Elizabeth's reign prayer book worship had become natural and right to many because it was the habit of the communities in which they were raised. By the 1580's the patterns of worship enforced by law in 1559 had penetrated to the grass roots" (Jones, *English Reformation*, 109). Lord Herbert's experience of prayer book worship as habitual and natural was therefore typical of his generation; only his transformation of this experience into a universal obligation and practice of humanity is unusual.

England—Roman Catholic recusants, Separatists, and Puritans—were increasingly tolerated by local practice, if not by law.[11] Herbert thus grew up in a church in which faith was shaped more by worship than by doctrine. Like others prominent in the Elizabethan Church, he regarded the bonds of unity between the Roman Catholic Church and the Church of England to be far stronger than any differences between them.[12] The larger society in which he lived was marked by a cluster of conflicting forms of Christianity. As a result, believers from different traditions who belonged to the same family, neighborhood, guild, or craft had to make repeated compromises and adjustments in their religious life.[13] An early form of religious diversity was thus a social condition indigenous to his society.

Three sorts of information flow together in my discussion of young Herbert's religious development: first, biographical information about his mother, Magdalen Herbert, especially her long relationship with her eldest son, Edward and the frequency of worship in her household; second, texts from the 1559 *Book of Common Prayer*, especially the service of *Morning Prayer* used in daily worship by members of Magdalen's household; and third, texts from Lord Herbert's mature writings, including his history of Henry VIII and his signature theological statement, the Common Notions of Religion, as developed in "A Layman's Faith."[14] The continuity between the worship experience of young Herbert and the mature theology of Lord Herbert become most apparent by juxtaposing these two disparate segments of his life with each other.

11. "James I observed that the law [prohibiting the practice of an illegal religion] would be better enforced if the [Catholic] recusants were not kin or friends of the judges" (Ibid., 142).

12. "I [Lord Herbert] conceived the points agreed upon on both sides [Roman Catholic and the Church of England] are greater bonds of amity betwixt us, than that the points disagreed on could break them" (*Life,* 154–55). John Donne, who had himself been raised as a Roman Catholic, expressed this same ecumenical view of blurred doctrinal differences:

> Rome, Wittenberg, or Geneva are all virtual beams of one Sun . . . They are not so contrary as the North and South Poles; and that [?] they are connatural pieces of one circle. (Donne, *Letters,* 25–26)

13. For examples of Roman Catholic and Puritan families in Elizabethan England negotiating their religious differences, see Jones, *English Reformation,* 50–53; for the effects of religious diversity on guilds, see ibid., 110ff.

14. Lord Herbert wrote *Henry VIII* between 1634 and 1639 and "A Layman's Faith" between 1639 and 1645.

Worship Habits of Magdalen Herbert's Household

As a product of Elizabethan England, Herbert's faith was formed and nourished by the Church of England, the 1559 *Book of Common Prayer*, and by a mother, Magdalen, who was as devoted to him as she was committed to the faith of that Church. Lord Herbert's father had died when he was only fifteen years old, shortly after he had begun his studies at Oxford.[15] As a result, his mother assumed the dominant role in shaping his faith and mind. Contemporary accounts of Magdalen emphasize two salient characteristics: 1) her devotion to her eldest son, Edward, and her unusually long and close relationship with him[16]; and 2) her devotion to God as known and worshiped in the faith and practice of the Church of England.

When Herbert was fifteen years old, Magdalen arranged for his marriage to a distant cousin, Mary Herbert. This marriage was intended to relieve the financial strains of Magdalen's husbandless family of ten children, and also to provide young Herbert with "a due remedy for that lasciviousness to which youth is naturally inclined."[17] When young Herbert returned to Oxford with his new wife, Magdalen took a second—and even more important—step. That step was to move her household of the remaining children plus servants from the family castle in Montgomeryshire to Oxford to create a home for him.[18] Izaak Walton (1593–1683), English biographer and friend of John Donne, has left an account of this mother's influential relationship with her son during his teen years at Oxford.

> In this time of her widowhood, she being desirous to give Edward, her eldest son, such advantages of learning, and other education . . . did remove from Montgomery Castle with him, and her younger sons [and daughters] to Oxford; and . . . she continued there with him . . . for she would often say, "That as our bodies take a nourishment suitable to the meat on which we

15. Herbert was only fourteen when he entered Oxford. Even in 1596, fourteen was a young age for matriculation in Oxford. Herbert's fellow matriculants were all sixteen, except for the only other fourteen year old, a brother of one of the sixteen year olds.

16. As late as 1617, when Edward was thirty-five and Magdalen had been remarried for almost a decade, she still addressed him as her "best-beloved son" (cited in Charles, *Life of George Herbert*, 60).

17. *Life*, 42.

18. "Not long after my marriage I went again to Oxford, together with my wife and mother, who took a house and lived there for some certain time" (ibid.)

feed; so our souls do as insensibly take in vice by the example or conversation with wicked company," and would therefore as often say," That ignorance of vice was the best preservation of virtue; and that the very knowledge of wickedness was as tinder to inflame and kindle sin and keep it burning." For these reasons she endeared him to her own company, and continued with him in Oxford.[19]

From a reading of Lord Herbert's advice to his posterity, it appears that he agreed with Magdalen's program for his moral development, especially her presence with him during his Oxford days. Besides his university tutors and the companionship of his wife and mother, Magdalen also extended Herbert's education by attracting the company "of any of eminent worth or learning," including John Donne, the poet and later Dean of St. Paul's; both Magdalen and Herbert subsequently became life-long friends of Donne.[20] Later, Magdalen's charm as a woman of wit and beauty enabled her to introduce Herbert to a growing circle of theological and literary figures in London. After young Herbert had completed his studies at Oxford, Magdalen moved her household of nine children, and sixteen servants, Herbert and his wife Mary, to London.[21] Indeed, young Herbert, his wife, and their several children lived virtually continuously in Magdalen's household until 1608 when he was about twenty-six years old.[22]

---

19. Walton, *Lives*, 275.

20. In the words of Izaak Walton, during her residence in Oxford, Magdalen "gained her an acquaintance and friendship with most of any eminent worth or learning that were at that time in or near that university; and particularly with Mr. John Donne, who then came accidentally to that place, in this time of her being there." (Walton, *Lives*, 275). For the long friendship of Magdalen and John Donne, see Bald, *John Donne*, 184. For letters from Donne to Magdalen, see *Life*, Appendix III, 316–17.

21. "When I had attained the age betwixt eighteen or nineteen years, my mother, together with myself and wife, removed up to London where we took house [along with six brothers and three sisters]" (*Life*, 80).

22. When Herbert was twenty-one, he officially moved to the family castle where he accepted the post of Sheriff of Montgomeryshire. *Life*, 86. In fact, however, he continued to reside most of the time in London at his mother's home. As Lee observes in a footnote, "From 1605 onwards, Lord Herbert's name appears on the roll of Montgomeryshire magistrates, but there is no evidence to show that he spent much time in the country. *Life*, 87 n. 1. Or, as reported in another source, "From about 1606 onwards Edward Herbert began to mix in literary as well as social circles in London. When in town he still resided with his mother at her house near Charing Cross (Bald, *John Donne*, 187).

Herbert's long residence in his mother's household played a very important role in his theological formation. His mother ran her household as if it were a seminary specializing in the spiritual formation of future clergy.[23] Each weekday began with the "Order for Morning Prayer" from the *Book of Common Prayer*; each day ended with the "Order for Evening Prayer" from the same book, and its extensive use of psalms for singing.[24] Besides the family members and servants, many guests and visitors knew the worship schedule of Magdalen's household. One of these long-term visitors was John Donne, who fled the London plague of 1625 and lived for six weeks in Magdalen's home in Chelsea. In his funeral sermon for Magdalen, Donne noted how she would come

> to this place, God's house of prayer, daily, not only every Sabbath, but even on those weekdays as often as these doors were opened. She ever hastened her family and her company hither with that cheerful provocation, "For God's sake let's go; let's be there at the Confession."[25] With her whole family, [she then ended] the day with a cheerful singing of psalms.[26]

Through these rituals Herbert learned the habit of giving thanks and praising God, or in the language of Thomas Aquinas, he cultivated the virtue of *religio*. Like Thomas, Herbert understood the practice of worship—giving God the honor, praise, and thanks that are his due—to be an obligation for all humanity. In his mature theology Lord Herbert identified the obligation for such worship of God as something "engraved upon the heart." Indeed, after spending his youth and young adulthood in the religious discipline of his mother's household, it would be surprising if he did not find such a practice "engraved upon his heart." For him it seemed self-evident that all humanity, not only those nurtured in his Christian tradition, shared such an innate disposition to worship God.

23. Edward's youngest brother, George Herbert, did in fact become a priest in the Church of England, though he remains best known for his poetry.

24. Subsequent references to these services and their source book will use the more familiar terminology: *Morning Prayer, Evening Prayer,* and *Prayer Book.*

25. "The Confession" to which Magdalen referred is "a General Confession . . .said by the whole congregation" soon after the priest reads a sentence from the Scriptures and exhorts the congregation to "confess our manifold sins" at the beginning of the service. *The Book of Common Prayer* (1559). Hereafter cited as *BCP.* All references are to the 1559 edition only.

26. Donne, "Sermon of Commemoration," 188.

Worship, however, was only one aspect of religion in Magdalen's household; the regular sharing of her goods with those in need was as much a part of the day's rituals as was the worship of God. Here also John Donne provides examples of her actions. In his eulogy he described Magdalen's evening ritual of almsgiving, as he had observed it in his long acquaintance with her.

> In which office [as God's steward, Magdalen] gave not at some great days or some solemn goings abroad, but as God's true almoners, the sun and moon, that pass on in a continual doing of good, as she received her daily bread from God, so daily she distributed and imparted it to others. In which office, though she never turned her face from those who, in a strict inquisition, might be called idle and vagrant beggars, yet she ever looked first upon them who laboured, and whose labours could not overcome the difficulties, nor bring in the necessities of this life; and to the sweat of their brows she contributed even her wine, and her oil, and any thing that might be useful to others, if it were not prepared for her own table.[27]

Magdalen's combination of daily almsgiving and worship taught Herbert that there were two forms of expression essential to religion, not one. To be sure, piety demanded daily worship and prayers, but Christian piety also required a generous heart, shown in the sharing of self and goods with others. A daily life of virtue belonged to the practice of religion, a lesson Lord Herbert had learned also from his mother.

In an abbreviated version of Lord Herbert's "Common Notions of Religion," the first Common Notion states simply, "There is a Supreme God;" the second calls attention to humanity's obligation to worship this God, while the third expands this obligation to include "virtue with piety [as] the most important part of religious practice."[28] In light of

---

27. Ibid., 192.

28. Lord Herbert first published his "Common Notions of Religion" in an appendix to the 1624 edition of *De veritate*. His formulation of these Common Notions varied considerably in his later writings. The version cited here and below appears in the 1645 edition of *De veritate,* Carré translation, 291–302.

The 5 Common Notions of 1645 read as follows:
1. There is a Supreme God.
2. This Sovereign Deity ought to be worshipped.
3. The connection of virtue with piety . . . is and always has been held to be, the most important part of religious practice.
4. The minds of men have always been filled with horror for their wickedness.

the practice of worship and charity in Magdalen's household, it is not difficult to surmise how a young man might have formed such ideas about religion.

From the period of Lord Herbert's residence in Magdalen's household, a brief note expressing his religious convictions has been discovered. Written in Herbert's own hand, it was dated by him, "1602."[29] In this note, he expressed his strong repudiation of two positions identified in the early seventeenth century as Stoic: "the Stoics tell more fabulous things than the poets, and would take away all happiness from men by their doctrine. They hold that there is nothing true or false in its own nature, but that as they are referred to our mind, and that things appear after one fashion to men that are sober, and another fashion to those that are drunken."[30] As a young man of twenty, Lord Herbert was already committed to an Augustinian theology of human destiny. Human beings are destined for a happiness that exceeds any pleasures this world can offer; the soul desires a happiness that is eternal. This is a theme central to all of his writings.

The Stoic's skepticism concerning the possibility of knowledge in general and, for Lord Herbert, knowledge of God and salvation, was the second claim he repudiated. In order that people may have the confidence concerning their ultimate future destiny to live a life of piety and virtue, they need to have reliable knowledge of God and God's way. They cannot be left in the confusion and strife created by the conflicting claims of clergy that became increasingly prominent in English church life. Lord Herbert understood his five Common Notions of Religion or "universal and catholic articles of religion" to provide the knowledge

---

Their vices and crimes have been obvious to them. They must be expiated by repentance.

5. There is reward and punishment after this life.

29. I am indebted to Julia Griffin for calling my attention to this early example of Lord Herbert's reflections in her Oxford PhD thesis, "Studies in the Literary Life of Lord Herbert," 22–23. The original copy of Herbert's written notes are now in the National Library of Wales, in an envelope taken from Parcel XXVI of the 1959 Powis Bequest.

30. Ibid. In 1569, Gentian Hervet published a popular edition of the works of Sextus Empiricus. Hervet was an anti-Calvinist who used the Pyrrhonian skepticism of Sextus as an antidote to the Calvinist search for knowledge of election (Jones, *English Reformation*, 190). The stoicism and skepticism, which young Herbert attributed to the Stoics, first came into England in Hervet's 1569 edition.

adequate for attaining the soul's desired destiny of eternal happiness with God.[31]

While evidence for young Herbert's own religious views is limited to the few examples cited above, there is a considerably larger body of texts for the religious views that he regularly absorbed as a participant in Christian worship. The services of *Morning Prayer*, which Magdalen's family attended regularly, were held at the nearby parish church. The children, servants, guests, and relatives of Magdalen's household were only part of a congregation gathered to begin the day with God in worship led by a local minister according to the rites of the Church of England. In her faith, Magdalen was formed by that combination of Scripture and church so distinctive in the Elizabethan Church. In the words of John Donne,

> For as the rule of all her civil actions was religion, so the rule of her religion was the Scripture; and her rule for her particu-lar understanding of the Scripture was the Church. She never diverted towards the Papist in undervaluing the Scripture, nor towards the Separatist in undervaluing the Church: but in the doctriine and discipline of that Church in which God sealed her to himself in baptism, she brought up her children, she assisted her family, she dedicated her soul to God in her life, and sur-rendered it to him in her death.[32]

While Lord Herbert expanded the scope of his theology far beyond the boundaries of the Church of England, the content of his church-less theology remained remarkably expressive of the faith he learned in the liturgical worship of his mother's church. Hence, in the next section I examine Lord Herbert's mature theology in light of the *1559 Prayer Book,* with a focus on repentance, the dynamic center of both *Morning Prayer* and Lord Herbert's theology.

31. The opposite side of this same piece of paper illustrates two Christian themes prominent in the preaching of the Elizabethan Church that Lord Herbert later ignored. "Our soul wanting therefore on earth the true looking glass wherein he [sic] may frame high beauty fit to be spouse of Christ, must turn his mind to that clear mirror of inac-cessible light, wherein we must not use our own light to be the medium of our sight, but for [sic] then we shall bee dazzled at the light, like as one should behold an infinite daz-zling light through a clear crystal, but wee must entreat that our most merciful Savior, with the hand of his mercy so to shadow that light as it may be so as our degenerate souls, may see to restore their deformed senses, to their true luster" (Griffin, "Studies in the Literary Life," 22–23).

32. Donne, "Sermon of Commemoration," 194.

Repentance in the Elizabethan Book of Common Prayer

While our knowledge of the young Lord Herbert's religious convictions is limited, if measured by his own writings, our knowledge of his worship practices during the first twenty-six years of his life is extensive. As already noted, *Morning Prayer* and *Evening Prayer* were virtually daily events in Magdalen Herbert's household. We also know the texts used in those services as preserved in the 1559 edition of the *Book of Common Prayer*. Finally, we know the authority of the *Prayer Book* as normative for the beliefs of Elizabethan Christians. The Church of England did not identify its theological norms with the writings of particular thinkers, such as Martin Luther or John Calvin, as in Lutheran or Calvinist churches. Nor did it construct systematic confessional statements, such as the Augsburg Confession of Lutherans or the several Confessions of Calvinist or Reformed churches. Rather, the norms of faith for Elizabethan Christians were given in the services of the *Prayer Book*. *Lex orandi-lex credendi*: "the law of praying is the law of believing."[33] For young Herbert, his family, and the larger company of Elizabethan Christians, the norms of faith were given in worship. As a result, in exploring Lord Herbert's theology, I first review the words he heard and the words he spoke as a participant in the prayers of the late sixteenth century English Church.

I begin with the words of his mother, "For God's sake let's go; let's be there at the Confession."[34] The "Confession" that marked for Magdalen the latest point of tardy arrival at church for the daily *Morning Prayer*, occurs at an early point in the service. Only the minister's reading of a sentence from Scripture and his exhorting the congregation to make a heart-felt confession of their sins to God precedes the general confession. Indeed, all of the first four elements in the *Morning Prayer* are built around the act of repentance.[35]

33. For a discussion of the role of the *Prayer Book* as a source of theological norms in the Church of England, see Stevenson, "LEX ORANDI-LEX CREDENDI."

34. For Magdalen's cheerful prodding of her brood, to move them to the church on time, see John Donne's funeral sermon above.

35. One of the suggested sentences from the Scriptures provides an example of the focus on repenting: "At what time so ever, a sinner doth repent himself of his sin from the bottom of his heart, I will put all his wickedness out of my remembrance, saith the Lord" (Ezekiel 18).

- The Minister's Reading of a Sentence from the Scriptures
- The Minister's Exhortation to Confession
- A General Confession to be said by the whole congregation
- The Minister's Pronouncement of Absolution

There is a fair amount of repetition between the sentences from Scripture, the confession of the congregation, and the words of the minister. All four elements stress the identity of God, the believer's condition, and the transaction between them. God is "gentle and merciful," "patient and forgiving," "our heavenly Father" or "most merciful Father." He is the same God who has given believers his "holy laws," who has blessed them with a multitude of "great benefits," and who expects them to be honest in "acknowledging and confessing their manifold sins and wickedness at all times, but especially when assembled together to give God thanks and praise."

Believers come to this God in their own sinful condition. They have "erred and strayed from God's ways," having committed many wrongs, their "manifold sins and wickedness," "following the desires of their hearts" instead of God's holy laws. They are burdened with the multitude of their "faults." They deserve nothing but God's most severe judgment and punishment, but because God is who God is, there occurs between believers guilty of so many wrongs and God a transaction quite different from their anticipated judgment and punishment. If they have brought to God their many wrongs, with a heart filled with sorrow for their sins, a heart that is "humble, lowly, penitent, obedient and pure," God will wipe their slate clean, blotting out all their offenses. Furthermore, the God who is experienced as other in forgiving is also the God who moves within the heart of believers, "granting them a true repentance and his Holy Spirit" so that they may "turn from [their] wickedness and live."

In this liturgical act, believers present their unclean thoughts and deeds to God who accepts them, cleanses them, and gives back the promise of a new life, freed from the burden and habit of past wrongs. To be sure, the believer's sincerity—the deep sorrow of the heart for the wrongs done—is one condition of this transaction, but even the believer unsure of her own heart may ask for God's help in being genuinely penitent. Indeed, believers are not left to their own fallible resources in repentance. The service invites them to seek God's help in resolving the ambiguities of their hearts as they contemplate past wrongs. They also need God's support for strengthening their resistance to such wrongdoing in the future. Repentance is not a transaction between equals, but it is a transaction, an event, which results in a changed condition for the believer. And that changed condition includes not only the renewal of the believer's moral life with others, but also the believer's hope for a communion with God that is eternal. God and believers are reconciled in this transaction; the past wrongs are cleansed and the future hope of an eternal communion with God is restored.

In *Morning Prayer*, repentance provides the dynamic center of the service. Later, in exploring Lord Herbert's mature theology, we will find that repentance plays the same role in his version of the religious life of all humanity. It is the believer's repentance, enabled by God's grace, which facilitates the reconciliation of the wrongdoing believer and the merciful God.

In this act of repentance, built into the daily *Morning Prayer*, it is important to note that the reconciliation of God and believers is not made conditional upon any cosmic event mediated by a third party, such as the atoning death of Christ.[36] The reconciliation appears to be conditional only upon God's merciful forgiveness, on the one hand, and the believer's deeply felt sorrow for past wrongs and promise to amend his life. Repentance is an event that transpires directly between the believer and God; only the sentence from Scripture and the minister's biblically based words of exhortation and absolution mediate between God and believers.

To be sure, the figure of Jesus the Christ is not absent from this transaction. As the minister petitions God, in his words of absolution, "restore thou those that are penitent, according to your promises declared unto mankind in Christ Jesus our Lord." It is Jesus who makes known God's identity as loving and forgiving; it is Jesus through whom

---

36. While there is no reference to the Anselmian doctrine of Christ's atoning death as the grounds for God's forgiveness of sin in the "Order for Morning Prayer," in the "Order for Holy Communion" we read, "Almighty God our heavenly Father, which of thy tender mercy didst give thine only Son Jesus Christ, to suffer death upon the cross for our redemption; who made there (by his one oblation of himself once offered) a full, perfect, and sufficient sacrifice, oblation, and satisfaction for the sins of the whole world" (*BCP* 263). In this same service, less explicit references to this same doctrine appear in the *BCP*, 255, 256, and 258.

God has promised forgiveness to humankind. Jesus is the messenger of God's true identity but Jesus here is not the explicit mediator who wins that forgiveness from God. Nor does Jesus ration that forgiveness of God, restricting it to the company of elect among Christians (which is how Lord Herbert understood the Calvinist doctrine of predestination). As a daily participant in this act of repentance for the first twenty-six years of his life, it is not surprising that Lord Herbert would identify repentance as the fourth of his Common Notions of Religion, a spiritual act he regarded as common to all humanity with the God made known to him in the daily worship of Magdalen's household.[37]

In *Morning Prayer*, it would appear as if God and the individual believer were the only parties involved in this transaction. Other services in the same *Prayer Book,* however, make it apparent that repentance is not merely a private transaction. Repentance may also involve other people, the others who had been the victims of wrongdoing. To set right such wrongs, some form of restitution may be necessary and so expected as a part of repentance. And if the wrong confessed takes the form of a broken relationship in need of healing, there may be need for mutual apologies and forgiveness among the estranged parties. In either case, the act of repentance may include any of those others with whom believers are knit together in a common life.

Repentance has clearly a prominent role in *Morning Prayer*, as it has in other services of the *Prayer Book*. Not surprisingly, in Lord Herbert's theology repentance is also the decisive spiritual event between humans and God. I turn now from the role of repentance in the Elizabethan *Prayer Book* to the role of repentance in Lord Herbert's mature theology.

Repentance in Lord Herbert's Theology

Two of Lord Herbert's mature writings illustrate the role of repentance in his theology, the first being his five Common Notions of Religion as developed in his theological essay, "A Layman's Faith." Secondly, this theme is taken up in his historical study, *The History of England under Henry VIII*. Herbert's Common Notions of Religion are his signature theological proposal. I have previously noted them in their abbreviated

---

37. "Wickedness, vice, or crime must be expiated by repentance" (Lord Herbert, *De veritate*, 301).

form. In "A Layman's Faith," he provided a more fully developed version of these Common Notions. My quotation from this text and commentary on it will focus on the fourth Common Notion of Religion: Repentance.

Not surprisingly, the fourth Common Notion on repentance is the one that requires the longest exposition of the five; it also provides the theological point in which Lord Herbert develops most fully his own religious convictions. The legacy of his worship in the Elizabethan Church is apparent in his exposition of this Common Notion.

As he wrote,

> repentance is a certain sign of God's Spirit working in us, [it is] the only remedy for sin that is declared publicly to all mankind, [it is] the most rational way to return to God and virtue, [and it is] by universal consent and agreement established everywhere without so much as the least contradiction.

He then introduced the question of the necessity for punishment for sin in order to satisfy God's justice. In dealing with this issue, he first reminded his readers of the identity and attributes of God.

> He who judges man is his Father and does look on man as a frail creature and obnoxious to sin. He [God] generally finds men sin out of this frailty [more] than out of any desire to offend his divinity.

God is the merciful common Father of all humanity. Lord Herbert worried that too much emphasis upon God's punishing role could lead believers to lose confidence in God's mercy and providential care.

> If man had been made inwardly prone to sin and yet destitute of all inward means to return to him [God] again, he had been not only remediles [without remedy] in himself, but more miserable than that. Could it be supposed that an infinite goodness did at first create and does still perpetuate humankind? Man can do no more on his part for the satisfying of divine justice then be heartily sorry and repent him of his sin and together endeavor through his grace to return to the right way from which through his transgressions he had erred. Or if this did not suffice for the making of his peace, the Supreme God, by inflicting some temporal punishment in this life, might satisfy his own justice. If temporal punishment in this life were too little for the sin committed, he [God] might inflict a greater punishment here-

after in the other life without giving yet eternal damnation to those who, if not for the love of goodness yet at least upon sense of their punishment, would not sin eternally. However, as these matters were controversial, I was constrained to insist upon this single proposition only, universally acknowledged: that repentance is the only known and public means which on our part is required for satisfying the divine justice and returning to the right way of serving God.[38]

Some temporary punishment, in this world or the life to come, might be appropriate without calling into question God's fundamental identity and attributes. Lord Herbert, however, will not tolerate any doctrine that would undermine repentance such as the limitation of salvation to only a few elect ones and the Calvinist doctrine of "eternal damnation" for the vast majority of the human species.

Lord Herbert's strong concern for the centrality of repentance to the religious and moral life of all people is prominent not only in his Common Notions of Religion, but also in his history of the early English Reformation under Henry VIII. According to Lord Herbert's historical account, in 1536 the king proposed to Parliament several articles of religion. These included the King's proposal to limit the sacraments of the English Church to three: not only Baptism and Communion, but also "Penance for satisfaction of faults after [Baptism] committed both towards God and our neighbor."[39] From Lord Herbert's point of view, the King's judgment in retaining Penance as a third sacrament was absolutely correct, regardless of what "the reformed [i.e., the Calvinists] might say for their only two sacraments."[40] An anonymous spokesman in his history of Henry VIII, who is Lord Herbert himself, presents three arguments for retaining the sacramental status of Penance. The arguments of this fictional speaker in an early sixteenth century Parliament repeat many of the same points made by Lord Herbert in "A Layman's Faith."

> 1) There is no other general way than aversion from sin and conversion to God, known to all mankind for making their peace with him and, obtaining pardon.

38. Herbert, "Lord Herbert of Cherbury's *Religio Laici*," 302–3. I have introduced changes in spelling and punctuation and added bracketed terms.

39. Herbert, *History of England Under Henry VIII*, 588.

40. Ibid.

2) The other two sacraments being particular rites only of the Christian Church are in their explication subject to so much difficulty and disputes, as no less than a man's whole age is required to study them;

3) [The sacrament of Penance is] an uncontroverted sign of the operation of God's spirit in our hearts [which] produceth such holy effects.[41]

For Lord Herbert, penance was therefore not only a sacrament of the ancient church rightly preserved in the Church of England by King Henry VIII, but a spiritual act "known to all mankind" and "the only general way for conversion to God, for making peace with him, and for obtaining pardon." To be sure, this sacrament would have to be cleansed from its abuse by the Roman papists, as would many other aspects of that church's legacy. Absolution was not to be given cheaply, as if both the sin and its forgiveness were not serious matters; the minister should pronounce God's absolution "only in case of such a serious repentance as might totally clear the fault and make the sinner a new man."[42]

Lord Herbert's arguments for the preservation of Penance as a third sacrament did not prove persuasive.[43] Baptism and Communion/Eucharist have remained the only two sacraments of the Church of England since 1562. However, the ancient church and its sacrament of Penance was only one of Lord Herbert's theological grounds for the retention of repentance as a sacrament. The doctrine of justification by faith, so prominent among continental Reformers, was a second source in his argument for the pre-eminent role of repentance in the religious life. In Herbert's revised form of this doctrine, God's justification of the believer could be appropriated only when faith was joined with repentance: "justification was attained by contrition or true repentance and faith."[44] Unlike Luther, his doctrine of justification was not "by faith alone" but required both faith and true repentance.

Lord Herbert's critique of indulgences, as developed in his history of Henry VIII, repeats his strong commitment to repentance or Penance.

41. Ibid., 590.

42. Ibid., 590–91.

43. Lord Herbert was not alone in advocating for the sacramental status of repentance. Martin Luther made similar arguments for the rite of absolution, a pronouncement central to Lord Herbert's drama of repentance.

44. Ibid., 588.

For him, the reduction of a strenuous spiritual act to a monetary trans-action, as in the sale of indulgences, had the religious effect of under-mining God's moral authority and spiritual rule. Such a transformation of genuine religion into a monetary transaction also undermined the authority of the Christian Church and its promise of salvation.

> For when men see what they are to pay for their faults, what will they care for other redemption? . . . Let us not then make the mysteries of salvation mercenary, or propose everlasting happi-ness on those terms, that it may be obtained for money.[45]

In addition, Lord Herbert also valued repentance as a public ac-tion, useful for the restraint of criminal activity. Repentance awakened fear of God's future punishment, as illustrated by warnings in the *Prayer Book* services of *Holy Communion* and *Commination*.[46] For Lord Herbert, the Church not only provided the means of salvation, but was also an agency for preserving social discipline. In one of his many con-structed quotations, inserted into the mouth of an anonymous actor of the past, he depicted the societal consequences of allowing indulgences to replace repentance as a means of church discipline.

> In England, one who was zealous for God's honor and the pub-lick good, observing that not only sins towards God were par-doned for money, but offences towards the law . . . spake after this manner to some of the principal clergy: That punishments might have been left to God but that they serve to deter others. But who would be afraid now, when he knows at what [cost] he may put away his crimes? At what use would our threatenings for sins be, if they grow so contemptible as a little sum of money would discharge them; is not this to make heaven venal, doth not this reflect so much on Christian faith, that it makes a new price for sin? Believe me, my lords, to make our faults cheap, is to multiply them.[47]

For Lord Herbert, repentance was an interior action of the human spirit necessary for the renewal of confidence in God's promise of salvation

---

45. Herbert, *Henry VIII*, 178.

46. The service of *Commination,* or Warning, was a service scheduled to fol-low *Morning Prayer* on Ash Wednesday and certain other holy days of the Church calendar.

47. Herbert, *Henry VIII*, 178.

and moral discipline as well as for the more mundane task of maintaining civil order.

Lord Herbert never lost the faith shaped by regular worship that he absorbed from the Elizabethan Church of England. In his mature theological writings, he presented the same God with the same attributes, the same gathering of believers engaged in a morally strenuous life but falling short, and the same dynamics of repentance: the interaction of believers, sorrowful for their wrong doing, with God's merciful response. To be sure, Lord Herbert located this drama of repentance in a worldwide context not confined to the Church of England and, as will become apparent, his expansion of the scope of faith required a reduction in its content. For an understanding of these changes in his theology, it will be necessary to examine the changing context of his church experience in the second half of his life.

From Naïve Believer to Believing Critic

In many ways, 1608 was a watershed in the life of Lord Herbert. For the first time in his life, he separated himself from his mother's house. To make that same point from another perspective, his mother separated herself from him. In 1608, she remarried; her new husband was Sir John Danvers—a man only slightly older than Herbert—and she moved from her home in Covent Garden to his home in Chelsea. Indeed, Herbert not only moved from his mother's home, but from his homeland, England. He made his first trip to the continent where he became a long-term guest and friend of Henri de Montmorency-Damville, that "brave old General" who had been named Grand Constable of France by King Henri IV.[48]

Herbert's trip to France in 1608–1609 was not a short holiday; he remained in France for about eight months. Nor was his time in France part of the Grand European Tour typically pursued by men of Herbert's class and age; he limited his travel to the distance between Paris and Montmorency's castle. During this transition in his life, he began to write poems, one of which was explicitly theological. It was entitled, *The State Progress of Ill [Evil]*.[49] The poem reflects the

48. Bald, *John Donne*, 91.

49. All quotations of this poem are from Lord Herbert's *Poems*, edited by Smith, 9–13.

influence of France's history: both the religiously inspired civil wars and the new religious policies of peace embodied in the kingship of Henri IV. It is also a poem in which Lord Herbert began to express his suspicion of clergy, especially those who have been politicized in the service of the state. In France he began to distance himself from the church in its political role, though not the church as a resource for the formation of faith. His time in France was thus a formative time of transition between his younger life as a naive Christian and his older life as a critical Christian. Lord Herbert's theological and political critique of a state-established church has its beginnings in his contacts with leaders of the *politiques* party in France.

Some information on the Duke of Montmorency is useful in understanding his influence on Lord Herbert. As a young man, Montmorency played a prominent role in quelling religious violence in the south of France. As an older man he was a close ally of King Henri IV whose new policies established religious peace in the whole of France.

During the sixteenth-century religious wars in France, one of the most heavily devastated areas was Languedoc.[50] Because of his outstanding military reputation, the Duke of Montmorency was appointed governor of Languedoc. Charged with the task of reducing its religious strife, he established religious peace in southern France. He also created a political model of limited religious freedom that proved persuasive for French political figures far beyond the borders of Languedoc. Indeed, by the time of Lord Herbert's visit, Montmorency had become a senior figure in a national political movement committed to the establishment of civil peace by tolerating some religious expression of the French minority (Huguenots). After 1564, this group was known by the name of *politiques* and they constituted a third political movement in sixteenth century France along with the Catholics and Huguenots.[51]

The policies of the *politiques* gained their most powerful expression during the reign of King Henri IV, a close ally of Montmorency. The "brave old general" had played a crucial role in winning the throne for Henri of Navarre and in keeping Languedoc within the French state.[52]

---

50. In the early thirteenth century, Languedoc (southern France) was also the center of religious strife; see the discussion of the Albigensian Crusade in chapter 2.

51. The term *politiques* first came into general use in 1564. Palm, *Politics and Religion*, 114.

52. Ibid., 264–65.

In France, the *politique* policy of limited freedom in religious matters reached its strongest expression in the 1598 Edict of Nantes.[53] Lord Herbert's sojourn with Montmorency occurred a decade later, during the reign of Henri IV while the Edict of Nantes was still in effect.

During his visit with Montmorency, Herbert wrote five poems, the longest of which is *The State Progress of Ill [Evil]*. This poem suggests that Herbert learned to view religion in a new perspective while he was in France. It appears as if he discovered the dangers to both parties in a church-state alliance. At least, this poem provides the first example of his politically-oriented reflection on religion. The poem is a satire exposing the religious State as an idol that extends the power of evil and suppresses the God-given gift of freedom.

The poem begins with the subject of evil in the metaphysical sense of that term: a great and mysterious power whose origins, while hidden, must lie in "causes great and far." It thus begins as if it were a poem in the metaphysical genre of early seventeenth century English poetry, so apparent in the work of John Donne and George Herbert, Lord Herbert's younger brother. This poem, however, quickly leaves the sphere of metaphysics and turns to politics, offering a theological critique of the State and its exploitation of religion. What concerned the poet was not evil in its primordial form, but evil in its secondary form of the religious state. While the state was intended to be an antidote to original evil, in actual fact, it extended that evil: "so States, to their Greatness, find No faults required but their own, and bind the rest." The state of which Lord Herbert wrote was not the modern secular and democratic state but the quasi-medieval religious state. Its authority was grounded in the God of that religion which the state supported. Similarly, the legitimacy of the ruler was not dependent upon the consent of the governed, but derived directly from God. Like God, this state appeared to be self-subsistent, not constituted by a contract of its citizens. Like God, this state was the means of "all our punishments" and was given the task of ruling the world.

> This [State] having some attributes of God,
> As to have made itself, and bear the rod
> Of all our punishments, as it seems, came
> Into this world, to rule it.

53. This Edict promised some measure of religious freedom to the Huguenots, such as the right to gather for public worship in certain areas of France, and civil liberties.

Like God, this state exercised its authority through its place in the hearts of men: "though it be him [the state] we love and God we fear." The state even claims for itself certain attributes of "the Godhead, [such] as Mercy." In short, the State in its religious disguise is an extension of evil for it is an ersatz god.

When the poem turns from the evil of the state to the sins of men, we hear once more the liturgical and theological language of the *Prayer Book*. The poet contrasts God's omniscient knowledge of all sins with human efforts to conceal them. In repentance for sins confessed, the poet finds the only means for their extirpation; to deny one's sins is to keep them alive and multiplied, extending their power beyond the death of the sinner. In the poet's discourse on God and sin is disclosed Herbert's own roots in Christian worship and its practices of faith.

> Mischief under doing of Good was veiled ...
> They only hide themselves from mortal eyes.
> Sins, those that both com-and o-mitted be,
> Are now such poisons, that though they may lurk
> In secret parts awhile, yet they will work,
> Though after death: Nor ever come alone,
> But sudden fruitful multiply e'r done.
> While in this monstrous birth they only die
> Whom we confess, those live which we deny.

Here, as elsewhere in this poem, Lord Herbert uses the language of the church's liturgy and bible to provide the framework and metaphors for his indictment of the state's exploitation of religion. Even Magdalen's practice of evening charity, for the sake of the poor and God finds a place in his text:

> All in the frame is equal; that desert
> Is a more living thing, and doth obey,
> As he gives poor, for God's sake (though they
> And Kings ask it not so).

The focus of the poem, however, is not upon God and sin, but upon the poet's new concern with the state as a quasi-religious entity and its role as an agent of evil. Anticipating the language of Karl Marx some centuries later, the poet chides the co-opted clergy who use their religious authority to solicit obedience to the state; they exploit the promise of a future heaven for the present subjection of the human spirit.

Meanwhile, suger'd Divines, next place to this,
Tells us, Humility and Patience is
The way to Heaven, and that we must there
Look for our Kingdom that the greatest rule here
Is for to rule our selves; and that they might
Say this the better, they to no place have right
By inheritance, while whom Ambition sways,
Their office is to turn it other ways.

The critique of religion entangled with the state, introduced in this poem, reappears throughout Herbert's later writings. His theology continually becomes increasingly anti-clerical, blaming the "suger'd Divines" for the divisive role of religions. They preach humility but pursue their own ambition by claiming for themselves exclusive rights to bestow God's promises. Over against a Calvinist vision of humanity's destiny determined by an eternal election, Herbert will celebrate human freedom as God's gift of grace. Theologically, the state has become an agent of evil because it has become an object of idolatry; the subjects of the state have projected onto it a cluster of attributes that belong to God alone. Similarly, the clergy—those "suger'd Divines"—have neglected their witness to God and his gift of freedom and become instead agents of the state, using God's authority to subject humans to that state. As a result, religious confusion reigns among the people and their clergy. The identity of God and the practice of faith, in confession and charity, are portrayed as consistent with God's gift of freedom; they provide the grounds for Herbert's critique of state idolatry.

Herbert's poem presumes a new model of the relationship between religion and the state. The state would be freed from the need for religious authority (God) to support the legitimacy of rulers and so the state would have no obligation to enforce the religion of that God. These were the political goals of the French *politiques*: to free the state from the self-destructive policy of enforcing the practice of one religion only. The sundering of faith and politics, still firmly joined in the courts of Elizabeth and James I, was a new discovery for Herbert. In retrospect, one can discern the beginning of the end of the Constantinian era in Lord Herbert's poetic critique of the state church.

The apparent victory of *politique* religious policies in France did not last long. In 1610, shortly after Herbert's visit with Montmorency, a militant Catholic assassinated King Henri IV.[54] Indeed, a decade after this first visit to France, when Lord Herbert was England's ambassador in 1621, the French military were once again active in killing Protestants. That, however, is another chapter in the formation of Lord Herbert's theology. For the transitional year of 1608–09, it is sufficient to note the beginnings of his separation of God and politics in his poetic critique of the religious state.

Theological Disputes and Intra-Christian Wars

Anti-Calvinist and anti-Clerical Roots of Herbert's Universalism

The union of Catholic worship and governance with Calvinist theology in the Church of England began to rupture in the second decade of the seventeenth century, shortly after Lord Herbert returned from France. The Calvinists had become sufficiently dominant in the English Church to press their case for further reformation.[55] Among other causes, they sought to eliminate from Church of England worship any characteristic of Roman Catholic worship, such as clergy robes, church altars, and other remnants of the "incomplete reformation" of Henry VIII. In addition, Calvinists urged James I to provide military support for their brethren in the faith on the continent.[56]

Some clergy and bishops reacted strongly against the Calvinist agenda for changes in worship, while James I repudiated Calvinist efforts to involve English troops in the religious wars of the continent. Those who were anti-Calvinists within the Church of England were called Arminians after Jacobus Arminius, the Dutch theologian who had proposed a conditional form of predestination rather than the ab-

---

54. A decade later, in 1621, Louis XIII resumed France's older policy of state-sponsored attacks on Huguenot strongholds. By 1629, the religious and civil liberty extended to Protestants in the 1598 Edict of Nantes had been annulled and in 1685 Louis XIV revoked the Edict of Nantes.

55. For evidence of and arguments for the church's solidly Calvinist identity, see Collinson, *Religion of Protestants*.

56. For the anti-Calvinist party in the English church struggle, see Tyache, *Anti-Calvinists*.

solute predestination of his orthodox Calvinist colleagues.[57] Arminians of the Church of England, however, did not share Arminius' concern for free will or a revised doctrine of predestination.[58] Rather, they wished to recover the centrality of sacramental church practice in theology as well as in worship.

The focus of this Calvinist/Arminian doctrinal dispute in the Church of England was on "the means of salvation." Two publications in the early stages of this conflict raised the issue. In 1613, Benjamin Carier published a pamphlet lamenting the sorry state of the English church which had driven him—the son of an English Protestant "preacher"— into the Church of Rome. In his long study of church history and the ancient fathers, Carier wrote, he had discovered that the English Church was teaching doctrines rejected by the ancient church. In his view, the Calvinist doctrine of absolute predestination made both priests and sacraments redundant. God's eternal election of some to salvation was the only "means of salvation" necessary. Two years later, in 1615, William Laud, the future anti-Calvinist Archbishop of Canterbury, published an essay focused on Church sacraments as the means of salvation. By omission, predestination became irrelevant. It was this quarrel concerning "the means of salvation" that prompted Lord Herbert's initial foray into the Calvinist/Arminian dispute.

Herbert's Correspondence with Sir Robeert Harley

The earliest evidence of Herbert's engagement with this argument appears in his 1617–1619 correspondence with Sir Robert Harley, a friend and distant relative.[59] Sir Robert played a significant public role in the

57. Arminius and the Dutch Remonstrants argued that the fulfillment of God's election of the saved was conditional upon the free response of believers in their faith and morality and not an absolute predestination to salvation.

58. Lord Herbert, however, was a bona fide Arminian. His library included all the works of Arminius (Fordyce and Knox, "Catalogue of Lord Herbert," 96) and leading Remonstrant theologians; he was a personal friend of Hugo Grotius and other leading Remonstrant figures; and his mature theological writings will repeatedly stress the role of a believer's free response in deeds of faith and virtue. For Herbert's theological library, see ibid., 75–76 and 96–102.

59. For Lord Herbert's five letters to Sir Robert Harley, see "Correspondence with Sir Robert Harley." Robert had studied at Oxford when Edward was there. Robert also knew Edward as a relative; his first wife, Anne, was Magdalen's niece. After Anne's death, Robert continued his close contact with Magdalen's family; for example, in one thirteen week period for which Magdalen's kitchen kept records, Robert dined with

English Church struggle before and during the civil wars of the 1640s; he was a militant advocate of Calvinist orthodoxy and critic of the anti-Calvinist Arminians.[60] He was a man of great piety, zealous in his desire to purify the Church of England of dress and decorations from its Catholic past, and willing to risk his wife, home, and family funds in the cause of establishing "true religion" in England. He was also the theological confidant of Lord Herbert who tested out his half-formed alternatives to orthodox Calvinism with his "dear friend," Sir Robert.

The central theological issue in their correspondence was the "means of salvation." Lord Herbert rejected both the Calvinist doctrine of election and Arminian sacramental theology as the "means of salvation." For him, neither of these positions was adequate to encompass the scope of God's grace or to express God's identity as merciful Father. Herbert's first letter to Sir Robert began by advising his friend not to be deceived by the name of Church in any country or time: "God's Church is all mankind. God does not make any whom he denies the means to come to him." For Herbert, the means of salvation would have to be universal: "God's Church is all mankind." Only some such universal means of salvation would be consistent with Herbert's theological norms: 1) that God is the merciful Father of all people and 2) that God the Creator of humanity is identical with God the Redeemer who has promised salvation or eternal happiness.

her family at least once a week (Charles, *Life of George Herbert*, 41). He seems to have been a particularly close friend of Edward. In his memoir, Edward twice referred to Sir Robert, once calling him "my dear friend."

60. In the 1628 Parliament and again in 1643, Sir Robert condemned the Arminianism of English intellectuals, especially Richard Montagu, whose books had opened up the case against Calvinism for a popular English audience. In 1628 Harley described the Arminians as a "threat to religious unity and consequently to national security" (cited by Tyache, *Anti-Calvinists*, 160). In the 1643 Parliament, Harley was entrusted with the preparation of an order to ban the minister's wearing of a surplice during worship (*Dictionary of National Biography* VIII 1283). In that same year, he was one of a three-man committee to collect information on "idolatrous monuments in Westminster Abbey and London churches with power to demolish the same" (ibid.). During the English Civil War, his wife, Brilliana, led the defense of Harley's castle against Royalist forces; she died during the second siege of that castle (ibid., VIII 1276). After the war, Harley did not rebuild his destroyed castle, but he did rebuild the church at Brampton Bryan (ibid. VIII 1284). Harley's library also discloses his theological position: he owned "the entire corpus of English puritan divinity" (Tyache, *Anti-Calvinists*, 97). Lord Herbert's library was equally revealing of his position: he owned all the writings of Jacobus Arminius, and the major Arminian theologians (Fordyce and Knox, "Catalogue of Lord Herbert," 96–102).

After postulating such a universal means of salvation, Lord Herbert then faced the question of specifying something that could serve as a means of salvation for all. What kind of God-given resource did all people have in common? Surely not church sacraments or God's election of a few. Lord Herbert rejected both of these options of the Arminian/Calvinist theological dispute. Instead, in this correspondence, he proposed that the several religions of the world were the means provided by God to lead all people into the way of salvation.

> For my part I believe that whoever loves God with all his heart, with all his mind and with all his strength and loves his neighbor as himself is capable of eternal happiness, and thus far in all religions one may go.[61]

In his reply to Lord Herbert, Sir Robert must have pointed out the difficulty of assigning such a role to religions that were often cruel, even bloodthirsty in their call for human sacrifice. For in his next letter, Lord Herbert acknowledged the ambiguities of the world's religions. He did not claim that "any man may be saved in any religion." While granting the deficiencies of many religions, he immediately repeated his confidence in them as a "means of salvation," though only because of a miracle of God's Providence.

> I think there is in every religion and always was and always will be enough taught to bring a man to happiness eternal if he follows it. I must never believe that God's Providence which extends to man and every creature besides would fail at the point which is both the most necessary [namely, the attainment of salvation or eternal happiness with God] and to which the rest are subordinate. If you ask me how this is wrought, I may say that I cannot tell, but the notion is written in my heart that God's providence is over all his works from which no ignorance of mine must make me depart, especially when all the works of God are miraculous. This is then the derivation of my belief. Yet by [this conviction] I take no liberty, since I imply all that can be expected in a pious life towards God and man, and which has been forever commanded in all laws and religions whatsoever.

61. Herbert's knowledge of "all religions" at this period of his life was very limited. Five years later, in the first edition of *De veritate*, he provided very little evidence to support his claims about religion in general. By the last edition of this book, twenty-four years later, he had accumulated a considerable body of knowledge of specific religions.

By the fourth letter, there is no longer any theological discussion of "the means of salvation." Herbert must have been severely rebuked by Sir Robert, as he mostly defends his piety: "no man is more zealous of the glory of God, or is more willing to lay down his life for it than myself." In the very brief fifth letter, it is apparent that the theological discussion has been completely terminated. Nor is Herbert even defending his own piety any longer. Now the stakes are more concrete: it is the friendship of these two men, their bonds of affection and mutual respect that is at stake.

> I must not contribute so much to the destruction of the friendship between us as to suffer it to fall on my part. Let me therefore awake you to those testimonies of affection which absence allows; or if nothing else, to cherish the memory of him who since he knew you first was, and if you please, ever will be your true friend.

Lord Herbert's correspondence with Sir Robert, in the midst of the Arminian-Calvinist dispute, provides the theological context for the origins of Herbert's five Common Notions of Religion that he will propose five years later. The Common Notions were as universal as the many religions that he first proposed to Sir Robert; but the Common Notions, as the norm for evaluating the validity of all religions, provided the answer to Sir Robert's objection concerning the cruelty of certain religions. After 1624, Herbert will identify the five Common Notions as the universal norm for evaluating the adequacy of any religion as a "means of salvation." In the five Common Notions, God made available to all people a set of norms for determining the truth of religion. Herbert did not intend for these Common Notions to be a substitute for the actual religions of the world, but rather to provide the measure of religious truth, and also to serve as a hermeneutical principle for interpreting the practices and beliefs of all religions.

An Ambassador in the Midst of Warring Christians: Protestant-Catholic Wars in Bohemia, France, and all Europe (1619–1624)

On January 23, 1619, shortly after Lord Herbert had written his last letter to Sir Robert Harley, King James appointed him to be the English ambassador to France. By May 1619, Herbert had completed the necessary financial and staffing preparations for his new position and he left England for Paris. In that same month, the Synod of Dort in the Netherlands proclaimed its five canons on predestination as absolute, and condemned the conditional predestination of Jacobus Arminius and the Remonstrant movement that adopted his cause[62]. Herbert thus left a theological quarrel in England and the Netherlands for incipient civil wars among Catholics and Protestants in Bohemia and France, and the beginnings of the European Thirty Years' War (1618–1648).

His arrival in Paris, however, was a joyous occasion. The new ambassador was celebrated by a large parade of coaches and "brave gentlemen on great horses" arranged by his former instructor in horsemanship at Montmorency's castle.[63] While this gala celebration was reminiscent of Herbert's earlier visit with the Duke of Montmorency, the political situation in France had changed dramatically in the decade since his visit in 1608–1609.

THE REPUDIATION OF RELIGIOUS PEACE IN FRANCE

In 1610 a militant Catholic assassinated King Henri IV and in 1614 Herbert's host and friend, the Duke of Montmorency died. The new young king, Louis XIII, was abandoning the *politiques* policies of his predecessor and reverting to the older policy of one religion, enforced by arms if necessary.[64] The chief advisor to the young king was Charles d'Albert de Luynes who strongly supported a return to the older policy of only one religion for all French citizens. As a result, Lord Herbert devoted much of his diplomatic work during his first term of service to the military crisis precipitated by the new leadership and policies of France.

62. "Five" came to be the standard number of propositions for both sides of the Dutch Arminian dispute. Herbert was probably indebted to the Synod of Dort for casting his version of theological polemics in terms of the Five Common Notions of Religion.

63. *Life*, 190–91

64. *Life*, 194 n. 1. The Duke de Luynes had arranged for the murder of his chief rival, Concini, who was a favorite of Marie de Medicis, the mother of the prince. He also managed to remove Marie from the court and install her in a prison at Blois. Like the Duke of Montmorency, the Duke de Luynes was named Grand Constable of France (*Life*, 194). "His [Luynes] advice to the king should be so prevalent, which also at last caused a civil war in that kingdom" (*Life*, 104).

The Preparation for a Protestant–Catholic war in Europe

Some background on earlier developments in Europe and recent changes in Prague may clarify Herbert's involvement with the emerging religious-political crisis in Bohemia. Such matters might appear to lie far *Why?* outside his field of responsibility as England's ambassador to France.

While Herbert had been a guest of Montmorency, the seeds of *Palatine* the Thirty Years' War were already being sown in Europe. In May 1608, Frederick IV, the Elector Palatine, succeeded in organizing a Union of Evangelical Estates. This Protestant Union of Lutherans and Calvinists was a military alliance for the common defense of Protestant territories against the growing power of Catholic forces. One year later, Bavaria, with the support of Spain and the Rhineland, organized a counter-force with a similar purpose. Named the Catholic League, it would combine military resources for the defense of Catholic territories. Alliances and armies were being readied for the military struggle of opposing Christian confessional communities.

Through marriage and treaties, England was becoming entangled in the preparations for religious conflicts of the continent. In 1610, Frederick IV, who had organized the [Protestant] Union of Evangelical Estates in 1608, died and was succeeded by his son, Frederick V. In 1612 England indicated its support of the [Protestant] Union of Evangelical Estates. A year later the younger Frederick married Elizabeth Stuart, the winsome daughter of James I. By 1618 Prague Protestants decided to free their country of Bohemia from the burden of their Catholic past. *Ejected* In the Prague castle, they ejected out of a window two of the Catholic council members.[65] After clearing the slate of Catholic rule, they offered to Frederick, the Elector Palatine and son-in-law of James I, the position of King of Bohemia.[66]

In his correspondence with King James, Lord Herbert expressed his strong support for Frederick's acceptance of "the perilous offer of the throne of Bohemia."[67]

65. Fortunately, there happened to be sufficiently "soft" material below this second-floor window to cushion the fall of both men.

66. In describing the intelligence he received from English agents scattered throughout Europe, Lord Herbert notes that from "his majesty's agent in Germany, on the behalf of his son-in-law, the Palatine, or King of Bohemia, I received all the news of Germany" (*Life*, 232).

67. For Lord Herbert's correspondence with King James I concerning the political and military situation of his son-in-law, see the Appendix of *Life*, 343–50.

> But God forbid that he should refuse it, being the apparent way . . . His Providence hath opened to the ruin of the Papacy. I hope therefore his majesty [King James] will assist in this great work.[68]

James I did not "assist in this great work." Indeed, Herbert's correspondence with the king repeatedly sought some public declaration from him, in order to support his task of sustaining French neutrality on the political-religious destiny of Bohemia. None was forthcoming. By January, 1620, Herbert warned the king that the French were leaning in the direction of supporting the [Holy Roman] Emperor's cause against Frederick V and that the Bohemian dispute was coming to be regarded as a great religious quarrel. He also wrote the king that the French, who Herbert had hoped would remain neutral, were complaining about the silence of the English king: "if the King of Bohemia's cause was a good one, James I would have publicly declared for it."[69] After another request for instructions on the Bohemian affair, Herbert warned the King that the Bohemian cause was in jeopardy: "all I have to comfort me, next God's Providence, is his Majesty's wisdom which I assure myself will temper all for the best."[70] In these negotiations concerning Bohemia, Lord Herbert found himself trapped between the isolationist foreign policy of King James—no English entanglements on the continent—and his role as an ambassador of Protestant England offering no support for the emerging Protestant Kingdom of Bohemia and Frederick V, King James' son-in-law. Negotiating treaties across religious, familial, and national lines turned out to be an extremely complicated business.

The struggle between King James and his ambassador to France provided only background noise for the far more costly drama emerging out of the Bohemian affair. By their actions, the Prague Protestants pulled the trigger on the war waiting to happen. There was now no turning back from the conflict for which both Protestant Christian and Catholic Christian nations had been preparing. In October 1620, the limited forces of King Frederick suffered a decisive defeat that ended his reign as King of Bohemia.[71] Of greater importance, however, was the role of this Prague folly in setting off the Thirty Years' War in Europe, a

---

68. Ibid., Herbert letter to James of September 1619.

69. Ibid., 348.

70. Ibid., 350.

71. *Life*, 196 n. 2.

war that cost the lives of at least one-third of the European population. *Source*
It began in 1618 in Prague; it ended with the Peace of Westphalia in 1648, the year of Lord Herbert's death.

THE RESUMPTION OF CIVIL RELIGIOUS WAR IN FRANCE

While Herbert was engaged in his unsuccessful efforts to win support for the King of Bohemia, the French were not only wavering in their neutrality on the Bohemian problem, but renewing the cause of war against French Protestants. The chief advisor of Louis XIII, Monsieur de Luynes, was a strong advocate of this cause. In describing the role of de Luynes, Herbert ascribed to him arguments that bear a strong resemblance to the words of Father Seguerend quoted at the beginning of this chapter. As Herbert reported,

> Monsieur de Luynes, continuing still the King's favor, advised him to war against his subjects of the reformed religion in France, saying, he would neither be a great prince as long as *Luynes* he suffered so puissant a party to remain within his dominions, nor could he justly style himself the most Christian king, as long as he permitted such heretics to be in that great number as they were, or to hold those strong places which by public edict were assigned to them; and therefore that he should extirpate them as the Spaniards had done the Moors, who are all banished into other countries[72]

By the fall of 1621, de Luynes had succeeded in persuading the teenage king to take military action against the Reformed religion. And King James had become convinced that his ambassador in Paris needed to take some action to restrain the French military. Indeed, Herbert was instructed "to mediate a peace" between the Catholic forces of the King and the French Protestants.[73]

Lord Herbert attempted to carry out the King's instructions, traveling to the trenches where Reformed and Royalist forces fought.[74] While his later meeting with King Louis XIII appeared to go well, he was not able to "mediate a peace." However, Herbert's efforts to counteract the war policy of Luynes so angered him that he demanded Herbert's recall. Since Luynes was, at this time, the chief advisor of Louis XIII, his

72. Ibid., 215–16
73. Ibid., 219–20.
74. Ibid., 223.

request was granted and Herbert was recalled to England. However, Luynes was stricken with an acute fever while engaged in battle with Protestant forces, and he died as a result. The young king acquired a new advisor and Herbert was invited to return to Paris as ambassador for a second term.

This second phase of Lord Herbert's life as a Christian was dramatically different from his younger experience of worship in the Church of England. Along with many other Englishmen, he became embroiled in the Calvinist/Arminian theological squabble concerning the means of salvation. Indeed, in this theological context, he first proposed the idea that God had provided the many religions of the world as a means of salvation for all of humanity.

While serving as England's ambassador to France, Lord Herbert witnessed the resumption of religious warfare in France and the beginnings of a long war between Protestant and Catholic forces in Europe. During the last years of his diplomatic service in France, Lord Herbert revised his original proposal drafted for Sir Robert. The many religions of the world could offer a means of salvation only when purified of their priestly corruptions. He therefore proposed his five Common Notions of Religion, inscribed in the conscience or heart of all people, as the norm for determining the God-given purpose of all religions.

Herbert saw no way to avoid religious violence so long as each of the differing churches and their clergy could claim God's authority for their cause. There had to be some norm for religious truth available to the reason of all people that was not a product of any particular religion. Like Ramon Lull, Herbert believed that he had identified such a God given standard. It was not Lull's magical garden, with Lady Intelligence and the word-inscribed flowers of five trees, but the five Common Notions of Religion inscribed upon the heart or conscience of human beings. If the religious and political leaders of Europe would resolve their theological disputes by the five Common Notions of Religion, they would not need to organize military alliances, raise armies, and initiate wars to resolve such disputes. Such was Lord Herbert's theological proposal for preserving religious peace by recognizing innate norms for religious truth.

Lord Herbert's Theological Legacy

This chapter has presented Lord Herbert as a reformer of political theology. Regular participation in Christian worship provided the context for his religious and intellectual development. His first visit in France introduced him to the dangers of blending religious authority with government and to a new type of political system that allowed some freedom of religion to citizens. Intra-Christian theological disputes and the wars they fueled provided the intellectual and religious challenge for his mature theology. The emerging cultural confidence in a new scientific form of rationality offered a primary resource for his reformulation of political theology. Like many other Christians of the seventeenth century, Lord Herbert was responding to the crisis of political theology precipitated by the many bloody and long-lasting religious wars of that era.

As a first step towards a reformation of political theology, Lord Herbert systematically undermined the authority of conflicting churches. He repudiated the supernaturalistic framework within which the narrative of Christian faith was set. He regarded the stories of miracles and divine revelation as nothing but a means to" establish some new government or religion."[75] In place of such stories and claims intended to buttress the authority of particular churches, he identified five Common Notions of Religion as the God-given authority for religious truth. Having dismissed miracle stories as a source of church authority, he could advise the layman "[to be so unconcerned with certain marvelous stories of past ages that it matters little to him whether they be true or false.[76] In contrast with the supernatural claims of particular churches, he set the Common Notions of Religion. They were not the property of any particular religion but were lodged in the mind of every person.

Similarly, in place of the claim of one church to be "God's interpreter," he set the "right Reason" of each individual.[77] For him, reason was the critical ally of faith, not its enemy. As a critic of traditional political theology, he, like Martin Luther before him, rejected the role of priests as mediators between the laity and God. Indeed, for him priests more

75. *De religione laici,* 97.

76. Ibid.

77. Ibid., 95.

often "diverted the soul from virtue to ceremonies and rites, [so that the laity] became bigoted and superstitious rather than good and honest.[78] For Herbert, a special corps of "God interpreters" was not needed for access to God. He relocated the means of recognizing God's truth from the realm of clergy-dominated churches to the individual's power of reason and its norms.

However, Lord Herbert's partially developed reform of political theology suffered from two great disadvantages. First, his limited theological education and experience often interfered with the clarity and consistency of his thought. Second, neither the Church of England nor the church of any European nation was ready to adopt his radical new theology; nor was any European government prepared to de-politicize its established church.

Lord Herbert's incipient reformation of political theology would have to wait a century and a half for leaders of a new nation to adapt and adopt his theology. Similarly, my discussion of Lord Herbert's theological legacy will have to wait until the next chapter. Only in the context of the American experiment in disestablishing religion does Herbert's theological legacy bear fruit; only by the separation of religion from government are the sources of religious violence dissolved.[79]

78. Ibid., 107.

79. The wars in which religion played a significant role during Lord Herbert's lifetime included the Puritan-Anglo-Catholic conflict within the Church of England and its role in the English Civil Wars of the 1640s; the multiple episodes of religious violence within sixteenth and seventeenth century France, and the Thirty-Year's War between the Union of Evangelical Estates and the Catholic League. Lord Herbert laid the foundations for a new political theology that would sunder the bonds between church and civil government and so neutralize the role of religion as a source of political violence. Such a theology was not fully developed until a century and a half after his death.

6

Disestablishing Religion and the Waning of Christian Violence

The Political Theology of Thomas Jefferson[1]

> The general foundation [of a state] is principally dependent on the establishment of religion, because the fear and reverence of religion keeps all subjects more effectively than even the presence of the prince. Therefore the magistrates must above all other things prevent the mutation of religion or the existence of diverse religions in the same state.[2]
>
> —Etienne Pasquier (1529–1615), French parliamentarian, lawyer, and historian

LIKE RAMON LULL AND LORD HERBERT, THOMAS JEFFERSON (1743–1826) was a lay theologian. By profession he was a lawyer and politician, one of the principal founders of the United States. He drafted the *Declaration of Independence* in 1776. The third president of the nation, he was twice elected to that office. Yet Jefferson did not regard his election and service as president as an achievement worthy of note. Instead, he requested that his gravestone record his authorship of "The Statute of Virginia for Religious Freedom" and the *Declaration of Independence* along with his role as "Father of the University of Virginia." Jefferson first

---

1. "Political Theology" first referred to a theological movement born in the 1960s and associated with the writings of Johann Baptist Metz, Dorothee Sölle, and Jürgen Moltmann. In this chapter, I use "political theology" to refer to a theory about the role of religion in civil society and the role of civil government in relation to religion.

2. Cited in Bouwsma, *Waning of the Renaissance*, 233–34. Pasquier published the first volume of his *Recherches de la France* in 1560; the last volume was published in 1620 after his death. I cite Pasquier's quotation at the beginning of this chapter not as a model to be endorsed but as a position typical of Christendom and much of the non-Christian world that was repudiated by Jefferson and Madison.

wrote a "Statute for Religious Freedom" and defended it in the Virginia Assembly before traveling to Philadelphia to draft the *Declaration*. While he was in Philadelphia, he wrote to the Virginia Assembly, trying to persuade them to include the "religious freedom" clause in a new constitution for Virginia. When he returned to Virginia, he argued on the floor of the Assembly for a disestablishment bill. Jefferson later described this experience as "the severest contest in which I have ever been engaged."[3] While Jefferson pursued a variety of other responsibilities for the new nation during the next decade, 1776–1786, he continued to work *in absentia* with colleagues in the Virginia Assembly (especially James Madison) for the adoption of this bill. In 1786 it was finally passed by the Virginia Assembly. Jefferson recounted a defeated amendment to the bill.

> An amendment was proposed so that [the preamble] should read; coercion is a departure from the plan of Jesus Christ, the holy author of our religion. This insertion was rejected by a great majority, in proof they meant to comprehend within the mantle of its protection, the Jew and the Gentile, the Christian and Mahometan, the Hindoo, and infidel of every denomination.[4]

This was not a man who took the issue of religion's political status lightly.

Reforming Political Theology

The tradition that Jefferson inherited was quite different from the religious freedom he proposed. In his *Notes on Virginia*, Jefferson recounted how the Virginia Assembly had established the Church of England in the colony of Virginia.

> The first settlers in [Virginia] were emigrants from England, of the Church of England, just at a point of time when it was flushed with complete victory over the religious of all other persuasions. Possessed of the powers of making, administering, and executing the laws, they showed equal intolerance in [Virginia] with their Presbyterian brethren, who had emigrated to the north. Several acts of the Virginia assembly of 1659, 1662, and 1693, had made [several religious practices of the Quakers to be a crime, punished by imprisonment or death]. If no capital

3. Jefferson, *Autobiography,* 62.
4. Ibid., 71.

execution took place here, as did in New-England, it was not owing to the moderation of the church, or spirit of the legislature.
The Anglicans retained full possession of the country about a
century. Other [religious] opinions began then to creep in, and
the great care of the government to support their own church,
having begotten an equal degree of indolence in its clergy, two-
thirds of the people had become dissenters at the commence-
ment of the present revolution.[5]

Virginia was not the only one of the American colonies to have an established religion. Nine of the thirteen colonies had an established church
in one form or another. The political theology of Etienne Pasquier cited
at the opening of this chapter was embedded in the American colonies
as well as in the European countries of the colonists' origins.

Pasquier was not the only European of his era who believed that
the authority of civil government was dependent on religion. Nor
was he the first to advocate government policies that would enforce
the uniformity of one state-established religion and defend it from
the intrusion of others. The political theology of Christendom had
long recognized the bond between civil authority and the church. As
a result, a civil authority, such as the king of France, would mobilize
knights of his kingdom to eliminate the religion of the Cathars in
the thirteenth-century Albigensian Crusade, and local authorities
of southern France would execute any individual convicted by the
Inquisition of Cathar beliefs.[6]

If the authority of government is dependent upon religion, that
government should take all steps necessary to protect its religion
against rivals. Eliminating any religion as a rival to the government's
established religion was in the self-interest of government. The policies
advocated by Pasquier were not unique. They were embodied in the
actions of his contemporaries who organized the Catholic Alliance and
the Union of Evangelical (Protestant) Estates.[7] This mutual dependence

---

5. Jefferson, *Notes on Virginia*, 157.

6. For the Albigensian Crusade along with the Inquisition's role in determining the
guilt of suspected heretics and their subsequent execution by a local civil authority, see
chapter 2.

7. Another contemporary of Pasquier, Lord Herbert, perceived this subordination
of the church to politics during his visit in France (see chapter 5). In the words of
Herbert's poem, while "suger'd Divines . . . tell us Humility and Patience are the way to
heaven" they neglect their witness to God and God's gift of freedom to human beings.

of government and religion was basic to traditional political theology; it antedated medieval Christendom and provides the dominant model of religion-government relations in many nations of the twenty-first century.[8]

The Peace of Augsburg 1555

The sixteenth century Reformation in Europe made only a slight modification in the political theology of Christendom. It recognized the division of Christendom (at this time) into two different religions: Catholic and Lutheran. However, the Peace of Augsburg preserved the basic principles of traditional political theology. It gave each European ruler the right to determine the religion of his territory: *cuius regio, eius religio* (whoever governs the territory decides its religion). In this peace agreement, the civil government determined what religion was to be the legitimate religion of citizens in that territory, and that there was to be only one religion.[9] These two principles of political theology—only one religion determined by civil government—were fundamental to European Christendom. They were repudiated most decisively in the new political theology of Thomas Jefferson.

Post-Reformation War Preparations

Martin Luther's Reformation in the early sixteenth century may not have focused on a new political theology, but it did begin the process of creating the political and theological conditions that would require such a reformation. Theologically, Luther denied the necessity for an ecclesiastical mediator between God and the individual. His critique

---

In his critique of the role of religion in cultivating fear among citizens, Lord Herbert was in the minority. Most thoughtful Europeans of the late sixteenth and early seventeenth century would have agreed with Pasquier.

8. "Political theology is the primordial form of political thought and remains a live alternative for many peoples today. [Those of us in the West] are living an experiment, we are the exceptions. We have little reason to expect other civilizations to follow our unusual path [in separating the powers of government and religion.]" (Lilla, *Stillborn God,* 308–9). Lilla uses the term "political theology" as if it developed in only one form: namely, what I call "traditional political theology" or some similarly qualified use of the term. For a discussion, and examples, of the many uses of "political theology," see Scott and Cavanaugh, *Blackwell Companion to Political Theology.*

9. Augsburg also gave citizens the right to emigrate to a territory ruled by a prince of their (Lutheran or Catholic) religion.

of the church for the sale of indulgences, clergy corruption, and the papal abuse of power also undermined church authority. His doctrine of justification by grace through faith created a radical new model of theology. However, in contrast with his new theology of justification, Luther's political theology was extremely conservative if not reactionary. His political theology portrayed rulers as the agents of God to whom Christians should be obedient.

Each of the Christian churches spawned by the Reformation (including the multiplication of Calvinist churches) developed a two-track strategy for protecting and increasing their constituencies. On the one hand, each pursued a development of doctrinal statements that established clear boundaries between themselves and other faith communities. For the Catholic Church, the Council of Trent, meeting in twenty-five sessions between 1545 and 1563, developed a series of doctrines, including their theological differences with Lutherans.[10] About a decade later, Lutheran theologians consolidated their doctrines in the Formula of Concord; among other matters, it specified their doctrine of the Eucharist over against the Calvinists. Dutch Calvinists (along with Calvinists from England, Switzerland, and Germany) met in the Synod of Dort in 1618–1619; they produced five criteria for Calvinist orthodoxy, making predestination absolute and condemning the conditional form of predestination advocated by Arminius. Each of these theological councils sought to clarify blurred differences between one church and others while making a persuasive case for the truth of that church's particular doctrines.

On the other hand, the several churches and their governmental counterparts formed military alliances binding together several states or principalities sharing a common confession of faith, or in the case of Lutherans and Calvinist, a common confessional opponent and threat. The fear of a Catholic effort to purge Europe of Christian "heresy" was sufficiently strong to enable Lutherans and Calvinists to overcome their theological differences and to form a single military alliance: the Union of Evangelical (Protestant) Estates.[11] Catholics formed a Catholic

10. In 1564 Pope Pius IV ratified the results of Trent for the Church. I am indebted to Professor Robert Daly, Boston College for my information on the Council of Trent.

11. "After [the Catholic Alliance] had established a position of strength, it will embark on a campaign to exterminate "heresy throughout Europe" (Parker, *Thirty Years' War*, 25 and 117–18). "Evangelical" is a translation of the German *Evangelisch*, which is still the name of the German Protestant Church consisting of both Lutheran

Alliance. By the first quarter of the seventeenth century, Europeans were poised to enact the political-military consequences of an unrevised political theology. The result was an event so destructive as to require a theological as well as political resolution: the Thirty Years' War.

The Thirty Years' War 1618–1648

I have already introduced the Thirty Years' War in the last chapter. Lord Herbert was engaged in diplomatic activities at the beginning of that war, attempting to win the support of King James for his son-in-law, the newly installed King of Bohemia, and trying to persuade the French to remain neutral in the defenestration fiasco in Prague.[12] He failed in both these efforts as the French became convinced that this was indeed a religious war. It turned out to be an extremely costly war in human lives and in its economic consequences. As one military historian has noted, "the Thirty Years' War was the longest, most expensive, and brutal war ever fought on German soil. The loss of lives was proportionately much greater than in World War II."[13] Approximately one-third of Europe's population lost their lives in the course of the Thirty Years' War, either as casualties of military action or because of war-related food shortages and epidemics. The economic consequences of the war persisted for a substantially longer period than the aftermath of World War II. The war demonstrated the dysfunctional role of Christian political theology in the post-Reformation era. The neutralizing of religious conflict as a causal agency of war was, in the judgment of Geoffrey Parker, one of that war's greatest achievements.[14]

Mark Lilla extends the legacy of the Thirty Years' War beyond the political-military conflict of seventeenth century Europe to encompass the basic political principles of the entire West. For him, the "Great Separation" of politics and religion is not an inevitable product of his-

---

and Reformed (Calvinist) congregations; it does not have the distinctive meaning of "Evangelical" as applied to churches in the American context.

12. Protestants ejected two Catholic counselors from the second story window of the Prague castle in order to elect as king the Protestant (Calvinist) Frederick V, Palatine Elector. Under terms of the Peace of Augsburg, the whole of Bohemia would have become Protestant if the King were Protestant.

13. Parker, *Thirty Years' War*, 215.

14. Ibid., 219.

torical development, but a particular response of Western nations to the destructive warfare of post-Reformation Christendom.

> The idea of separating political discourse from theological discourse was a novelty conceived to meet a particular predicament of Christian history . . . Though Britain and the United States can pride themselves on having cultivated the ideas of toleration, freedom of conscience, and a formal separation of church and state, their success has depended upon a wholly unique experience with Protestant sectarianism in the seventeenth and eighteenth centuries. . . . Our most basic political principles arose in response to the unique theological challenges of Christendom.[15]

The worst of the religious wars noted in this book also played an essential role in transforming the political theology of Christendom, a political theology and political status of religion that made religious warfare virtually inevitable.

The Peace of Westphalia 1648

In October 1648, after thirty years of fighting between a changing set of participants from a number of European nations, representatives of France and Sweden, Spain and the Holy Roman Empire, together with their numerous allies, signed a pair of treaties creating the Peace of Westphalia.[16] That peace agreement ended the Thirty Years' War. Even more important, that peace agreement ended the four centuries of European religious warfare recounted in this book and initiated the movement towards a new political theology. Except for a post-Westphalia transitional era, a few persistent exceptions, and the new wave of religious violence in the late twentieth century, Europeans have enjoyed an environment of religious peace for the past three hundred years.[17]

The Peace of Westphalia also created the beginning of the modern religious history of Europe. That agreement marked the end of one of its

---

15. Lilla, *Stillborn God,* 298, 304, and 306.

16. While I and others refer to a Thirty Years' War as if it were a single war, there were in fact a series of connected wars with the most intense fighting in the early 1630s (Parker, *Thirty Years' War*).

17. Religious peace refers to the absence of a particular kind of war, not all wars. Europeans have had more than their share of territorial, racial, and ideological wars in the past century.

main signatories, the Holy Roman Empire; it also quietly and inauspiciously signaled the abandonment of the political theology of Augsburg that presumed each civil government would enforce some form of religious uniformity. A state-sanctioned limited religious diversity became the new political model for European religions after Westphalia.

For the sake of religious peace, Westphalia proposed a new model of limited religious diversity to replace the older model of religious uniformity. Article 28 of the Peace Agreement affirmed the right of Lutheran and Reformed Christians "to have the free exercise of their religion in public churches." Previously, in territories ruled by Catholics, the public exercise of any Protestant form of worship was banned, as was Catholic worship in Protestant territories. Similarly, Article 49 set forth religious freedom as a general principle: "it has been found expedient to confirm and ratify the liberty of the exercise of religion by this present treaty." As best I could determine, the principle of religious liberty for all citizens was not implemented by the Westphalia Agreement. Catholic, Lutheran, and Reformed (Calvinist) churches were the only three religions represented in these peace negotiations and the only three whose religious rights were explicitly recognized. Nevertheless, while the Peace of Westphalia did not offer religious freedom for all Christians, to say nothing of Jews, Muslims, and unbelievers, it did establish a new political context for religious life in the West. One state-supported religious monopoly was replaced by a variety of state-sanctioned churches. The theological, philosophical, and political thinkers of the Enlightenment were given a new context for thinking through the complicated issues of religion and politics inherited from their problematic past. After Westphalia, political theology had to confront a new agenda of issues like religious diversity, toleration, and freedom of conscience.

Jefferson's Heterodox Theology and Jesus Piety

Jefferson's commitment to the disestablishment of religion in Virginia and the United States was rooted in his religious commitment as well as his political pragmatism. He fought for the freedom of religion from the jurisdiction of government in order to protect the integrity of religion. Insofar as religion was established by government, it was a means of governing and served the purposes of the civil order. As a result, the Christian Church would necessarily be tied to government policies of coercion and violence alien to its own ministry. In pursuing this disestablishment project, Jefferson sought a resolution to the dynamics of religious violence consistent with the ministry of Jesus, though he would come to learn this only later in his life. Like so many of us, Jefferson, the great rationalist among the founders of America, lived a life that repeatedly transcended the bounds of his reason.

Jefferson's disorderly theological reflections blended together church teachings, Enlightenment rationalism, and the ethics of Jesus. These three dimensions of his religious development provided the building blocks for his political theology. Because of his life-long engagement with religious issues and his formative role in shaping the public status of religion in this country, I will first review these three dimensions of his theology before focusing on his political theology.

Jefferson and the Church of England[18]

As a child and young adolescent, Jefferson was regularly exposed to church teachings. His religious life appears to have been conventional for his time and place: regular participation in the Sunday worship of the Church of England, a daily exposure to the scriptures and prayers of that church as part of his early education in a church academy, psalm singing with family at home, and prayers with his mother.[19] While his religious beliefs later wandered far beyond the limits of Christian orthodoxy, his behavior was consistent with the piety of his childhood. He regularly attended worship in his home parish in Virginia or other locations while traveling. He and his children were the beneficiaries of Christian rituals of baptism, marriage, and funerals. During the last several decades of his life, Jefferson often ended each day by reading from a digest of the four Gospels that he had himself assembled. As he was dying, his family heard him recount the scriptural prayer, "Lord, now lettest thou thy servant depart in peace." The priest of his local parish conducted his funeral shortly after. He was not a man who separated himself from the church of his origins.

---

18. In 1787, the name of this church was changed to the Episcopal Church.

19. Jefferson studied with the Rev. William Douglas from 1756–1758 and with the Rev. James Maury from 1758 to 1760. Holmes, *Faiths of the Founding Fathers,* 79. *The Book of Common Prayer* provided the source for the prayers taught Jefferson by his mother.

Jefferson as a Deist

In his beliefs, however, Jefferson was not as consistent with his church origins as he was in his practice. At the age of seventeen, Jefferson enrolled in the College of William and Mary. Shortly thereafter, he began to change his mind about Christian beliefs. In the person of William Small, professor of mathematics and natural science, Jefferson encountered the intellectual revolution of English deists. These were the philosophers and scientists who set forth the new scientific view of nature and the new empirical method of reasoning. Jefferson soon adopted the scientific worldview and rejected the supernatural worldview of traditional theology. Like other deists, he also extended the empirical method to theological reasoning; by reflecting on the intricate interconnections observed in nature, a rational mind would be led to recognize the hand of the Creator in the creation. From the age of seventeen to his early thirties, Jefferson read extensively in the literature of deism and classical authors; he copied large portions of these readings in a diary of learning called *The Commonplace Book*.[20] His entries included large sections of material from Lord Bolingbroke, one of his favorite English deist sources, and also from some of the French *philosophes*; Jefferson was one of the few Americans of this generation who was fluent in French.

After the prior chapter on Lord Herbert, I need not develop in any detail the Enlightenment theology that occupied Jefferson. I regard Jefferson as a second-generation disciple of Lord Herbert. To the best of my knowledge, Jefferson had not read any of Lord Herbert's writings. However, he was familiar with the writings of those who had read Lord Herbert and used Herbert's material freely in their writings. Jefferson's library included the *Miscellaneous Writings* of Charles Blount (1654–93), Herbert's most devoted disciple;[21] Lord Bolingbroke, who had appropriated much of Lord Herbert's theology, was one of the most frequent sources of hand-copied material in Jefferson's *Commonplace Book*. Like Lord Herbert, Jefferson found Calvin's theology to be the most offensive; they both characterized Calvin's God as a form of Demonism and recommended atheism as an alternative theologically superior to Calvinism. Like Lord Herbert, Jefferson's theology was unitarian, not

20. Jefferson, *Jefferson's Literary Commonplace Book*.
21. Gilreath, *Thomas Jefferson's Library*.

trinitarian. Like Herbert, he rejected any claim for supernatural agency in miracles and divine inspiration in scripture; he advised his nephew to read the biblical text in the same way that he would read any history from the ancient world. Like Herbert, he used "priests" as a pejorative term and almost always included Calvinist clergy in the company of "priests."

Jefferson knew only one God as creator and ruling providence of history. He referred to the doctrine of the Trinity as a species of tritheism unacceptable to any rational person. He regarded Jesus as a reformer of Jewish monotheism, and most certainly not a human incarnation of God. He did not regard the scriptures as divinely inspired or as a reliable source of our "opinion" of God. In contrast to the church's Bible, Jefferson found the creative hand of God disclosed in the laws of Nature. For him, any person who observed the intricacies of nature and reflected rationally upon what had been seen would be very likely to conclude that a purposive rational mind was involved in the creation of the world. It is such a theology of creation and Creator that informs the first paragraph of the *Declaration of Independence.*

> When in the course of human events it becomes necessary for one people to dissolve the political bonds which have connected them with another and to assume among the powers of the earth, the separate and equal station to which the Laws of Nature and of Nature's God entitle them.

It is the God of nature, not the biblical God, to whom Jefferson appeals for legitimating the separation of the American colonies from Britain. Jefferson was a firm believer in the role of Nature to provide the evidence which, by way of the argument from design, disclosed God as Creator.

Like his doctrines of God and Jesus Christ, Jefferson's views of human nature fell considerably outside the boundaries of orthodox Christianity. He rejected any doctrine of original sin as undermining the spirit of democracy. In his view, a democratic republic needs to instill confidence in its citizens for their judgments; it did not need a doctrine that undermines such confidence. For the same reason, he rejected the Christian drama of salvation in which citizens were made dependent upon God's grace for their salvation. Jefferson believed in some form of life after death that included punishment and rewards in accordance with one's behavior in this life. Somewhat similar to Lord

Herbert's innate five criteria for religious truth, Jefferson believed that
God had provided innate moral criteria within each person for guidance in making moral decisions between right and wrong, good and
evil. He also claimed that God had endowed each human being with a
cluster of innate rights.

In the language of the *Declaration's* second paragraph,

> We hold these truths to be self-evident, that all men are cre-
> ated equal, that they are endowed by their Creator with [innate]
> unalienable Rights, that among these are Life, Liberty and the
> pursuit of Happiness. To secure these rights, Governments are
> instituted among Men, deriving their just powers from the con-
> sent of the governed.[22]

All people are created equal and equally endowed by their Creator with
certain innate and unalienable rights. Governments are instituted to
preserve these rights of individuals, not to preserve the dominance or
exclusivity of any particular religion. Jefferson never repudiated these
Enlightenment theological themes, just as he never repudiated the worship, Scriptures, and prayers of the Church of England.

There is one Enlightenment judgment, however, that he did come
to repudiate. When he was a young law student, Jefferson copied into
his *Commonplace Book* the judgment of Lord Bolingbroke that the ethic
of Jesus was inferior to the moral teachings of classical philosophers
of Greece and Rome. While this negative judgment did not appear in
Jefferson's own words, it was one of the points he had learned from
Lord Bolingbroke and recorded in his *Commonplace Book*. When he
made this entry as a law student, there is no question that he shared
Bolingbrook's judgment:

> It is not true that Christ revealed an entire body of ethics, to
> which recourse might be had on every occasion. Moral obli-
> gations are occasionally recommended and commanded, but
> nowhere proved from principles of reason, and by clear deduc-
> tions. Were all the precepts of this kind that are scattered about
> in the whole New Testament, collected, like the short sentences
> of ancient sages in the memorials we have of them, and put
> together in the very words of the sacred writers, they would
> compose a very short, as well as unconnected system of ethics.

22. Jefferson wrote "that they are endowed by their Creator with innate unalienable
rights"; Congress replaced "innate" with "certain."

> A system thus collected from the writings of ancient heathen
> moralists—of Tully, of Seneca, of Epictetus, and others, would
> be fuller, more entire, more coherent, and more clearly deduced
> from unquestionable principles of knowledge.[23]

Insofar as this was the judgment of Jefferson as well as Bolingbroke, it provides an important marker for his theological journey in and beyond the Enlightenment.

Jefferson's Jesus

A third dimension of Jefferson's theology began to appear during the late seventeen-nineties and first term of his presidency (1801–1805). Several factors coincided to lead Jefferson to a long-term engagement with the ethic of Jesus: 1) an historical study of Jesus by Joseph Priestly that enabled Jefferson to take seriously Jesus's ethics; 2) experiences of political conflict that appeared to pose serious threats to the future well-being of this new nation; and 3) personal conversations with a Christian friend that led Jefferson to appreciate the potential role of Jesus's ethic for a democratic republic.

Sometime after 1793, Jefferson read a two-volume book by Joseph Priestly (1733–1804), the scientist and Unitarian minister he greatly admired.[24] Priestly offered a new version of Jesus as a rational reformer. Many deists had characterized Jesus as a victim of illusions of grandeur; they knew no other explanation for his repeated statements of identity with God. Preistly's book, *An History of the Corruptions of Christianity,* provided an alternative explanation for Jesus's apparent self-attributions of divinity. According to Priestly, the "real Jesus" never claimed for himself any divine attributes or origins. This divinizing of Jesus was a product of the work of others: his "ignorant followers" who were entrusted with the task of recording his words, which they had never understood, and the "Platonizing mystics" of the early church. In correspondence of the early 1800s, Jefferson repeatedly told his friends how much Priestly's book meant to him: "I have read [Priestly's two volumes] over and over again, and I rest on them . . . as the basis of my own faith." In spite of the historical naiveté of Priestly's arguments, they

23. Jefferson, *Jefferson's Literary Commonplace Book,* 35. In his introduction to Jefferson's *Commonplace Book,* Douglas Wilson provides the approximate date of 1765–1766 for this entry from Lord Bolingbroke (Wilson, Introduction, in ibid., 8).

24. Priestly, *History of the Corruptions of Christianity* in two volumes.

did convince Jefferson that "the historical Jesus" (as we might say today) never claimed any unique identification with God. As a result, Jefferson adopted Priestly's new view of Jesus: he was not the mentally deranged victim of grandiose illusions, but a morally serious reformer of Jewish monotheism.

The presidential campaign of the late 1790s was the first political contest in which Americans were sufficiently divided to regard each other as enemies.[25] The attacks on Jefferson were often personal and focused on his religion. Voters were warned that Jefferson was an anti-Christian; they should hide their Bibles because, if elected, he would order all of them to be confiscated. Clergy were particularly active in the campaign against Jefferson. The people who had been united against the British now found themselves divided against each other. For Jefferson, as for many other Americans, the campaign of 1798–1799 for the presidency of the United States created a host of disturbing problems, personal as well as political.

During this time—after reading Priestly and in the midst of campaign conflicts—Jefferson was also engaged in conversations about the Christian religion with his friend, Benjamin Rush. Rush was a Philadelphia physician and colleague of Jefferson from the Continental Congress. Rush believed that Jefferson's apparent lack of religion weakened his leadership abilities, especially in dealing with social conflict. Rush, like many other founders, also believed that the United States needed some resource for sustaining public morality and social harmony and that the Christian religion was best suited for this task. Hence, in one of these conversations in 1798–99, he asked Jefferson about his religious beliefs and made his case for the political utility of the Christian religion. Jefferson apparently promised to write him his religious views in general and his view of the Christian religion in particular. As Rush wrote Jefferson in 1800,

> You promised me when we parted . . . to send me your religious Creed. I have always considered Christianity as the strong ground of Republicanism. Its Spirit is opposed not only to the splendor, but even to the very forms of monarchy and many of its precepts have for their objects republican liberty and equal-

25. In addition to the political differences between the two parties, the two candidates for the presidency—John Adams and Thomas Jefferson—had been friends and colleagues in the liberation and formation of this new nation.

ity as well as simplicity, integrity and economy in government. It is only necessary for republicanism to ally itself to the Christian religion to overturn all the corrupted political and religious institutions of the world.[26]

In March of 1801, a mere six months after receiving this letter from Benjamin Rush, Jefferson wrote a letter to a political colleague from Vermont that included comments resembling the advice of Rush.

> I am in hopes that . . . they will find that the Christian religion, when divested of the rags in which they [the clergy] have involved it, and brought to the original purity and simplicity of its benevolent institutor is a religion of all others most friendly to liberty, science, and the freest expansions of the human mind.[27]

Events of 1798–1799 persuaded Jefferson that this new nation was in jeopardy. His conversations with Rush led him to explore the ethical resources of a rationalized Jesus. In the next few years, he tested out the acceptability of a rationalist version of Jesus for what he perceived to be the nation's growing divisions and partisan conflicts.[28] As a result of this change of heart and mind, Jefferson immersed himself in a study program that eventually produced three documents.

SYLLABUS: JESUS COMPARED WITH OTHERS

In the winter of 1798–99 Jefferson promised his friend, Dr. Rush, that he would send him his views of "the Christian system." Four years later, Jefferson wrote Rush a letter accompanied by a syllabus titled, *An*

26. Benjamin Rush to Thomas Jefferson 8/22/1800. All letters concerning Jefferson's religious views are taken from the Dickinson Adams edition of *Jefferson's Extracts from the Gospels.*

27. Thomas Jefferson to Moses Robinson 3/23/1801

28. Garry Wills calls attention to the fact that Jefferson's engagement with Jesus was personal as well as political (Wills, *Head and Heart,* 159). During the bitterly fought and divisive political campaign of 1798–1799, Jefferson had to deal with his own anger in response to personal attacks as well as a newly divided nation. On the basis of Jefferson's life in retirement, I would agree with Wills. "Jefferson changed his attitude toward Jesus's moral standard in the 1790s, when he was embroiled in the heightening animosities of partisan politics. Trying to temper his own emotions, he noticed what he thought the most striking thing about Jesus's teachings—that earlier moralists had enjoined love for one's friends but Jesus commanded that one loves one's enemies . . . [Jefferson] obviously felt a personal need in this period of intense conflict to find a calming influence on his own attitudes, and found it in Jesus" (ibid., 159).

Estimate of the Merit of the Doctrines of Jesus Compared with Those of Others The "Others" considered in this syllabus were writings from the Hebrew Bible and philosophers from Greece and Rome. In his letter to Dr. Rush, Jefferson recalled his promise to provide him with an account of his view of the Christian religion.

> You may recall our conversations in the evenings of 1798–99 which served as an Anodyne to the afflictions of the crisis through which the country was then laboring. The Christian religion was sometimes our topic, and I then promised you that, one day or other, I would give you my views of it. They are very different from the Anti-Christian system imputed to me by those who know nothing of my opinions. To the corruptions of Christianity I am indeed opposed; but not to the genuine precepts of Jesus himself. I am a Christian, in the only sense he wished anyone to be; sincerely attached to his doctrines in preference to all others; ascribing to himself every human excellence, and believing he never claimed any other. In confiding [this Syllabus] to you I know it will not be exposed to the malignant perversions of those who make every word from me a text for new misrepresentations and calumnies. I am, moreover, averse to the communication of my religious tenets to the public, because it would countenance the presumption of those who have endeavored to draw them before that tribunal and to seduce public opinion to erect itself over the rights of conscience, which the laws have so justly proscribed.[29]

Jefferson had been wounded by misrepresentations of his religious views during the presidential campaign and did not wish to repeat those experiences. While he never developed the Syllabus beyond the outline provided in his letter to Benjamin Rush, it marked the beginning of his new engagement with Jesus. By 1803, Jefferson had not only completed at least the outline of his comparative study of ancient moralists, but had also reached a conclusion concerning their relative merits: "The moral precepts of Jesus are more correct and sublime than those of the

---

29. Thomas Jefferson to Rush, 4/21/1803. Jefferson's description of his first two Jesus projects as strictly confidential was only partially true. He was circulating to a limited number of persons in his cabinet, family, or friends copies of these early religious documents as "trial balloons" to see if a positive rationalistic version of Jesus would be acceptable to American Christians.

ancient philosophers."[30] The Syllabus then specified the reasons for the superiority of Jesus's moral teaching:

> And [his moral doctrines] were more pure and perfect than those of the most correct of the philosophers. And they went far beyond [both Jewish traditions and Greek philosophers] in inculcating a universal philanthropy, not only to kindred and friends, neighbors and country men, but to all mankind gathering all into one family, under the bonds of love, charity, peace, common wants and common aids...[This is] the peculiar superiority of the system of Jesus over all others.

By 1803 Jefferson had not only rejected the judgment of Bolingbroke that he had so carefully recorded in his *Commonplace Book*, but he recognized a resource in the ethic of Jesus for dealing with the most pressing personal and political problem of social conflict and enmity.

Jefferson assembled his second Jesus project the next year (1804). In later correspondence, he described the context in which this work was done: after "the evening task of reading the letters and papers of the day."[31] The title of this second Jesus study suggests a different focus from the first:

The Philosophy of Jesus

The original of this volume no longer exists. Its full title is *The Philosophy of Jesus of Nazareth Extracted from the Account of his Life and Doctrine as given by Matthew, Mark, Luke, and John Being an Abridgement of the New Testament for the use of the Indians*[32] *unembarrassed with Matters of Fact or Faith beyond the level of their Comprehension.*[33] Much of the content is known from Jefferson's correspondence and a reconstructed text is available in *Jefferson's Extracts from the Gospels.* Using two English Bibles of the same edition, he cut out those passages from the four Gospels which he judged to be the authentic teaching of Jesus. He then pasted these snippets on the pages of a book as if they were one

---

30. Thomas Jefferson to Edward Dowse, 4/19/1803.

31. Thomas Jefferson to William Short, 10/31/1819.

32. Jefferson never intended that this volume would be distributed to the "Indians" or any other general group of readers. "Indians" was a code word for his political opponents, the Federalists.

33. For a reconstructed text of *The Philosophy of Jesus,* see Jefferson, *Jefferson's Extracts from the Gospels,* 1–46.

continuous text. In later correspondence, he expressed his confidence in anyone's ability to recognize the true teaching of Jesus and distinguish it from the "folly of the evangelists'" misrepresentation of him. In his Jesus book he intended to include

> the very words only of Jesus paring off [the Evangelists'] own misconceptions as his dicta and expressing unintelligibly what they had not understood themselves. There will be found re-maining the most sublime and benevolent code of morals which has ever been offered to man. I have performed this operation for my own use, by cutting verse by verse out of the printed book, and arranging the matter which is evidently his and which is as easily distinguished as diamonds in a dung hill.[34]
>
> Probably you have heard me say I had taken the four Evangelists, had cut from them every text that had recorded of the moral precepts of Jesus . . . although they appeared as frag-ments, yet fragments of the most sublime edifice of morality which had ever been exhibited to man.[35]

He is explicit in noting that he prepared this book, like the previous Syllabus, only for himself, not for the general public. It was only forty-six pages in length.

THE LIFE AND MORALS OF JESUS OF NAZARETH

His third Jesus project, *The Life and Morals of Jesus of Nazareth,* had eighty-three pages of pasted texts, with parallel columns in Greek, Latin, French, and English. Its full title is: *The Life and Morals of Jesus of Nazareth Extracted from the Gospels in Greek, Latin, French & English.* He again cautioned readers to keep his religious views private. "I not only write nothing on religion but barely permit myself to speak of it."[36] Jefferson completed this third and longest of his Jesus projects in 1820, after he was no longer president.

In the published edition of this book, the pasted character of cut snippets is apparent, including, now and then, a phrase or two pasted vertically on the page because there was no room for another horizontal line. While working on this larger project, Jefferson continued to write others effusively about the marvel of Jesus's ethics.

---

34. Thomas Jefferson to John Adams, 10/12/1813.

35. Thomas Jefferson to Charles Clay, 1/29/1815.

36. Ibid.

A more beautiful or precious morsel of ethics I have never seen; it [his collected sayings of Jesus] is a document in proof that I am a real Christian, that is to say, a disciple of the doctrines of Jesus, very different from the Platonists who call me infidel and themselves Christians and preachers of the gospel, while they draw all their characteristic dogmas from what its Author never said at all.[37]

The story of Jefferson's involvement with the figure of Jesus did not end with the completion of this last project. As he confided to a friend, after finishing *The Life and Morals of Jesus,* "I never go to bed without an hour or half-hour's previous reading of something moral whereon to ruminate in the intervals of sleep.[38] This, in part, is why I use the category of "Jesus Piety" for this last dimension of Jefferson's theological pilgrimage.

A Constitutional Reform of Political Theology

Jefferson was not able to shepherd his bill for religious freedom through the Virginia Assembly. He was most often absent from the Assembly. It was therefore James Madison (1751–1836) who oversaw the Bill's journey to adoption. It was also Madison who wrote the two brief phrases in the First Amendment of the United States Constitution—the so called "Establishment Clause" and "Free Exercise Clause"—that translated the complex struggle for religious freedom in Virginia into political structures shaping the relation of religion and government in the United States as a whole.

Congress shall make no law respecting an establishment of religion, or prohibiting the free exercise thereof.[39]

Madison, however, was not merely a decade-younger replica of Jefferson. He shared Jefferson's passion for disentangling the traditional relationship of religion and government, which was already firmly established in Virginia, but he brought to this task a different perspective.

37. Thomas Jefferson to Charles Thomsen, 1/9/1816.

38. Jefferson's own *Life and Morals of Jesus of Nazareth* was one of these books for nightly readings according to Adams, "Introduction," in *Jefferson's Extracts from the Gospels,* 38.

39. When Jefferson first read the Constitution, without the first amendment, he was somewhat disappointed: "I found articles which I thought objectionable [including] the absence of express declarations ensuring freedom of religion" (*Autobiography,* 118).

Madison was not a graduate of William and Mary. That church-related college had become sufficiently notorious for its deist inclinations to persuade Madison's family—like Jefferson's, members of the Church of England in Virginia—to send James up north, to the College of New Jersey or Princeton. Better that he emerge a Presbyterian than a deist.[40]

At Princeton, Madison became sufficiently interested in the Christian religion to spend an extra year in the study of Hebrew, Greek, and ethics. His professor, John Witherspoon was also then the president of Princeton. Witherspoon combined orthodox Presbyterian theology with Scottish Common Sense philosophy.[41] When Madison returned to Virginia, he led worship services for his family, signaling his more orthodox approach to religion. However, Madison did not have time in Virginia to become complacent with his practice of religion. Shortly after his return, in a neighboring county, the established church of Virginia had identified religious dissenters who were being arrested and jailed by local authorities. Madison was 22 years old when he witnessed these consequences of the establishment of religion. To the task of creating a new political theology and its embodiment in government structures, Madison brought the resources of his theological studies in the bible and ethics. Disestablishing the church in Virginia now had a more orthodox champion in Madison as well as the heterodox Jefferson.[42]

For his own political reasons, Jefferson was also concerned with the preservation of vital religious communities. He saw himself as a restorationist standing in the tradition of Martin Luther and "the Glorious Reformation." Luther freed God-talk from the institutional bondage of the church, but not from the authority of civil government. Civil government then prescribed the one and only legal religion for all citizens that was supported by the tax revenues from all citizens. As Jefferson argued in his (1776) first presentation of the Bill for Religious Freedom in Virginia, an established religion is the product of "the impious presumption of legislators and rulers, civil as well as ecclesiastical, who

---

40. Madison's college choice was also influenced by Reverend Thomas Martin in whose academy he studied immediately before beginning college.

41. John Witherspoon was also the only clergy signer of the *Declaration of Independence.*

42. Within the limits of this chapter, I cannot develop adequately the legacy of Calvin's covenantal theology that Madison brought to the task of disestablishment.

have assumed dominion over the faith of others."[43] The presumption is "impious" because men are presuming to take the place of God. For Jefferson, "our rulers can have authority over such natural rights only as we have submitted to them. The rights of conscience we never submitted, we could not submit. We are answerable for them to our God."[44]

While Jefferson, like Lord Herbert, spoke disparagingly of priests, Jefferson spoke with equal scorn of "legislators and rulers." For him, civil government agents were as guilty of corrupting the teachings and practice of religion as were church authorities. For him, the only valid mediating agency in the practice of religion was the conscience of the individual believer. Jefferson was an exponent of an unqualified religious individualism.

In his first argument for religious freedom in the Virginia Assembly, Jefferson located the right to worship God in each individual; it is not a right that has its locus in a civil government. Nor can any person surrender this right to a civil government because the right is also an obligation of each person to God. As Madison expressed this same point in his *Memorial and Remonstrance,*

> We hold it for a fundamental and undeniable truth, "that religion, or the duty which we owe to our Creator and the manner of discharging it, can be directed only by reason and conviction, not by force or violence."
>
> It is unalienable also, because what is here a right towards men, is a duty towards the Creator. It is the duty of every man to render to the Creator such homage and such only as he believes to be acceptable to him. This duty is precedent, both in order of time and in degree of obligation, to the claims of Civil Society... We maintain therefore that in matters of Religion, no man's right is abridged by the institution of Civil Society and that Religion is wholly exempt from its cognizance.[45]

43. Jefferson's Statue for Religious Freedom (Wills, *Head and Heart,* 193). Critics of church-state separation sometimes suggest that the church was divested of war-making potentialities because the state would be a more reliable custodian of such matters. The past two centuries disproved any such folly nor did Jefferson and other founders presume that political leaders were more virtuous or innocent than their ecclesiastical counterparts.

44. Jefferson, *Notes of Virginia,* 159.

45. Madison, *Memorial and Remonstrance.* Unless otherwise indicated, all Madison quotations are taken from his this work.

In the American political theology of Jefferson and Madison, we meet again the definition of *religio* introduced by St. Thomas and discussed in Chapter two.[46] *Religio* is "a virtue because it pays the debt of honor to God" (*ST* II-II 80, 1). Every person is responsible for giving honor and thanks to God, for paying their debt to their Creator. In the language of Jefferson and Madison, every one is responsible for cultivating their own virtue of *religio* in a manner consistent with conviction and judgment; *religio* is not a virtue that can be developed by coercion or violence. Like Aquinas, Jefferson and Madison presupposed that all people had the obligation to give God their Creator the honor, praise, and thanks, which they owed God.

This theological recovery of the grounds for *religio* also had consequences for the language of "religious tolerance." John Locke had argued persuasively for the toleration of differing religions. George Mason, a member of the Virginia Assembly, introduced Locke's concept of religious tolerance into Jefferson's Bill for Religious Freedom. Jefferson, by mail, rejected the addition of "religious tolerance" to his bill and Madison, by argument, won its exclusion from the text. Jefferson and Madison rejected the notion of toleration because it presumed that the right of religion was lodged in the civil government, not in the individual person. To adopt a policy of toleration would leave the government in the position of authority concerning what religion or religions would be legally open to citizens. Civil governments would then be the responsible "other" in human dealings with God, not people in their individuality. A state that tolerated several religions, as happened in Europe after the Peace of Westphalia, would still have the same theological status as the civil government that supported and required the practice of one religion only.

Furthermore, "religious freedom" and "toleration" have quite different political consequences as illustrated in chapter three. After the Christian re-conquest of Spain, King James I of Aragon-Catalonia-Majorca adopted the policy of tolerating the worship of Jews and

---

46. Thomas Aquinas defined *religio* as "a virtue because it pays the debt of honor to God" (ST II-II 80, 1). The recognition of *religio* as a virtue fulfilling a universal God-given obligation, duty, or debt has been attached to this concept through its long history from St. Thomas to Thomas Jefferson and his colleague-successor, James Madison. Obviously, *religio* in the political context of religious liberty takes a multitude of forms not imaginable in the single-religion context of Thomas Aquinas.

Muslims in their synagogues and mosques.[47] The King also supported the missionary activities of Ramon Lull who sought to convert Muslims and Jews to Christianity. However, when Aragon-Catalonia-Majorca no longer needed the economic skills of Muslims and the professional talents of Jews, and when significant numbers of them had not converted to Christianity, their religious rights were gradually eroded until both groups were expelled. Religious toleration depends upon the discretion of the ruler. Unlike political experiments in religious tolerance, Jefferson and Madison rejected the assumption of any civil government's jurisdiction in matters of religion. They also rejected any attempt to preserve covertly, through the language of toleration, the assumption of governmental sovereignty in religion.

The claim of governments to religious authority not only posed a barrier between people and God; they also involved God-fearers in violent acts that contradicted the explicit teachings of Jesus. For Jefferson, the ethic of Jesus was superior to that of the philosophers of classical antiquity because of its unlimited inclusiveness. Jefferson found this universal concern for others made explicit in the Sermon on the Mount, especially its injunction to love the enemy, which Jefferson expressed as including the enemy in "the circle of benevolence." It was this unlimited benevolence of Jesus that Jefferson found especially distinctive; a love of others not confined to friends, family, neighbors, and fellow countrymen, but extended even to enemies. As Jefferson wrote in his *Syllabus* of 1803,

> In developing our duties to others [the philosophers of Greece and Rome] were short and defective. They embraced indeed the circle of kindred and friends, and inculcated patriotism. As a primary obligation: towards our neighbors and countrymen, they taught justice, but scarcely viewed them as within the circle of benevolence. Still less have they inculcated peace, charity,

47. In response to a Saracen uprising on Majorca, King James finds a plausible reason to abandon his policy of religious tolerance of Muslims. "It pleases me much, for if, on account of the treaties made with the Saracens I did not drive them out of this country, should they now have done anything owing to which I should be justified in driving them out, I would be delighted to be the means of destroying them entirely and their accursed sect, and that those temples where the name of Mohammed has long been proclaimed and invoked should be retrieved for the faith of Christ" (James I, *Chronicles* II 475–76).

and love to our fellow men, or embraced with benevolence the whole family of mankind.[48]

Over against this teaching of Jesus, Jefferson saw the ugly history of Christianity as an established religion: "Millions of innocent men, women, and children, since the introduction of Christianity, have been burnt, tortured, fined, imprisoned."[49]

For Jefferson, such measures of violence executed by civil government for the established church could only create religious hypocrites, not the virtue of *religio* or the worship of God. For both Jefferson and Madison, religious freedom was the necessary political precondition for the practice of *religio*, for giving God our Creator the honor, praise, and thanks that we owe. The recognition of religious freedom by civil government was not only essential to the political unity of a new nation with several different established religions; it was also essential to the vitality and integrity of the Christian religion.

Madison also argued that the establishment of the Christian religion was not necessary for its survival and growth.

> To say that [the Christian religion requires state support] is a contradiction to the Christian religion itself, for every page of it disavows a dependence on the powers of this world; it is a contradiction to fact, for it is known that this Religion both existed and flourished, not only without the support of human laws, but in spite of every opposition from them.

If the establishment of religion is not necessary for the benefit of religion, neither is it necessary for the preservation of the state. Madison unequivocally rejected Pasquier's position cited at the beginning of this chapter. For Madison, the well being of a society and its government did not depend upon the right worship of its people. As he wrote in his *Memorial and Remonstrance,* "the establishment in question is not necessary for the support of Civil Government." Indeed, established religions in the past may have been more of an enemy of a free republic than an ally: "rulers, who wished to subvert the public liberty, may have found an established Clergy convenient auxiliaries. A just Government instituted to secure & perpetuate [public liberty] needs them not."

---

48. A colleague familiar with classical philosophy has suggested that Jefferson's view of classical philosophy was incorrect.

49. Jefferson, *Notes on the State of Virginia,* 160.

Throughout his *Memorial and Remonstrance,* Madison's critique of an established church was theological as well as political: if the state employs religion "as an engine of civil policy, it is an unhallowed perversion of the means of salvation."

While Jefferson and Madison argued strongly for the separation of any particular religious organization from the government, neither denied the mutual dependence of religion and government on each other. The generic category of religion simply permitted them to substitute a mix of independent self-supporting voluntary associations for the single government-supported religion which required some form of participation by all citizens. Jefferson and his fellow founders were convinced of the essential role played by religion, especially for a republic of free citizens. They recognized that a democratic republic was vulnerable to self-destruction because human beings were not designed to live peaceably with each other. The task of cultivating public virtue was therefore essential to the survival and growth of a free republic, and this was not a task which could be effectively accomplished by any agency of government. Religions may need the government to use its coercive resources to preserve law and order, but the government needed religious communities to cultivate a moral environment that sustained political stability, social harmony, and the free interaction of citizens. Jefferson and other founders were thus explicit in acknowledging the reliance of government on religions to form, by example and teaching, a public morality appropriate for the common life of free citizens.[50] The institutional separation of religion and government did not deny the mutuality that united religion and government. Theirs was simply a political theology appropriate to a post-Reformation era in the West when religion was no longer one, but many.

While Jefferson did not discover the unique features of the ethic of Jesus until late in his political career, it was a discovery that was simultaneously political. and personal for him Living with enemies was not a social condition that ended with the defeat of British forces. The political dynamics of a free republic generated conflicts which could rupture the bonds of political union or personal friendship. In Jesus's circle of benevolence which included enemies, Jefferson found a moral resource of inestimable value. His circle of benevolence, like that of

50. For a discussion of the centrality of ethics in the founders' discussions of religion, see Noll, "Evangelicals in the American Founding," 156ff.

John Adams, eventually grew to include the other, however much enmity may have passed between these two founders during the bitter campaign of 1798–1799. The two of them shared advice and encouragement through their lengthy and frequent letters and even managed to die on the same date: July 4, 1826, fifty years after they signed the *Declaration of Independence.*

Epilogue

Reclaiming the Peace Mandate of Jesus
for the Twenty-first Century

This book presents a series of studies in church history and historical theology. Chapters two through six depict a variety of church actions in supporting religious warfare, on the one hand, and a tradition of peace-oriented theological alternatives, on the other. All episodes of religious violence and peacemaking efforts discussed in these chapters are located within the boundaries of the late medieval and early modern periods, the thirteenth through the eighteenth centuries. During these later centuries of the Constantinian era, the Church was both a dependent and an ally of government, whether that government was an empire, a feudal principality, or an emerging nation-state. As a matter of course, these Constantinian bonds between government and Church severely restricted the range of the Church's peace witness. So it is no accident that these chapters do not include any studies of broadly based nonviolent movements for justice or opposition to war. While such events have occurred with some frequency in the era of modern democratic states, they were unlikely if not impossible during the Constantinian era.[1] However, these chapters did demonstrate that, even within the restrictions of the Constantinian era, the Church did foster a theological tradition that was continuous with the peace ministry of Jesus.

In this epilogue, I extend into a modern context my exploration of the two themes basic to the first six chapters of this book: 1) the

---

1. Modern history offers many examples of peace movements inspired by a Christian witness: for example, Martin Luther King's civil rights movement in the United States, Nelson Mandela's leadership in abolishing apartheid in South Africa, and the success of the People Power movement in their nonviolent ouster of President Ferdinand Marcos in the Philippines.

role of church-government alliances that inhibit or distort the church's peace witness and 2) the necessity of a theology that embraces the peace mandate of Jesus for the church's peace witness. The epilogue offers two case studies of church responses to issues of war and peace: one from a French Reformed congregation of the mid-twentieth century and another from an American Evangelical Church of the early twenty-first century. Both examples demonstrate the debilitating role of government alliances for a church's peace witness. Both examples also illustrate the necessary role of a peace-oriented theological tradition for church leaders seeking to reclaim the peace mandate of Jesus.

The epilogue thus permits readers to examine these two issues of violence and peace, fundamental for the church in the Constantinian era, as they reappear in the more familiar contexts of the recent past. Hopefully, they will set the historical trends we have examined in chapters two through six in clear relief and also underline the importance of this kind of historical study.

The Peace Witness of Le Chambon-sur-Lignon, France, 1940–1944[2]

In the midst of an expanding reign of violence during World War II, a congregation of the French Reformed (Huguenot) Church mobilized an extensive and effective nonviolent campaign against the Nazi killing of non-combatants. As a result of their efforts, the lives of over 2500 Jewish adults and children were saved along with an unknown number of other Europeans. I begin by describing the role of the pastor, the congregation, and the people of the village of Le Chambon with a focus on the question: how did this witness happen? What were some of the factors that made it possible? What were some factors that could have undermined it?

---

2. I first came to know the wartime story of Le Chambon during the nineteen-seventies when my wife and I lived for a time in that village. One of our sons was then studying at the international school (College Cévenol) founded by the French Reformed congregation. When I returned to the United States, I continued to pursue the story of this village as presented in a 1979 book by Hallie, *Lest Innocent Blood Be Shed*, and a 1989 documentary movie by Pierre Sauvage, *Weapons of the Spirit*. Much of the information about Le Chambon in this epilogue is from Hallie's book.

Pastor André Trocmé

In the judgment of the people of Le Chambon, André Trocmé provided the leadership and inspiration for the transformation of their village into a haven of refuge. By his words and the example of his own commitment, he persuaded others to risk their lives, individually and collectively, in the project of saving the lives of people destined for death. These were people whom they first met as strangers seeking help. Without Trocmé, Le Chambon might have been just another French village seeking its own survival in the midst of a devastating war and the systematic persecution of diverse groups of people. Trocmé's appropriation of a peace-oriented theology was clearly one essential factor in the peace witness of Le Chambon.

André Trocmé was the pastor of the Reformed (Huguenot) congregation in Le Chambon. While that was his official position it is a misleading description of his identity and role in Le Chambon if understood as the whole picture. He was not a typical pastor of the French Reformed Church. In his spiritual identity, he was much more like a leader of one of the peace churches (such as the Quakers, Mennonites, or Church of the Brethren) than a pastor of the Reformed tradition. When he was a young boy, he had his first encounter with a Christian pacifist: a German soldier leaving French territory at the end of the First World War. The German explained to André that he carried no weapon, though he wore the uniform of a German soldier. "God has revealed to us that a Christian should not kill, ever. We never carry arms." While working as a young man with a group of French map-makers in Morocco, André followed the example of the soldier he had met many years earlier. He refused to carry the loaded pistol provided him for protection against bandits. As a young man studying theology at the University of Paris, André joined the Fellowship of Reconciliation, an international Christian pacifist movement. Later, from 1948 to 1960, he served as the European Secretary of the International Fellowship of Reconciliation. While he was ordained by the French Reformed Church and served in several of their parishes, his theology and practice were more consistent with such Christian pacifists than with Christians of the Reformed tradition.

As a result, his different orientation sometimes created conflicts with the larger church of which he was a part. The French Reformed Church rejected Trocmé's pacifist theology, in part, because of its potential for conflict with government policies. The Reformed Church believed that Christians should obey the laws of the government, including the laws of the Vichy French government prohibiting the concealment of Jews. Shortly after Trocmé began his ministry in Le Chambon in the late nineteen-thirties, officials of the Reformed Church demanded that he renounce his status as a conscientious objector and cease speaking about nonviolence in his congregation. His "doctrinal errors" were perceived to be dangerous for the well being of his congregation and the Reformed Church in France. In response to this demand, Trocmé submitted a letter of resignation to the lay elders of his congregation with an explanation of his theological conflict with the national synod. They refused to accept his resignation. Again, in the nineteen-forties, after Le Chambon had become known throughout Europe as a haven for Jews and others fleeing the Nazis, a senior official of the Reformed Church visited him in Le Chambon with the same complaint—along with the demand that he give up his ministry of hospitality for persons otherwise condemned to death. He again submitted his resignation which the council of lay leaders again refused to accept.

The leadership response of the French Reformed Church is a reminder that Churches or denominations are large and complex ecclesial organizations often averse to offending many of their constituency or the government. The disappearance of the Constantinian legal bond between church and government in the modern era did not eliminate other means by which governments could exert pressure on churches.[3] If Trocmé had been a more obedient servant of the French Reformed Church, the peace witness of Le Chambon might not have happened, nor would it have happened without local support. Trocmé carried out his anti-violent, nonviolent ministry in Le Chambon in spite of the national church he served, but with the strong backing of his own congregation.

Pastor Trocmé's spiritual and intellectual identity was formed, in good part, by Christian pacifist theological resources of the early twentieth century. From his own writings and from his reports of teaching experiences with church members, it is apparent that he had become familiar with studies of the historical Jesus prominent in European theological literature of the nineteenth and early twentieth century. In

---

3. Chapter 6 recounts the end of the Constantinian era through the repudiation of the legal and constitutional basis for any fusion of church and government.

his book, *Jesus and the Nonviolent Revolution,* Trocmé grounded the identity and teachings of Jesus in the Jewish traditions of the Hebrew Bible and first century Palestine.[4] According to Trocmé, Jesus borrowed the biblical promise of "the remission of debts" from the Jewish year of Jubilee for his own proclamation of "Good News" including "God's forgiveness of sins." Trocmé also linked the politics of Jesus with the effective nonviolent Jewish protests against the early policies and actions of Pontius Pilate.[5] According to Trocmé, Jesus called for a revolution that was economic and political, as well as spiritual; that is why he was arrested and killed.

In the early nineteen-thirties, Trocmé was discussing a new theological book with a group of miners who were members of his congregation in Sin-le-Noble. The book argued that Jesus was a fiction created by Paul's theology. In the course of refuting that claim, Trocmé suddenly blurted out some probing questions:

> If Jesus really walked upon this earth, why do we keep treating him as if he were [nothing but] a disembodied ethical theory? If he was a real man, the Sermon on the Mount was made for real people on this earth. And if Jesus existed, God has shown us in flesh and blood what goodness is for flesh and blood people.[6]

Trocmé's discovery of the humanity of Jesus, in contrast with the "mythical" Jesus proposed in the book under discussion, led him to take seriously the ethics of Jesus, including the renunciation of violence and the commandment to love our enemies. His spontaneous questions in the midst of this book discussion inspired his group of miners to begin a spontaneous prayer session. Their prayers, in turn, initiated a

---

4. *Jesus and the Nonviolent Revolution* was first published in French in 1961. It later appeared in an English translation in 1972 and a second English edition, edited by Charles E. Moore, in 2004. This latter edition is now available as a free download from www. Bruderhof.com. Chapter 1 is "Jesus the Jew," chapter 2, "Jesus Proclaims Jubilee," chapter 3, "Implications of Jubilee," and chapter 4, "The Politics of Jesus." The middle section of the book is focused on the political movements that were the contemporaries of Jesus including nonviolent protests against Pilate and Zealot aspirations to free Palestine from Roman rule by violent means.

5. See chapter one of this book for my discussion of one of these effective nonviolent Jewish protests against Pontius Pilate. When I wrote about the peace ethic of Jesus in chapter one of this book, I had not yet read *Jesus and the Nonviolent Revolution.* I did not know that I was citing one incident among the several discussed by Trocmé more than a half century earlier.

6. Hallie, *Lest Innocent Blood Be Shed,* 68–69.

three-month long Awakening in the congregation and village of Sin-le-Noble.

In the mind and life of Trocmé, there is a strong theological continuity from this teaching experience of the early nineteen-thirties through his ministry in Le Chambon to his 1961 writing of *Jesus and the Nonviolent Revolution*. Trocmé not only embodied Jesus' theology of nonviolence in his ministry at Le Chambon, but he wrote a book about it to share with other pastors. I will presently note some of the ways in which Trocmé's theological legacy has informed the ministry and theological reflection of church leaders in the twenty-first century.

The Reformed congregation of Le Chambon.

A majority of Le Chambon's residents in the nineteen-forties were members of the Protestant "temple."[7] A sizeable number of these people had Protestant ancestors who had been persecuted by the French government in the sixteenth and seventeenth centuries because of their religion.[8] The congregation itself was a product of the French Revolution that gave Protestants again the right to worship, a right first given them in the Edict of Nantes by Henri IV, an edict revoked in 1645. They were people who had experienced the threat to their lives and faith while living as a persecuted minority in Catholic France. Their own historical experience of government persecution empowered them to resist the bureaucratic authority of their government or their church. It also prepared them to welcome European Jews who came to Le Chambon seeking refuge. They not only supported Pastor Trocmé's theological position against the authority of his church superiors, but they also were themselves actively engaged in the work of hiding and caring for people condemned to death. For example, Trocmé recruited a small group of young men in the congregation to lead bible discussions in the homes of church members and, when needed, to deliver a warning to the outlying farms hosting refugees so that their guests could hide in the near-by woods before a suspected "round-up" of foreigners.

---

7. As I learned by the highway signs on the outer edge of the village, French Protestants worshiped in a "temple"; only Catholics worshipped in a church (*une église*).

8. For a discussion of the civil wars of religion in France along with the Edict of Nantes that first gave Protestants religious freedom and its repudiation in practice and revocation as law, see chapter five.

Trocmé did not need to persuade members of his congregation of the human need for safety and hospitality while living under the rule of an unjust government. He only needed to remind them of God's commands against killing and for saving the lives of the innocent from their pursuers "lest innocent blood be shed in your land" (Deut 19:10). The spiritual complexion of his congregation was as unusual as the spiritual formation of Trocmé himself.

The people of Le Chambon

If it takes a village to raise a child, it most certainly took a whole village to shelter and feed thousands of European Jews and other condemned groups. The life-saving ministry of Le Chambon was not a project of the Protestant temple and its pastor alone; it required the engagement of the resources of the whole village, along with a variety of supporters outside the village.

A group of Christians known as Darbyites constituted about one-third of the Protestant population of Le Chambon. These people were followers of a nineteenth century English preacher named John Darby; they were also the most radical Protestants in France. They rejected even the minimal church authority exercised by the Reformed Church in France. While they were not members of Trocmé's congregation, they provided strong and unwavering support for him, his wife and family, and his congregation. When Trocmé was arrested in 1943, a group of Darbyites sent him off with food and Bible verses scrawled on a roll of toilet paper. Most of them lived on farms outside the village; their isolated homes provided ideal locations for hiding the most vulnerable refugee families.

In addition to the Darbyites, American Quakers played a significant role in the peace ministry of Le Chambon. In the early 1940s, Trocmé traveled to Marseilles to meet with Burns Chalmers, a representative of the American Friends Service Committee. Chalmers had been looking, without success, for a somewhat isolated French village that could shelter European Jews and other refugees. Together Chalmers and Trocmé worked up a tentative plan for Le Chambon to play such a role, with some financial assistance from American Quakers. In addition to this support, American Congregationalists, Roman Catholics, the World Council of Churches, Jewish groups and the governments of Sweden and Switzerland also provided financial support for the expenses of feeding and housing Jewish refugees, children and adults. As a result, there were seven "funded" houses in the village, some of which functioned as dormitories for refugee students at College Cévenol while others housed Jewish families on their way to Switzerland.

While the small Catholic parish in Le Chambon did not play an active role in the village's ministry of saving lives, Catholics in other villages and other parts of France were allies who received overflow refugee families from Le Chambon.

In addition to these diverse Christian and Jewish sources of support, the people of Le Chambon also included Communists and a variety of non-religious citizens who fed and sheltered refugee families. The village's real estate included a group of *pensions* or boarding houses that were originally built to feed and house tourists who came to Le Chambon during the summer months. After 1942, all of them were turned into housing for the town's refugee population.

In addition to the funded houses, the *pensions,* and the Darbyite farms, a number of private homes in the village also housed one or more refugee families. The numbers of refugees arriving on the 1:00 p.m. train became so large that they could not be accommodated in any one housing cluster. It took the whole village and its environs to open their homes.

It also took the radical silence of the village to protect its law-breaking citizens from arrest, imprisonment, and death. Everyone knew the large number of refugees who arrived each day by train; anyone could observe the arrival of a new family or two in any given living unit. Yet, by the 1970s when I was in Le Chambon, I was able to learn the name of only one man in town who was even suspected of being an informer. Other visitors and written studies of Le Chambon have given similar reports. What the people knew was obviously not a subject for gossip. Their realistic sense of danger suppressed the curiosity of all; no one, wisely, wished to know too much of what was happening.[9] While the whole of the village was engaged, in one way or another, with the dangerous and illegal activity of concealing Jews, to say nothing of cre-

---

9. Hiding Jews was against the law of Vichy France, which ruled the south of France including Le Chambon from 1940–1942, as well as the German Occupation, which ruled this area directly from 1942–1944.

ating the false ID and ration cards provided these guests, only a few of the most prominent leaders were ever arrested, imprisoned, or killed.[10]

The Political-Theological Crisis of an American Evangelical Congregation in 2004

Unlike the French Reformed congregation in Le Chambon, most American Protestants have long fused their loyalty to America with their faith in God. In this marriage of faith and national identity, America acquired a special status as God's favored nation. Many Christian Americans believed that their nation's wars were fought for God's causes such as overthrowing the rule of royalty, abolishing slavery, defeating evil empires, and extending God's gift of freedom to all nations. Within this blended script of God and nation, American Christians did not experience their government as an enemy of their church, as did the people of Le Chambon. Indeed, the church was widely envisioned as the religious guardian of the government.

This "civil religion," as it is called, led some people to believe that they acquired a particular political responsibility when they became Christians. They felt obliged by their faith to vote for leaders of their government who were themselves Christian and who would keep America aligned with God's laws and God's causes. While this political theology has long played a role in American history, it became particularly prominent among Evangelical Christians in the late twentieth century.

Indeed, by the beginning of this century, this political theology had become a powerful force in American politics. In part, this was a result of many conservative Christians feeling as if the increasingly pluralistic and secular America was losing its religious purpose as God's ally; in part, it reflected the political energy that American Evangelicals and Pentecostals devoted to limiting or banning the right to an abortion or a same-sex marriage. It also reflected the exploitation of such moral

10. Pastor Trocmé, Édouard Theis who was a half-time pastor of the Reformed Temple and head of the College Cévenol, and Roger Darcissac, head of the state school in Le Chambon were arrested in 1943 and imprisoned for several months. The reason for their release was not known. Roger Trocmé, the pastor's second cousin and head of one of the funded houses in Le Chambon was arrested and killed as was a physician committed to nonviolence who took up residency in this village during the war years.

issues for the purpose of winning elections, a prominent strategy of the White House during the presidency of George W. Bush.

For Gregory Boyd, founder and pastor of the 5,000-member Woodland Hills Church in St. Paul, Minnesota, the political pressures of the 2004 election provoked a theological critique of this American political theology.[11] During this presidential election campaign, he found himself under increasing pressure "to shepherd my flock into voting for the right candidate" and "the right position."[12] (The presidential election of 2004—"for the right candidate"—was also perceived by many as a referendum—"for the right position"—on the controversial Iraq war.) In the words of Pastor Boyd, he had come under increasing "pressure from a number of right-wing political and religious sources ... to hand out leaflets, to call attention to certain political events, to have members of his church sign petitions, make pledges, and so on."

In April, 2004, Pastor Boyd decided that he needed to warn his congregation of the spiritual dangers involved in fusing together faith and politics. So he preached a series of six sermons entitled "the Cross and the Sword" in which he contrasted the ways of God's Kingdom with the ways of worldly kingdoms, including the American kingdom. Some members of the congregation were very appreciative of these sermons. Others, however, gave him "the most intensely negative feedback" that he had ever received. As many of these protesters suggested, to preach such sermons, Boyd must be "a liberal, a compromiser, wishy-washy, unpatriotic, afraid to take a stand, or simply on the side of Satan."[13] Indeed, the negative response to these sermons was so strong that about twenty percent of the congregation (roughly a thousand people) simply left the church. Introducing theological differences between the Kingdom of God and the kingdom of America was not the kind of message that these members expected to hear from an Evangelical pastor. Severing the bonds between the Kingdom of God and the kingdom of America that exposed the claim of a Christian America as nothing but a myth was a threatening message for many.

11. Pastor Boyd described the conflict created by his theological critique of "civil religion" in his book, *Myth of a Christian Nation*. In this book, he included the controversial sermons he preached, responses of congregation members, and a series of studies in church history and historical theology focused on issues of violence and peace.

12. Boyd, *Myth of a Christian Nation*, 9.

13. Ibid., 10.

Boyd's theological critique of the church's alliance with government is multi-faceted. Most often, he objects to the identification of God's kingdom with any worldly option—however good and desirable some political system might appear in comparison with other options—because such a fusion of "goods" undermines the radical character of faith as an alternative to all worldly possibilities. However, he also writes at length about the church's implicit endorsement of violence that accompanies any church affiliation with government. He documents the church's long history of violence during the Constantinian era from its beginnings with the conversion of the Roman Emperor, Constantine, to the Christian massacre of Native Americans in the European settlement of North and South America. A brief sample of his version of church history suggests some points of continuity between Boyd's account of his anti-political sermons and the prior chapters of this book.

> The first recorded instance of Christians killing pagans occurred shortly after . . . Constantine legalized Christianity. [During the medieval era,] the Holy Roman Empire was about as violent as the Roman Empire it aspired to replace. Christian sectarian groups . . . such as the Cathars were massacred by the towns. Every group of the Reformation fought each other and Catholics and martyred Anabaptists and other "heretics" by the hundreds.[14]
>
> The American myth [of a Christian nation] is simply a version of the myth that has dominated Christianity since the fourth century when Christianity emerged from its persecuted past and "triumphed" as a global force. From Constantine on, the church has more often than not seen itself as the religious guardian of the empire—with disastrous consequences for the gospel and *often for the empire*.[15]

Indeed, Boyd's critique of the violence intrinsic to church-government bonds leads him to embrace a pacifist theological tradition extending back almost a half-century to the work of André Trocmé.[16] Boyd apparently discovered Trocmé's writings through his reading of John Howard Yoder, the Mennonite theologian whose work has exerted so much influence among a wide variety of Christian theologians in the

14. Ibid., 77–79.

15. Ibid., 189 (italics original to quotation).

16. See, for example, Boyd's discussions of Trocmé in chapter 3 and again in chapter 5 of *Myth of a Christian Nation*.

late twentieth and early twenty-first century. Boyd quotes more exten-sively from Yoder than from any other author.[17]

The title of Yoder's classic, *The Politics of Jesus*, appears to be bor-rowed from the title of Trocmé's fourth chapter, "The Politics of Jesus," in *Jesus and the Nonviolent Revolution*. Similarly, the title of chapter three in Yoder's book, "The Implications of the Jubilee," is virtually the same as the title of chapter three, "Implications of Jubilee," in Trocmé's book. Indeed, as Yoder notes, his chapter three is "adapted freely with the author's permission from André Trocmé's book, *Jesus and the Nonviolent Revolution*." Similarly, Yoder's chapter five, "The Possibility of Nonviolent Resistance," is an abbreviated borrowing from Trocmé's chapter nine, "The Seeds of Nonviolence." In Yoder's words, his "expo-sition [of Trocmé's chapter nine] parallels and expands a segment of André Trocmé's *Jesus and the Nonviolent Revolution* [with title in origi-nal French in Yoder's note].

The continuity of this theological tradition among a diversity of denominational spokesmen—from a French Reformed pastor through a Mennonite theologian to an American Evangelical pastor—suggests something of the breadth of recovery of the peace message of Jesus in the late twentieth and early twenty-first centuries. And there are many other voices also indebted to the work of Yoder, such as Stanley Hauerwas, that could be added to this company of witnesses. Theological literature of the twenty-first century once again gives voice to the peace ethic of Jesus, as did a long tradition of Christian theology including the theologians of the Constantinian era documented in the first six chapters of this book.

I do not wish to suggest that the theologians discussed in these chapters have had any direct effect on the thought and lives of church leaders like Trocmé and Boyd or on the work of theologians like Yoder and Hauerwas. However, I wrote this book in response to both the rela-tively new and widespread Christian peace witness in our time and the growing public concern with religious violence. I am convinced that Christians engaged in the present struggle with issues of religious vio-lence and peace can benefit from some familiarity with their historical predecessors who, in the most inhospitable of times, bore witness to God's peaceable kingdom. Those of us who find ourselves committed

17. Boyd's end notes (189–207) include more than fifteen citations to the writings of Yoder, most of which refer to Yoder's *Politics of Jesus*.

today to the peace ethic of Jesus can learn from the failings as well as the courage of theologians from the Constantinian era: Thomas Aquinas, Ramon Lull, Nicolas of Cusa, Lord Herbert, and Thomas Jefferson.

Bibliography

Abelard, Peter. *Dialogus inter philosophum, Judaeum, et Chtristianum.* Edited and translated by John Morenbon and Giovanni Orlandi. New York: Oxford University Press, 2001.

Alverny, Marie Therese de. "Le cosmos symbolique du XIIe siècle." *Archivs d'histoire doctrinale et littéraire du Moyen Age* 20 (1953) 31–81.

Asad, Talal. *Genealogies of Religion: Discipline and Reason of Power in Christianity and Islam.* Baltimore: Johns Hopkins University Press, 1993.

Babinger, Franz. *Mehmed the Conqueror and His Time.* Translated by Ralph Manheim. Princeton: Princeton University Press, 1978.

Bacon, Roger. *The Opus Majus of Roger Bacon.* 2 vols. Edited by John Henry Bridges. Oxford: Clarendon, 1897–1900.

Baer, Yitzhak. *A History of the Jews in Christian Spain.* Philadelphia: Jewish Publication Society, 1966.

Bald, R. C. *John Donne: A Life.* Oxford: Oxford University Press, 1970.

Ballentine, Karen. "Beyond Greed and Grievance: Reconsidering the Economic Dynamics of Armed Conflict." In *The Political Economy of Armed Conflict,* edited by Karen Ballentine and Jake Sherman, 259–83. London: Lynne Rienner, 2003.

Beierwaltes, Werner. "Cusanus and Eriugena." *Dionysius* 13 (1989) 115–52.

Bell, Daniel M. Jr. "State and Civil Society." In *The Blackwell Companion to Political Theology,* edited by Peter Scott and William T. Cavanaugh, 423–38. Blackwell Companions to Religion. Malden: Blackwell, 2007.

Benedict XVI, Pope. "Pope's Speech at University of Regensburg." *Catholic World News,* September 15, 2006. No pages.

Betz, Hans Dieter. *The Sermon on the Mount.* Minneapolis: Fortress, 1995.

Biechler, James E. "A New Face Toward Islam: Nicholas of Cusa and John of Segovia." In *In Search of God and Wisdom,* edited by Gerald Christiansen and Thomas Izbicki, 185–202. Leiden: Brill, 1991.

The Book of Common Prayer 1559. Edited by John E. Booty. Washington, DC: Folger Shakespeare Library, 1976.

Bouwsma, William J. *The Waning of the Renaissance, 1550–1640.* The Yale Intellectual History of the West. New Haven: Yale University Press, 2000.

Boyd, Gregory. *The Myth of a Christian Nation: How the Quest for Political Power is Destroying the Church.* Grand Rapids: Zondervan, 2005.

Burman, Thomas E. "Exclusion or Concealment: Approaches to Traditional Arabic Exegesis in Medieval-Latin Translations of the Qur'an." *Scripta Mediterranea* 19–20 (1998–1999) 182–97.

———. "*Tafsir* and Translation: Traditional Arabic Qur'an Exegesis and the Latin Qur'ans of Robert of Ketton and Mark of Toledo." *Speculum* 73 (1998) 703–32.

Busa, Robert, S. J. *Index Thomisticus.* Milano: Editoria Electronica Editel, 1992.

Bush, George. W. "Bush Speech Transcript." *Associated Press*, September 20, 2001. No pages.

Byrne, Peter. *Natural Religion and the Nature of Religion.* London: Routledge, 1989.

Carroll, James. No Title. *The Boston Globe.* October 9, 2001.

———. *Constantine's Sword.* Boston, MA: Houghton-Miflin, 2001.

———. *Constantine's Sword. The Church and the Jews: A History.* DVD Documentary Movie. Online: http//www.Constantinessword.com.

Cavanaugh, William T. "A Fire Strong Enough to Consume the House: the Wars of Religion and the Rise of the State." *Modern Theology* 11 (1995) 397–420.

Charles, Amy. *A Life of George Herbert.* Ithaca: Cornell University Press, 1977.

Chase, Kenneth R., and Alan Jacobs. *Must Christianity Be Violent? Reflections on History, Practice, and Theology.* Grand Rapids: Brazos, 2003.

Chejne, A. G. *Ibn Hazm.* Chicago: University of Chicago Press, 1992.

Chittick, William C. *The Sufi Path of Knowledge.* Albany: Suny Press, 1989.

Cicero. *The Nature of the Gods.* Translated by P. G. Walsh. New York: Oxford University Press, 1997.

Cobban, Helena. "Religion and Violence." *Journal of the American Academy of Religion* 73 (2005) 1121–39.

Cohen, Jeremy. *The Friars and the Jews: The Evolution of Medieval Anti-Judaism.* Ithaca: Cornell University Press, 1982.

Collier, Paul. "Doing Well out of War: An Economic Perspective." In *Greed and Grievance: Economic Agendas in Civil Wars,* edited by Mats Berdal and David Malone, 91–111. Boulder, CO: Lynne Rienner, 2000.

Collinson, Patrick. *The Religion of Protestants: the Church in English Society, 1559–1625.* Oxford: Oxford University Press, 1984.

Colomer, Eusebio. *Nikolaus von Kues und Raimund Llull aus Handschriften der Kueser Bibliothek.* Berlin: Walter de Gruyter, 1961.

———. *Nikolaus von Kues und Ramon Lull: ihre Begegnung mit den nichtchristlichen Religionen.* Trier: Paulinus-Verlag, 1995.

Cullmann, Oscar. *The State in the New Testament.* New York: Scribners, 1956.

Cusanus, Nicholas. *Apologia Doctae Ignorantiae.* Vol. 2 of *Nicolai de Cusa Opera Omnia.* Edited by R. Kilbansky. Leipzig: Felix Meiner, 1932. English title: *A Defense of Learned Ignorance.* In *Nicholas of Cusa's Debate with John Wenck.* 3rd ed. Translated by Jasper Hopkins. Minneapolis: Arthur Banning, 1988.

———. *The Catholic Concordance.* Translated by Paul E. Sigmund. Cambridge: Cambridge University Press, 1991.

———. *De Coniecturis.* Vol. 3 of *Nicolai de Cusa Opera Omnia.* Edited by Josef Koch. Hamburg, 1972. English title: *On Conjectures.* In *Toward a New Council of Florence.* Translated by William F. Wertz. Washington, DC: Schiller Institute, 1993.

———. *Cribratio Alkoran.* Vol. 8 of *Nicolai de Cusa Opera Omnia.* Edited by L. Hegemann. Hamburg: Felix Meiner, 1986. English title: A *Sifting of the Koran.* In *De pace fidei and Cribratio Alkoran.* 2nd ed. Edited and translated by Jasper Hopkins, 75–189. Minneapolis: A. J. Banning, 1994.

———. *De docta ignorantia.* Vol. 1 of *Nicolai de Cusa Opera Omnia.* Edited by E. Hoffman and R. Kilbansky. Leipzig-Hamburg, 1932. English title: *On Learned Ignorance.* In *Nicholas of Cusa: Selected Spiritual Writings,* edited and translated by Lawrence Bond, 87–206. New York: Paulist, 1997.

————. *Idiota de Sapientia et de Mente*. Translated by M. L. Führer. *The Layman on Wisdom and the Mind*. Ottawa: Dovehouse, 1989.

————. *De Pace Fide*. Vol. 7 of *Nicolai de Cusa Opera Omnia*. Edited by R. Kilbansky and H. Bascour. Hamburg: Felix Meiner, 1970. English title (with Latin text): *Nicholas of Cusa on Interreligious Harmony*. Translated by James Biechler and Lawrence Bond. Lewiston, NY: Edwin Mellen, 1990.

————. *Nicholas of Cusa: Selected Spiritual Writings*. Edited and translated by H. Lawrence Bond. The Classics of Western Spirituality. New York: Paulist, 1997.

Dawson, Christopher, editor. *The Mongol Mission*. London: Sheed & Ward, 1955.

Dictionary of National Biography. Edited by Leslie Stephen and Sidney Lee. Oxford: Oxford University Press, 1937–1938.

Donne, John. *Letters to several Persons of Honor*. Edited by Charles Merrill Jr. New York: Russell & Russell, 1910.

————. "A Sermon of Commemoration of the Lady Danvers, late wife of Sir John Danvers and Mother of George Herbert, preached at Chelsea where she was lately buried, July 1, 1627." In *Devotions*, 158–97. London: W. Pickering, 1840.

Doukas, Michaelis. *Decline and Fall of Byzantium to the Ottoman Turks*. Translated by Harry J. Magoulias. Detroit: Wayne State University Press, 1975.

Dupuis, Jacques, S.J. *Toward a Christian Theology of Religious Pluralism*. Maryknoll, NY: Orbis, 1997.

Encyclopedia of Islam: New Edition. Leiden: E. J. Brill, 1971.

Eriugena, John Scotus. *Periphyseon* or *The Division of Nature*. Translated by I. P. Sheldon-Williams and revised by John J. O'Meara. Washington, DC: Dumbarton Oaks, 1987.

Fernandez-Palmer, Gabriel. *Encyclopedia of Religion and War*. Routledge Encyclopedias of Religion and Society. London: Routledge, 2004.

Flint, V. I. J. "Honorius Augustodunensis of Regensburg." In *Authors of the Middle Ages: Historical and Religious Writings of the Latin West,* edited by Patrick Geary, 2:89–183. Brookfield, VT: Ashgate, 1995.

Fordyce, C. J., and T. M. Knox. "Catalogue of Lord Herbert of Cherbury's Books." In *The Library of Jesus College, Oxford*, 75–115. Oxford: Oxford University Press, 1987.

Gayà, J. Estelrich. "Honori d'Autun i Ramon Llull. Ràons per a una hipòtesi." *Estudis Baleàrics* 29–30 (1988) 19–24.

Gilreath, James, editor. *Thomas Jefferson's Library*. Washington, DC: Library of Congress, 1989.

Given, James B. *Inquisition and Medieval Justice*. Ithaca, NY: Cornell University Press, 1997.

Gómez, Luis Martínez, SJ. "From the Name of God to the Name of God: Nicholas of Cusa." *International Philosophical Quarterly* 5 (1965) 80–102.

Griffin, Julia. "Studies in the Literary Life of Lord Herbert of Cherbury." PhD diss., Oxford University, 1993.

Griffiths, Paul J. *An Apology for Apologetics: A Study in the Logic of Interreligious Dialogue*. Maryknoll, NY: Orbis, 1991.

Gurr, Ted. "Peoples against States: Ethnopolitical Conflict and the Changing World." *International Studies* 38 (1994) 347–77.

Hallie, Philip. *Lest Innocent Blood Be Shed: The Story of the Village of Le Chambon and How Goodness Happened There*. New York: Harper & Row, 1979.

Harrison, Peter. *"Religion" and "Religions" in the English Enlightenment.* Cambridge: Cambridge University Press, 1990.

——. "Science and Religion: Constructing the Boundaries." *Journal of Religion* 86 (2006) 81–97.

Hauerwas, Stanley. *The Hauerwas Reader.* Edited by John Berkman and Michael Cartwright. Durham, NC: Duke University Press, 2001.

——. *Matthew.* Brazos Theological Commentary on the Bible. Grand Rapids: Brazos, 2006.

——. *The Peaceable Kingdom: A Primer in Christian Ethics.* Notre Dame: University of Notre Dame Press, 1983.

——. *Performing the Faith: Bonhoeffer and the Practice of Nonviolence.* Grand Rapids: Brazos, 2004.

Hengel, Martin. *Die Zeloten.* Leiden: Brill, 1961.

Heim, David. "Voters and Values." *Christian Century,* August 8, 2006.

Heim, Mark. *Salvations: Truth and Difference in Religion.* Faith Meets Faith. Maryknoll, NY: Orbis, 1997.

Herbert, Edward, Lord. *The Autobiography of Edward, Lord Herbert of Cherbury.* Edited and partially written by Sidney Lee. London: J. C. Nimmo, 1860.

——. "The Correspondence with Sir Robert Harley." In *The Manuscripts of His Grace the Duke of Portland,* 3:8–10. London: Royal Commission on Historical Manuscripts, 1899.

——. *The Expedition to the Isle of Rhé.* London: Whittingham & Wilkins, 1860.

——. *The History of England under Henry VIII.* London: A. Murray, 1870.

——. "Lord Herbert of Cherbury's *Religio laici.*" Edited by H. G. Wright. *Modern Language Review* 28 (1933) 296–307.

——. *The Poems English and Latin of Edward Lord Herbert of Cherbury.* Edited by G. C. Moore Smith. Oxford: Clarendon, 1923.

——. *De Religione Gentilium Errorumque apud eos Causis.* Amsterdam: Typis Blaeviorum, 1663. Reprint edited by Günter Gawlick. Stuttgart: Bad Cannstatt, 1967. English translation: *The Ancient Religion of the Gentiles and Causes of Their Errors.* London: John Nutt, 1705.

——. *De Religione Laici.* Edited by H. R. Hutcheson. New Haven, CT: Yale University Press, 1944.

——. *De Veritate.* Reprint edited by G. Gawlick. Stuttgart: Bad Cannstatt, 1966. Translated by Meyrick H. Carré. *On Truth.* Bristol: University of Bristol, 1937.

Hick, John. *A Christian Theology of Religions.* Louisville: Westminster John Knox, 1995.

Hill, Eugene. *Edward, Lord Herbert of Cherbury.* Boston: Twayne, 1987.

Hillgarth, J. N. *Ramon Lull and Lullism in Fourteenth Century France.* Oxford: Clarendon, 1971.

——. *The Spanish Kingdoms, 1250–1516.* 2 Vols. Oxford: Clarendon, 1976–1978.

——. "An Unpublished Lullian Sermon by Pere Deguí." In *Aristotelica et Lulliana magistro doctissimo Charles H. Lohr septuagesimum annum feliciter agenti dedicata,* edited by Fernando Domínguez. The Hague: Nijhoff, 1995.

Holmes, David L. *The Faiths of the Founding Fathers.* Oxford: Oxford University Press, 2006.

Hopkins, Jasper. "Introduction." In *De pace fidei and Cribratio Alkoran,* 2nd ed. Minneapolis: A. J. Banning, 1994.

———. editor and translator. *Nicholas of Cusa's Debate with John Wenck.* Minneapolis: Banning, 1981.

Horsley, Richard. *Jesus and the Spiral of Violence: Popular Jewish Resistance in Roman Palestine.* San Francisco: Harpers, 1987.

Hughes, Philip. *The Church in Crisis: A History of the General Councils.* New York: Image, 1960.

Hughes, Philip, editor. *Religion and the New Republic.* Lanham, MD: Rowman & Littlefield, 2000.

James I. *The Chronicle of James I, King of Aragon.* 2 vols. Translated by John Forster. London: Chapman & Hall, 1883.

Jayne, Allen. *Jefferson's Declaration of Independence.* Lexington: University of Kentucky Press, 1998.

Jefferson, Thomas. *Autobiography of Thomas Jefferson: 1743–1790.* Introduction by Paul Leicester Ford. New York: Putnam, 1914.

———. *Jefferson's Extracts from the Gospels.* Edited by Dickinson W. Adams. Princeton: Princeton University Press, 1983.

———. *Jefferson's Literary Commonplace Book.* Edited by Douglas Wilson. Princeton: Princeton University Press, 1983.

———. *Notes on the State of Virginia.* Edited by William Peden. New York: Norton, 1972.

John of Plano Carpini. "History of the Mongols." In *The Mongol Mission,* edited by Christopher Dawson, 3–72. London: Sheed & Ward, 1955.

Johnson, Luke Timothy. *The Writings of the New Testament.* Philadelphia: Fortress, 1986.

Johnson, Roger A. "Natural Religion, Common Notions, and the Study of Religions: Lord Herbert of Cherbury." *Religion* (1994) 213–24.

Johnston, Mark D. *The Evangelical Rhetoric of Ramon Llull.* Oxford: Oxford University Press, 1996.

Jones, Norman. *The English Reformation.* Oxford: Oxford University Press, 2002.

Josephus, Flavius. *The Jewish War: I–II.* Translated by H. St. John Thackeray. Cambridge: Loeb Library, 1937.

Juergensmeyer, Mark. *Terror in the Mind of God: the Global Rise of Religious Violence.* Berkeley: University of California Press, 2000.

Kimball, Charles. *When Religion Becomes Evil.* San Francisco: HarperCollins, 2003.

Knitter, Paul. *Introducing Theologies of Religion.* Maryknoll, NY: Orbis, 2006.

———. "Karl Rahner and Beyond: a New Meeting of World Religions." In *Critical Issues in Modern Religion,* 2nd ed., edited by Roger A. Johnson. Englewood Cliffs: Prentice-Hall, 1990.

———. *No Other Name? A Critical Survey of Christian Attitudes towards the World Religions.* Maryknoll: Orbis, 1985.

———. "Toward a Liberation Theology of Religions." In *The Myth of Christian Uniqueness.* Edited by John Hick and Paul Knitter. Maryknoll: Orbis, 1987.

Kritzeck, James. *Peter the Venerable and Islam.* Princeton: Princeton University Press, 1964.

Lambert, Malcolm. *Medieval Heresy: Popular Movements from Bogomil to Hus.* New York: Holmes and Meier, 1976.

Lansing, Carol. *Power and Purity: Cathar Heresy in Medieval Italy.* New York: Oxford, 1998.

Lash Nicholas. *The Beginning and the End of 'Religion.'* Cambridge: Cambridge University Press, 1996.

Lawson, Thomas, and Robert McCauley. *Rethinking Religion: Connecting Cognition and Culture.* Cambridge: Cambridge University Press, 1990.

Lee, Sidney. *Autobiography of Edward, Lord Herbert of Cherbury.* London: J. C. Nimmo: 1860.

Lilla, Mark. *The Stillborn God.* New York: Knopf, 2007.

Lindbeck, George. *The Nature of Doctrine: Religion and Theology in a Postliberal Age.* Philadelphia: Westminster John Knox, 1984.

Lohr, Charles. "Christianus arabicus, cuius nomen Raimundus Lullus." *Freiburger Zeitschrift für Philosophie und Theologie* 31 (1984).

———. "Die Exzerptensammlung des Nikolaus von Kues aus den Werken Ramón Llulls." *Freiburger Zeitschrift für Philosophie und Theologie* 30 (1983) 373–84.

———. "Metaphysics." In *The Cambridge History of Renaissance Philosophy*, edited by Charles B. Schmitt, Quentin Skinner, et al., 537–638. Cambridge: Cambridge University Press, 1988.

———. "Ramón Lull und Nikolaus von Kues: Zu einem Struktvergleich ihres Denkens." *Theologie und Philosophie* 56 (1981) 218–31.

Lovin, Robin. "Faith, Ethics, and Evil." In *Strike Terror No More: Theology, Ethics, and the New War*, edited by Jon Bergquist. St. Louis: Chalice, 2002.

Lucentini, Paulo. "Le annotazioni di Nicola Cusano alla Clavis physicae." In *Platonismo medievale,* 77–109. Firenze: La Nuova Italia, 1980.

———. *Honorius Augustodunensis Clavis physicae.* Roma, 1974.

Lull, Ramon. *Blanquerna.* Translated by E. Allison Peers. London: Jarrolds, n.d.

———. *Book of the Gentile and the Three Wise Men.* In *Selected Works of Ramon Llull,* 1:91–304. Introduction and translation by Anthony Bonner. Princeton: Princeton University Press, 1985.

———. *The Book of the Lover and the Beloved.* Translated by Eva Bonner. In *Doctor Illuminatus* (below).

———. *Doctor Illuminatus: a Ramon Llull Reader.* Edited and translated by Anthony Bonner. Princeton: Princeton University Press, 1993.

———. *Felix.* Translated by Anthony Bonner. In Vol. 2 of *Selected Works of Ramon Llull,* 647–1105. Princeton: Princeton University Press, 1985.

———. *Liber Tartari et Christiani and Disaputatio Raymundi christiani et Hamar saracenci in Raymundi Lulli Opera omnia.* Edited by Ivo Salzinger. Reprint edited by F. Stegmüller. Frankfurt: MOG, 1965.

———. *Libre de Gentil.* Vol. 1 of *Obras de Ramón Lull.* Edited by Jerónimo Rosselló. Palma, 1901.

———. *Le livre du gentil et des trois sages.* Edited by Armand Llinares. Paris: Presses Universitares de France, 1966.

———. *Obres Selectes de Ramon Llull.* Edited by Antoni Bonner. Mallorca: Moll, 1989.

———. "Petitio Raymundi pro conversione Infidelium (1294)." In *Raymundi Lulli Opera omni.* Frankfurt: MOG, 1966.

———. *Selected Works of Ramon Llull.* 2 vols. Edited and translated by Anthony Bonner. Princeton: Princeton University Press, 1985.

———. *Vita coaetanea.* Translated by Anthony Bonner. In vol. 1 of *Selected Works of Ramon Llull,* 13–52. Princeton: Princeton University Press, 1985

MacDonald, Duncan. *Muslim Theology, Jurisprudence and Constitutional Theory.* New York: Scribners, 1903.

Madison, James. *Memorial and Remonstrance Against Religious Assessments.* No Pages. Online: http://religiousfreedom.lib.virginia.edu/sacred/madison_m&r_ 1785.html.

Marty, Martin. "Is Religion the Problem?" *Tikkun,* March–April, 2002.

Marx, Jacob. *Verzeichnis der Handscriftensammlung des Hospitals zu Cues.* Trier, 1905.

May, John D'Arcy. *Transcendence and Violence: The Encounter of Buddhist, Christian, and Primal Traditions.* London: Continuum, 2003.

McCutcheon, Russell. "The Category 'Religion' in Recent Publications: a Critical Survey." *NUMEN* 42 (1995) 284–309.

McTernan, Oliver. *Violence in God's Name: Religion in an Age of Conflict.* Maryknoll: Orbis, 2003.

McTighe, Thomas P. "Nicholas of Cusa's Unity-Metaphysics and the Formula *Religio una in rituum varietate.*" In *In Search of God and Wisdom.* Edited by Gerald Christiansen and Thomas Izbicki, 161–74. Leiden: Brill, 1991.

Mohler, Ludwig. "Einführung." In *Über den Frieden im Glauben: De Pace Fidei* by Nicholas Cusa, 42–61. Leipzig: Felix Meiner, 1943.

Moore, R. E. *The Formation of a Persecuting Society.* Oxford: Blackwell, 1987.

Moore, R. I. *The Birth of Popular Heresy.* Toronto: University of Toronto Press, 1995.

Moran, Dermot. *The Philosophy of John Scottus Eriugena.* Cambridge: Cambridge University Press, 1989.

Nelli, René. *Écritures Cathares.* Paris: Éditions Planète, 1968.

Nelson-Pallmeyer, Jack. *Is Religion Killing Us?* New York: Continuum, 2003.

New Catholic Encyclopedia. Washington D.C.: Catholic University of America, 2003.

Noll, Mark. "Evangelicals in the American Founding and Evangelical Political Mobilization Today" (137–58). In *Religion and the New Republic,* edited by James Hutson. Lanham, MD: Rowman & Littlefield, 2000

Noll, Mark, and Lyman Kellstedt. "Religion, Voting for President, and Party Identification, 1948–1984." In *Religion and American Politics: from the Colonial Period to the 1980s,* edited by Mark Noll, 355–79. New York: Oxford University Press, 1990.

Pailin, David. "Herbert of Cherbury and the Deists." *Expository Times* (1983) 196–99.

Palm, F. C. *Politics and Religion in Sixteenth Century France.* Boston: Ginn, 1969.

Palmer-Fernandez, Gabriel, editor. *Encyclopedia of Religion and War.* New York: Routledge, 2004.

Parker, Geoffrey. *The Thirty Years War.* London: Routledge, 1987.

Peers, E. Allison. *Ramon Lull.* London: SPCK, 1929.

Peters, Edward. *Heresy and Authority in Medieval Europe: documents in translation.* Philadelphia: University of Pennsylvania Press, 1980.

Polo, Marco. *De Condicionibus et Consuetudinibus Orientalium Regionum.* Translated by Francisco Pipino. 1445.

Priestly, Joseph. *An History of the Corruptions of Christianity.* London: J. Johnson, 1793.

The Qur'an. *The Meaning of the Glorious Koran.* Translated by M. M. Pickthall. New York: New American Library, 1953.

Richardson, Louise. *What Terrorists Want.* New York: Random House, 2006.

Rogers, Eugene F. Jr. *Thomas Aquinas and Karl Barth.* Notre Dame: University of Notre Dame Press, 1995.

Runciman, Steven. *The Fall of Constantinople, 1453.* Cambridge: Cambridge University Press, 1990.

———. *The Medieval Manichees.* Cambridge: Cambridge University Press. 1960.

Sanford, Charles B. *The Religious Life of Thomas Jefferson.* Charlottesville: University Press of Virginia, 1984.

Sanford, Eva Marie. "Honorius, Presbyter and Scholasticus." *Speculum* (1948) 397–425.

Schaff, Philip. *The Creeds of Christendom.* 1919. Reprint, New York: Kessinger, 2009.

Schiff, Stacy. *A Great Improvisation: Franklin, France, and the Birth of America.* New York: Holt, 2005.

Scholem, Gerschom. *Major Trends in Jewish Mysticism.* Jerusalem: Schocken, 1941.

Schottroff, Luise, Reginald H. Fuller, Christoph Burchard, and M. Jack Suggs. *Essays on the Love Commandment.* Philadelphia: Fortress, 1978.

Scott, Peter, and William T. Cavanaugh, editors. *The Blackwell Companion to Political Theology.* Blackwell Companions to Religion. Malden: Blackwell, 2007.

Sherwood, Terry. *Herbert's Prayerful Art.* Toronto: University of Toronto Press, 1989.

Sigmund, Paul E. *Nicholas of Cusa and Medieval Political Thought.* Cambridge, MA: Harvard University Press, 1963.

Skinner, Quentin. *The Foundations of Modern Political Thought.* Cambridge: Cambridge University Press, 1973.

Smith, Wilfred Cantwell. *The Meaning and End of Religion.* New York: Macmillan, 1963.

Stark, Rodney. *One True God: Historical Consequences of Monotheism.* Princeton: Princeton University Press, 2001.

Stevenson, W. Taylor. "LEX ORANDI-LEX CREDENDI." In *The Study of Anglicanism,* edited by Stephen Sykes and John Booty. Minneapolis: Fortress, 1988.

Sumption, Jonathan. *The Albigensian Crusade.* London: Faber & Faber, 1978.

Swierenga, Robert. "Ethnoreligious Political Behavior in the Mid-Nineteenth Century: Voting, Values, Cultures." In *Religion and American Politics: from the Colonial Period to the 1980s,* edited by Mark Noll, 146–171. New York: Oxford University Press, 1990.

Swift, Jonathan. *Miscellanies.* 6 vols. London: Benjamin Motte and Charles Bathurst, 1736–38.

Thomas, Aquinas, Saint. *Summa Contra Gentiles.* Notre Dame: University of Notre Dame Press, 1975.

———. *Summa Theologiae.* New York: McGraw-Hill, 1964.

Thouzellier, Christine. *Catharisme et valdéisme en Languedoc à la fin du XIIe et au début du XIIIe siècle. Politique pontificale controversies.* Louvain: Éditions Nauwelaerts, 1969.

Torrell, Jean-Pierre. *Aquinas's Summa: Background, Structure, and Reception.* Translated by Benedict M. Guevin. Washington, DC: Catholic University of America Press, 2005.

———. *Saint Thomas Aquinas.* Translated by Robert Royal. Washington, DC: Catholic University of America Press, 2005.

Trocmé, André. *Jesus and the Nonviolent Revolution*. Farmington, PA: The Bruderhof Foundation, 2004.

Tugwell, Simon, editor and translator. *Albert & Thomas: Selected Writings*. Classics of Western Spirituality. New York: Paulist, 1988.

———, editor. *Early Dominicans: Selected Writings*. Classics of Western Spirituality. New York: Paulist, 1982.

Tyache, Nicholas. *Anti-Calvinists: The Rise of English Arminiaism*. Oxford: Oxford University Press, 1987.

Urvoy, Dominique. *Penser l 'Islam: les présupposés islamique de l 'Art ' de Lull*. Paris: J. Wrin, 1980.

———. "The 'Ulama' of al-Andalus." In *The Legacy of Muslim Spain*, edited by Salma Khadra Jayusi, 849–78. Leiden: Brill, 1992.

Van Nieuwenhove, Rik, and Joseph Wawrykow, editors. *The Theology of Thomas Aquinas*. Notre Dame: University of Notre Dame Press, 2005.

Walters, Kerry S. *The American Deists*. Lawrence: University of Kansas Press, 1992.

Walton, Izaak. *The Lives of John Donne, Sir Henry Wotton, Richard Hooker, George Herbert and Robert Sanderson*. Oxford: Oxford University Press, 1900.

Weisheipl, James A. *Friar Thomas d 'Aquino*. Washington, DC: Catholic University of America Press, 1983.

Weiss, René. *The Yellow Cross: The Story of the Last Cathars*. New York: Alfred Knopf, 2001.

William of Tudela and an Anonymous Successor. *The Song of the Cathar Wars: a History of the Albigensian Crusade*. Translated by Janet Shirley. Brookfield: Ashgate, 1966.

Wills, Garry. *Head and Heart: American Christianities*. New York: Penguin, 2007.

Wink, Walter. *Engaging the Powers: Discernment and Resistance in a World of Domination*. Minneapolis: Fortress, 1992.

Yates, Frances. "Ramon Lull and John Scotus Erigena." *Journal of Warburg and Courtauld Institutes* 23 (1960) 1–44.

———. "Ramon Lull and John Scotus Erigena." In *Lull & Bruno: Collected Essays*. London: Routledge & Kegan Paul, 1982.

Yoder, John Howard. *The Politics of Jesus*. 2nd ed. Grand Rapids: Eerdmans, 1994.

Name Index

Abelard, Peter, 55
Adams, John, 210n25, 214n34, 222
Albert the Great, 38, 116n16
Aquinas, Thomas, 3–4, 6–7, 13n21, 33–72, 75, 85n25, 87, 218–19
Aristotle, 34, 37–38, 43–45
Arminius, Jacobus, 185
Augustodunesis, Honorius, 93n34, 123n32

Bacon, Roger, 55
Betz, Hans Dieter, 21–22, 25n47, 27n50, 28n51
Blount, Charles, 206
Bolingbroke, Lord, 206, 213
Boyd, Gregory, 232–34
Bush, George W., 8, 232

Cavanaugh, William, 12n17
Cicero, 127, 137–38, 140–41
Cusanus, Nicholas, 5–7, 107–58

Dionysius (Pseudo-), 122n31
Donne, John, 166–69, 171, 182
Dupuis, Jacques, 155–56

Eckhart, Meister, 122n31
Eriugena (Erigena), Johannes Scotus, 92–93, 93n35, 94, 97, 123

Frederick V, 162, 191

Hallie, Philip, 224n2, 227
Harley, Sir Robert, 186–88
Harrison, Peter, 114

Hauerwas, Stanley, 234
Heimericus de Campo, 116
Herbert, Edward of Cherbury, 5–7, 157, 159–96, 197, 199n7, 206–8, 217
Herbert, George, 168n23, 182
Henri IV, King of France, 180–84, 228
Hick, John, 115n13, 154

Ibn al-Arabi, 97n44–45
Ibn Haxm, 100n51
Ibn Tumart, 100

James I, King of Aragon-Catalonia, 74, 76n10, 84n23, 85, 104, 218–19
James I, King of England, 184–85, 192
James II, ruler of Majorca, 77–78
Jefferson, Thomas, 6–7, 21n35, 197–222
John of Plano Carpini, 112n5, 156
Jurgensmeyer, Mark, 9n10

Knitter, Paul, 115,n14

Louis IX, King of France, 33, 73
Louis XIII, King of France, 193
Lovin, Robin, 2–3
Lull or Llull, Ramon, 5–6, 55, 73–106, 113, 115–17, 120–23, 135–36, 157, 197, 219
Madison, James, 215–17, 220–21
Marty, Martin, 14

McTernan, Oliver, 10, 18n29
Mehmed II, 15, 107–9
Montmorency-Damville, Henri de,
      180–83

Nelson-Pallmeyer, Jack, 16n25
Nicholas of Cusa,
      see Cusanus, Nicholas
Noll, Mark, 11, 221n50

Palmer-Fernandez, Gabriel, 16n25,
      19n31
Peter I, King of Aragon, 75–76,
Polo, Marco, 55, 112n6, 144, 156
Pontius Pilate, 22, 227n5
Pope
      Benedict XVI, 13n20
      Innocent III, 39n13
      Eugene IV, 119
      Gregory IX, 42
      Nicholas V, 119
      Pius II, 109, 119
Priestley, Joseph, 209–10

Richardson, Louise, 15, 17–18, 20
Rush, Benjamin, 210–12

Smith, Wilfred Cantwell, 114
Stark, Rodney, 10n13
Swift, Jonathan, 1

Trocmé, André, 225, 233–34
Yates, Dame Frances, 92–93n34,
      96n41
Yoder, John Howard, 23n41,
      233–34

Subject Index

Albigensian Crusade, 2, 39–42, 63,
    71, 75–76, 199
Anti-Calvinists in Church of
    England (Arminians),
    161–62, 184, 194
Anti-Judaism and Anti-Semitism,
    7, 230n9
Anti-Muslim stereotypes, 13n21,
    67–68

Cathars (Manichees) (Manichean
    Heresy), 4, 34–37, 63, 199,
    233
Christian Concepts of Religion,
    Antecedents:
    Thomas's Moral Virtue of
        Religio, 6, 46–54, 168,
        218, 218n46, 220
    Lull's Monotheistic *Secta*
        (Sect) and *Lex* (Law),
        81n18, 113
    Universal Generic Concepts:
    Cusanus' NeoPlatonic
        concept, 111, 123–31,
        143
    Islamic elements, 121,
        134–35, 137–40, 142
    Ciceronian elements,
        140–41
    Herbert's Elizabethan and
        Enlightenment con-
        cept, 161–68
    Christian theological
        elements, 168,
        175–80

Anti-clerical, anti-
    ecclesiastical
    elements, 183–90
Political anti-war
    elements, 162–63,
    181, 191–95
Scientific worldview
    elements, 195
Jefferson's Political
    Enlightenment con-
    cept, 205, 208
Pragmatic political ele-
    ments, 198–99
Christian theological
    elements, 204–5,
    216–17, 219–21
Scientific worldview
    elements, 206–7
Constantinian Era, 2n2, 3, 7, 39,
    184, 223–24, 226, 233
Constantinople in 1453, 15, 107–10

Disestablishment of Religion 6,
    196, 197–99, 204–5, 215–17

Elizabethan Church of England,
    161, 164–75
English Civil Wars of 1640s, 5, 162

Historical Jesus, 20n35, 25n45

Inquisition, 4, 35, 42n17, 63, 199
Inter-religious Dialogue in Lull, 82,
    84n22
    and NeoPlatonic Rationality,
        83–88, 89–96

Inter-religious Dialogue in Lull
    (cont.),
    and Islamic Rationality, 88–89,
        100–101

Inter-religious Dialogue in Lull
    (cont.),
    exclusion of scriptural/
        doctrinal norms, 88–89
    exclusion of objections/
        interruptions, 89–90, 104
Islamic Studies, 5, 79–80, 98–103,
    120–21

Law of equal Retribution
    (*ius talionis*), 26–28,

Mongols (Tartars) in 13th century
    Europe and Asia, 69–71
    as prospective Christian
        converts, 81n19, 86,
        150–51

NeoPlatonism
    in Lull and Cusanus, 90–96,
    Eastern Patristic Sources,
        93n35
    Eriugena and Honorius, 92–95,
        123
    in Cabalistic Judaism, 96–98
    in Islamic Sufism, 96–98, 100
Nonviolent Alternatives to
    Religious Violence, 3–4, 20,
    43–45, 71–72, 106

Pacifists, 6, 225
Pacifist Theologies, 225–26, 233
Peace Mandate of Jesus, 6, 20–32,
    223
Peace Churches and Organizations,
    225
Peace Witnesses, 2–3, 4–7, 20–21,
    32, 235
    Aquinas, 44–45, 71–72

Lull, 78, 80–84, 86, 88, 106
    Cusanus, 110–11, 114, 118, 124,
        132–33, 152, 156–58
    Herbert, 162–63, 180–82, 184,
        193, 196
    Jefferson, 198–99, 204–5,
        216–17, 219–21
    Village of Le Chambon, 224–31
    Trocmé, 225–28, 234–35
    Boyd, 232–34
The *politiques* party in France, 181,
    184

Religious Diversity in
    13th-century France and Italy,
        34–35
    13th-century Iberia, 75–77
    15th-century world, 108–11
    16th-century England,
        165nn11–12
    17th-century Europe, 203–4
    18th-century America, 6,
        198–99
Religious Violence
    Sermon on the Mount, 30–32
    objections to concept, 8–14
    complexity of, 12, 14–18
    increasing frequency of, 18–20
    particularity of religious vio-
        lence, 8
    Majorca, 74–75
    France, 180–81, 193–94,
        228n8
Repentance in
    Church of England, 172–75
    Lord Herbert's Theology
        of Religion, 175–80, 183

Saracen, 74, 77n14, 78, 81, 98,
    102–5
Sermon on the Mount
    Beatitudes of, 21–22
    Antitheses of, 22, 24–32
    Non-retaliation, 24–28

Non-retaliation versus nonresistance, 25–26n47
Loving the religious enemy,
6–7, 29–32, 211n28,
212–13, 219, 221–22
Loving others as God loves,
29–32

Theology of Religion, 5, 111–15,
153–58
Similarities of Religions, 115
Christian Norms in Religions,
145–50
Theological Agnosticism, 128–29
The Thirty Years' War, 2, 162,
191–92, 202–4

Made in the USA
Columbia, SC
25 May 2019